Child Abuse and Human Rights

CHILD ABUSE AND HUMAN RIGHTS

(In 2 Volumes)

Current Trends in Child Abuse

(Volume-1)

Editor

Jyotsna Tiwari

ISHA BOOKS

DELHI-110 033

Child Abuse and Human Rights

Rs. 1600 (Set)
Rs. 800 (each volume)

ISBN: 81-8205-071-5 (Set)
ISBN: 81-8205-072-3 (Vol. 1)

Reprinted in 2011 in India by
Isha Books
B-63, Ist Floor
New Gupta Colony
Near DDA Market
Delhi-110009

Printed at: G. Print Process, Delhi

Contents

Preface

Our children are our most valuable and vulnerable resource. Child abuse is a huge issue for our community, as big an issue as that of protecting our environment. Child abuse is the misuse of power by adults over children that endangers or impairs a child's physical or emotional health and development. It includes: physical abuse; emotional abuse; neglect; sexual abuse or exploitation.

Each day, the safety and well-being of a considerable number some children across the world are threatened by child abuse and neglect. A range of factors in our society—including increased family breakdown, accelerated social and technological change, toleration of violence, financial stress and other pressures upon parents and caregivers—are contributing to an environment conducive to an increase in child abuse and neglect.

For long the issue of child abuse has been a neglected one. In the last decade or so the situation has changed dramatically. Child abuse and neglect have been attracting growing international attention, and greater awareness has been created among common people. Never before in history have societies been so outspoken about the violations of 'human rights' and protection of 'the rights of the child'. International organizations, governments and advocacy groups are creating and implementing strategies and initiatives to address the issues of child abuse. The UN Convention on the Rights of the Child (CRC), drawn up in 1989 gives guiding principles to protect child rights. It has been ratified by almost all countries in the world.

The present volume addresses the scope, causes, and consequences of child abuse and neglect. It also presents an overview of prevention efforts and the child protection process. Because child protection is a multi-disciplinary effort, the book describes the roles and responsibilities of different professional groups and offers guidance on how the groups can work together effectively to protect the safety, permanency, and well-being of children. The primary audience for this book includes parents, teachers, child protective services, professionals and concerned community members.

Editor

1

Understanding Child Abuse

Our children are our most valuable and vulnerable resource. Child abuse is a huge issue for our community, as big an issue as that of protecting our environment. Child abuse is the misuse of power by adults over children that endangers or impairs a child's physical or emotional health and development.It includes :

— physical abuse

— emotional abuse

— neglect

— sexual abuse or exploitation

Physical Abuse: punching, slapping, shaking, burning, biting, throwing a child, strangulation.

Emotional Abuse: constant criticism, scapegoating, name-calling, belittling, excessive teasing, ignoring a child, punishing normal social behaviours, exposure to domestic violence, withholding praise and affection.

Neglect: failing to meet the child's basic needs for adequate supervision, food, clothing, shelter, safety, hygiene, medical care, education, love and affection and failure to use available resources to meet those needs. In its extreme form, abandonment.

Child abuse is usually a pattern or cycle, not a one-off incident. Child sexual abuse is any sexual act or sexual threat imposed upon a child. Coercion (physical and emotional) is intrinsic to child sexual abuse. This distinguishes it from consensual peer sexual activity. Sexual abuse can include: exposure, indecent phone calls, fondling, voyeurism, persistent intrusion of a child's privacy, penetration, rape, incest, involvement with pornography, child prostitution.

Secrecy, misuse of power and the distortion of adult-child relationships are key factors in the sexual abuse of children. Most abusive behaviour is perpetrated by someone the child knows and trusts (a parent, step-parent, relative, family friend or care provider). Only a small proportion of child sexual abuse is by a stranger.

This makes the child vulnerable to tricks, bribes and threats. The perpetrator may slowly introduce the child to behaviour which becomes more sexualised. This is called a 'grooming' process.

Common emotional responses to child abuse and neglect include:

— Shock

— Denial

— Sympathy and pity

— Frustration

— Anger

— Distress and Anxiety

— Guilt and self recrimination

— Blame

— Sadness or depression

— Revulsion, horror and disgust

— Revenge and desire for punishment

Sympathy and pity can lead to adults supplying food, baths, etc., rather than reporting to the authorities so that underlying causes are addressed. It is important to show children that not all adults are caught up in a conspiracy of silence.

Anger can stop us from gaining co-operation with a negligent parent and can even add to that parent's low self esteem, stress and isolation, and thus place children in greater jeopardy. Substance abuse and poverty are major factors in relation to child abuse and are directly linked to family violence.

It is now acknowledged that children who witness their mother being beaten could suffer as much as if they themselves were being hit. Family violence between spouses is a major precursor to child homocide. Families in which harm to children is occurring are often isolated from extended family, neighbours and the broader community. Families in which harm to children is occurring tend to participate less in community organisations and make less use of available economic, health and social resources.

Role reversal (parenting the parent) can occur in family settings where there is harm to children. Some study shows that while some parents who were abused as children go on to abuse their own children (intergenerational abuse), the majority do not. Evidence suggests that parents who were abused as children and who broke the cycle of abuse :

— experienced a significant positive relationship with someone during childhood

— were open and angry about the abuse they received in childhood

— made a conscious resolve not to repeat their histories

— had a supportive spouse/partner

— had developed friendships

— had a broader network of resources and were skilled at using community agencies

— developed different family patterns of interaction to their families of origin

Behavioural psychologists have observed that preschoolers typically demand that their caretakers deal with some kind of need or desire at an average rate of three times a minute. Under ideal circumstances, mum or dad might respond cheerfully. But when a parent is stressed or otherwise distracted, a child's incessant demands can seem too difficult to deal with appropriately.

It should be noted that this demanding behaviour may be age appropriate yet can still add more stress to an already over burdened parent. The individual's response to stress is a major issue in child abuse. Families in which a child has a disability are particularly vulnerable because:

— Parents often feel isolated and/or shunned by family and friends

— Families often lack adequate community resources and support such as respite care

— The dependency needs of the child are often very high

— Financial difficulties can result - parents often cannot maintain employment

— The child may be unable to communicate needs

Carers are often very stressed because of these problems System abuse can be characterised by one or more of the following:

— unavailability of appropriate services for the child

— failure to effectively organise and coordinate existing services

— institutional failure to consider the child's needs

— abuse - perpetrated within agencies and institutions responsible for the care of children

When children are abused by a system meant to offer them care, they learn to distrust all adults and have difficulties developing relationships. Behavioural disorders often result. Child abuse and neglect within educational settings may include :

— overly restricting access to toilets for young children the use of fear-inducing techniques (ex hurling books, tipping chairs, pulling a child's ears)

— verbal abuse, esp. labelling and name calling

— scapegoating and rejecting a child

— failure of teachers to deal with allegations or suspicions of child maltreatment

— bullying by peers.

Following are the short and long term consequences of child abuse and neglect:

— death

— disability/permanent physical injury

— developmental delay

— failure to thrive

— low self esteem

— learning problems

— behavioural problems

— inability to maintain relationships

— psychiatric problems

— eating disorders

— anxiety

— depression

— substance abuse

— homelessness

— prostitution and criminal behaviour

— suicide

The younger the child is, the more vulnerable they are and the more serious the consequences are likely to be. Point out the extensive cost in human lives, wasted potential and financial and other resources involved in treating these consequences after the damage has been done.

Prevention of child abuse and neglect is important because:

— It is the humane and socially just thing to do

— It costs much less to prevent than to try to 'fix' it afterwards

The child's physical and social environment is chaotic and non-child-safe. A chaotic, unsafe and unclean environment can pose risks to a child's health including exposure to hazards such as hot water, stairs, swimming pools and heights.

Children may be at risk of harm through exposure to multiple unknown adults if there is inadequate parental supervision. Departmental officers who undertake assessments will consider protective factors such as:

— There is a person present who is able and willing to protect the child.

— The child is able to access supports

— The family is supported by a community agency

— Extended family members meet the child's protective needs

— Medical treatment has been sought

The parent acknowledges the incident, takes responsibility for change and/or has the capacity to prevent recurrence. The child is at an age where they can protect themselves to some degree. The impact of abuse on a particular child will be influenced by:

— the severity of the harm

— the period of time over which the harm occurred

— the age, gender and personality of the child

— the existence of positive relationships within/or outside the family

— the relationship of the perpetrator to the child

— the timing and quality of the intervention.

There are 4 key areas to the prevention of child abuse and neglect:

— Parenting Support and Skill Development

— Personal Safety Education for Children

— Development of Social Infrastructure

— Community Awareness Campaigns

Adequate social infrastructure to prevent child abuse and neglect includes the provision of affordable:

— child care services

— playgroups

— respite care

— transport

— housing

— medical and dental care

— counselling/family therapy

— legal services

— recreational activities

When a child discloses abuse or neglect:

— try to remain calm - do not express shock, panic or disbelief

— find a private place to talk

— use the child's vocabulary and encourage them to discuss their feelings

— reassure the child that they have done the right thing by telling

— reassure the child that it is not his/her fault

— do not push for details - the child will face interviews after referral to protective services

— tell the child that support and protection is available

— do not confront the parents/perpetrator

— do not make promises you can't keep

— seek expert advice

— let the child know what will happen when the report is made

A range of factors in our society - including increased family breakdown, accelerated social and technological change, toleration of violence, financial stress and other pressures upon parents and caregivers - are contributing to an environment conducive to an increase in child abuse and neglect.

We can all play a part in breaking the silence surrounding child abuse and neglect and in challenging the power of offenders who sexually abuse children. A strong, caring community can make a great difference to a family by offering support networks, parent drop-in centres, parenting programs, family fun days and other initiatives to ease the burdens on stressed families. At the community level:

— Developing integrated community services

— Creating safe and supportive environments (in neighbourhoods and communities)

— Developing co-ordinated networks (of all programs and services for families and children)

— Universal and Intensive/Targeted programs and services.

Co-ordinated community networks can provide universal programmes and services (to assist all families) and intensive programs and services (for those having problems in creating safe and healthy environments for their children).

— An integrated response should include:

— essential parenting information and support

— support for parents at transition points (e.g. birth, home to school, childhood to adolescence)

— intensive support and advice on parenting and health issues and access to support services for parents with high needs (e.g. socially isolated parents, women experiencing domestic violence, parents of children with disabilities, parents with substance abuse issues.

— Programs and strategies can be implemented to support families at developmental transition points prenatal/perinatal (eg. pre-marital/cohabitation education, home visiting programs, family support strategies);

— infancy (eg. parent training and early education);

— preschool (eg. child training and teacher training, personal safety training);

— school (e.g. peer group training, self esteem programmes, social skills programs);

— adolescence (e.g. anti-bullying programs and community youth support schemes, values based education, sexuality and relationship education);

— adulthood (e.g. social and economic development and building social networks, employment programs, stress management training, relationship counselling).

Some agencies have developed 'one stop shops'. Others have used the school setting as an appropriate site to develop community centres. Often people are simply unaware of what services are available to support families and for the assessment and referral of children at risk or who have been abused.

It is important to know what services are available in your community to support parents who are stressed and children who are at risk or who have already experienced abuse or neglect. The well-being of families and of children involves a range of services including the health, education and welfare sectors.

These sectors are increasingly collaborating in order to provide more effective and efficient services for families and children. When developing projects or programmes within a community it is important not to duplicate already existing services. Sometimes the establishment of networks or collaboration about what is being done is more important than providing a new service. It is especially important to refer a family or individual to another agency or a specialist services if they have issues that you are not comfortable or experienced in working with, or if they need assistance from a member of their own cultural or special needs group.

The Office of Child Protection offers a range of books, videos, posters and pamphlets for purchase or loan to professionals and community organisations. The Families, Youth and Community Care Queensland provides programs, as well as funding to community organisations, to support families and children through a broad range of strategies and services. These include both prevention and intervention programs, comprehensive therapeutic services, shared family care and a range of other intiatives.

The Department also offers a child protection service. This service engages in collaboration with a range of government and non-government agencies. Stress the importance of being familiar with the various organisations involved in the welfare of children and families.

Role of Parents

One of the hardest tasks of parenthood, but also one of the most important and rewarding, is teaching a child about sexuality. What do I say? When do I start? We live in a sexually open society where movies, songs, and conversations often include references to sex. Advertising sells products with sex, and radio and TV programs use sexual situations to entertain us.

You can begin to help your daughter understand that many of these depictions or illustrations of sex are shallow. Commercialized sex is misleading because it shows sex only as glamorous and trouble-free. By helping your daughter understand the special significance of our sexuality, you can begin to develop conversations with her about sex as well as help her to make positive sexual choices.

Try to remember your own early curiosity about sex. What did you want to know? How did you find answers to your questions? What do you wish had been different about your education or experiences? You may remember that much of what you learned from friends, or pieced together yourself, often turned out to be untrue.

Even though our society probably treats sexuality differently today than when you were a teen, young people still have many of the same questions and needs that you did. What your daughter really needs is for you to provide answers to her questions, to be there to listen, and to help her to form educated opinions and decisions. This can be accomplished through everyday conversations with her.

In fact, when sexuality is discussed as a part of everyday situations, rather than having the "big talk," parents (and youth) often find the experience more comfortable. To help you with this, consider the following issues as you guide your daughter in understanding her sexuality and sexual decisions.

Girls need to understand that changes are normal and happen at different rates for different girls. The awkwardness will not last. They also need to know what to expect in terms of a growth spurt, hair growth, and menstruation. Parents should also familiarize themselves with, and teach their daughters, the following terms: fallopian tubes, ovaries, menstruation, uterus, urethra, clitoris, labia majora, labia minora, vulva, hymen, vagina, anus, rectum, and cervix. There are many resources for parents and teens about these changes and terms listed at the end of this brochure.

Girls wonder exactly what it is, how it feels, and when it is okay to have intercourse. They also need to know the place of intercourse within a loving relationship. Explain that intercourse occurs when a man places his erect penis inside a woman's vagina, and that this can lead to pregnancy.

Teens also need to understand that it is never okay to have intercourse unless both partners understand the consequences and willingly agree. Girls need to know that this is one way that many people handle their sexual feelings and pressures. If you are uncomfortable addressing this issue with your daughter, give her resources to explore this issue on her own. Reassure your daughter that getting familiar and comfortable with her own body, how it functions, and how it responds to touching is a normal part of understanding herself.

Girls need to learn how to handle their desires and pressures that some friends may put on them to become sexually active. Your daughter will be tempted in many situations over the course of her adolescent years. Learning to handle sexual feelings and to make mature decisions is part of growing up.

One of the most important choices your daughter will make is when to have intercourse. Delaying intercourse until maturity is beneficial for teens, but most of them need help and support to do so. Of course, the teen years are filled with lots of decisions about risky behaviors. Coping with the consequences of good and poor decisions is an important step to maturity.

Girls sometimes feel tremendous pressure to participate in sexual acts by both friends and boyfriends. They fear being made fun of or rejected by peers. Talk to your daughter about making responsible decisions as well as the difference between positive and negative popularity.

If your daughter decides to delay having sex, this does not mean that the decision will stay made. Young people have to make this decision over and over again, which may become increasingly difficult. Therefore, it is essential to talk with your daughter about protecting herself and her partner, and how to use birth control correctly.

This part of sexuality education is as essential as all others, even if she intends to delay intercourse. Some parents fear that discussing contraception will encourage sexual activity, but the opposite is true. Many parents assume that their daughter knows all about birth control, where to get it, and how to properly use it. Unfortunately, she probably does not.

The resources will help you and your daughter familiarize yourselves with methods and their effectiveness. Important topics are abstinence, birth control pills, IUD/intrauterine devices, diaphragms, foam, condoms, and natural family planning. Many parents include the risks of sexually transmitted diseases, including HIV/AIDS, when discussing contraception.

Perhaps the most important part of teaching your daughter about sex and her own sexuality is not the facts that you present to her, but the manner and sincerity with which you deliver those facts. Letting her know your values is very important. Despite how you may sometimes feel, teens still look to parents as an important source of guidance and boundaries.

Regardless of what values are taught in the home, young people will consider many attitudes and opinions before they decide on their own sexual values. Be patient and understanding as your daughter explores and makes decisions. And always keep the lines of communication open. In addition, keep the following points in mind.

All children need to feel that their ideas or concerns about sex are worth listening to. Look for natural opportunities to talk to your daughter. Don't wait until she comes to you with questions or comments about sex. Take advantage of natural openings to talk about sexuality (e.g., television programs, newspaper stories or in the car). Listen carefully for hidden feelings. Many times children have trouble saying exactly what they mean, especially when it comes to sex.

Try to avoid judging your child. Making harsh judgments or criticizing your daughter's attitudes about sex will often cut off communication. Let your daughter express her feelings freely. Many young people have values or opinions about sex that are different from those of their parents. Remember, these may not be firmly held ideas or values, but only part of the sorting-out process.

First, listen to what your child has to say. If you agree, say so. If you disagree, clearly state your own viewpoint and why you feel that way. Don't cut off communication. Parents sometimes lose the chance to help their child think and talk about sex because they begin to nag, preach or moralize. Your child needs to know that talking about sex is two-way communication. Pose questions to your daughter that, when she answers, will help make the best decision obvious.

Avoid over-/under-answering questions. Answer questions directly, in words she understands. Don't assume that a simple question about sex needs an answer far beyond what was asked. Ask your daughter to share back with you what she understands has been said. Help your daughter develop strong self-esteem.A healthy self-concept is important for teens to make good decisions about sexual issues. A well-known educator has said, "Hope is the best contraceptive."

Remember that there are plenty of resources for you as parents to help you talk effectively with your daughter about sexuality. You do not need to be an expert to talk effectively with your children. You may want to keep a reference book in your home, not only for your own knowledge but also as a resource for your children when they want to explore issues on their own.

If you do not have a partner of the other sex, consider asking a trusted friend to talk occasionally with your daughter from that perspective. The resources listed below, and many others available from your library or online, will give you information and encouragement to answer many of the questions that you or your daughter might have.

Boys need to understand that the changes they are feeling are normal and happen at different rates for different boys. The awkwardness will not last. They also need to know what to expect in terms of a growth spurt, hair growth, genital growth, and "wet dreams."

Parents should also familiarize themselves with, and teach their sons, the following terms: ejaculation, erection, hormones, penis, prostate gland, scrotum, semen, sperm cell, testicle, and testosterone. In addition, boys need to know the physical changes that girls experience in puberty.

Boys wonder exactly what it is, how it feels, and when it is okay to have intercourse. They also need to know the place of intercourse within a loving relationship. Explain that intercourse occurs when a man places his erect penis inside a woman's vagina, and that this can lead to pregnancy. Teens also need to understand that it is never okay to have intercourse unless both partners understand the consequences and willingly agree.

Boys need to know that this is one way that many people handle their sexual feelings and pressures. If you are uncomfortable addressing this issue with your son, give him resources to learn about this on his own. Reassure your son that getting familiar and comfortable with his own body, how it functions, and how it responds to touching is a normal part of understanding himself.

Masturbation is very common among males and females. Contrary to some old beliefs, it does no physical harm. Young men need to learn how to handle the pressures friends will put on them to become sexually active. Your son will be tempted in many situations over the course of his adolescent years. Learning to handle sexual feelings and to make mature decisions is part of growing up.

Many teens are very intolerant of differences among their friends, including narrow definitions of how "real men" behave. This pressure can be very troubling to boys who may not fit that stereotype. One of the most important choices your son will make is when to have intercourse. Delaying intercourse until maturity is beneficial for teens, but many of them need help and support to do so.

Of course, the teen years are filled with lots of decisions about other risky behavior, too. Coping with the consequences of good and poor decisions is an important step to maturity. Many boys feel a tremendous pressure to "score" with girls as a way of proving their manhood. They fear being called "gay" or "sissy" if they don't put sexual pressure on girls.

Talk with your son about making responsible decisions as well as the difference between positive and negative popularity. If a young person decides to delay having sex, this does not mean that the decision will stay made. Young people have to make this decision over and over again, which may become increasingly difficult.

Therefore, it is essential to talk with your son about protecting himself and his partner, and how to use birth control correctly. This part of sexuality education is as essential as all others, even if your child intends to delay intercourse. Some parents fear that discussing contraception will encourage sexual activity, but the opposite is true. Many parents assume that their son knows all about birth control, where to get it, and how to properly use it.

Unfortunately, he probably does not. It will help you and your son familiarize yourselves with methods and their effectiveness. Important topics are abstinence, birth control pills, IUD/intrauterine devices, diaphragms, foam, condoms, and natural family planning. Many parents include the risks of sexually transmitted diseases, including HIV/AIDS, when discussing contraception.

Perhaps the most important part in teaching your son about sex and his own sexuality is not the facts that you present to him, but the manner and sincerity with which you deliver those facts. Letting your children know your values and expectations is very important.

Despite how you may sometimes feel, teens still look to parents as an important source of guidance and boundaries. Regardless of what values are taught in your home, young people will consider many attitudes and opinions before they decide on their own sexual values. Be patient and understanding as your son explores ideas and makes decisions.

Child Marriage

Birth, marriage and death are the standard trio of key events in most people's lives. But only one - marriage - is a matter of choice. The right to exercise that choice was recognized as a principle of law even in Roman times and has long been established in international human rights instruments. Yet many girls, and a smaller number of boys, enter marriage without any chance of exercising their right to choose. Some are forced into marriage at a very early age. Others are simply too young to make an informed decision about their marriage partner or about the implications of marriage itself. They may have given what passes for 'consent' in the eyes of custom or the law, but in reality, consent to their binding union has been made by others on their behalf.

The assumption is that once a girl is married, she has become a woman - even if she is only 12. Equally, where a boy is made to marry, he is now a man and must put away childish things. While the age of marriage is generally on the rise, early marriage - marriage of children and adolescents below the age of 18 - is still widely practised. While early marriage takes many different forms and has various causes, one issue is paramount. Whether it happens to a girl or a boy, early marriage is a violation of human rights.

The right to free and full consent to a marriage is recognized in the 1948 Universal Declaration of Human Rights (UDHR) and in many subsequent human rights instruments - consent that cannot be 'free and full' when at least one partner is very immature. For both girls and boys, early marriage has profound physical, intellectual, psychological and emotional impacts, cutting off educational opportunity and chances of personal growth.

For girls, in addition, it will almost certainly mean premature pregnancy and childbearing, and is likely to lead to a lifetime of domestic and sexual subservience over which they have no control. Yet many societies, primarily in Africa and South Asia, continue to support the idea that girls should marry at or soon after puberty. Their spouses are likely to be a few years older than they are, but may be more than twice their age. Parents and heads of families make marital choices for daughters and sons with little regard for the personal implications. Rather, they look upon marriage as a family-building strategy, an economic arrangement or a way to protect girls from unwelcome sexual advances.

Social reformers in the first part of the 20th century were concerned about early marriage, especially in India,and influenced the UDHR and other human rights conventions of the 1950s and 1960s. In the latter part of the 20th century, interest centred on the behavioural determinants fuelling rapid population growth, for obvious reasons.Early marriage extends a woman's reproductive span, thereby contributing to large family size, especially in the absence of contraception.

More recently, advocates of safe motherhood have turned their attention to this issue. Pregnancies that occur 'too early' - when a woman's body is not fully mature - constitute a major risk to the survival and future health of both mother and child.Concern with the special health needs of adolescents has also recently been growing in a world where young people are particularly vulnerable to HIV/AIDS.

However, from a demographic and health perspective, early marriage is seen primarily as a contributory factor to early child-bearing. And sometimes, even in this context, its role is overlooked: the phrase 'teenage pregnancy' is typically understood to mean pregnancy outside marriage. Yet far more adolescent or teenage pregnancies occur within marriage than outside it.

During the past decade, the movement for 'Education for All' has stressed the need to enrol more girls in school and to keep them from dropping out before completion. In this context, the custom of early marriage is acknowledged as one of the reasons for girls' exclusion from school, especially in cultural settings where girls are raised for a lifetime confined to household occupations and are expected to marry very young.

Very recently, the situation of children in need of special protection, notably girls vulnerable to sexual abuse and HIV/AIDS, suggests that early marriage is being used as a strategy to protect girls from sexual exposure,or to pass the economic burden for their care to others. Thus, early marriage lingers on as a culturally and socially sanctioned practice according to some traditional sets of values and, among some highly stressed populations, it may even be on the rise.

Despite the efforts of reformers in the early part of the 20 century, early marriage has received scant attention from the modern women's rights and children's rights movements. There has been virtually no attempt to examine the practice as a human rights violation in itself. Children and teenagers married at ages well below the legal minimum become statistically invisible as 'children'.

Thus, in the eyes of the law, an adult male who has sex with a girl of 12 or 13 outside marriage may be regarded as a criminal, while the same act within marriage is condoned. To date, most studies on the effects of early marriage have focused on premature sex and pregnancy and school drop-out.

Marriages that take place under the age of 18 - the upper age limit for protection under the 1989 Convention on the Rights of the Child (CRC). It examines early marriage from the human rights perspective in order to offer guidelines for much-needed analysis and action. The CRC and the 1979 Convention on the Elimination of all forms of Discrimination Against Women (CEDAW) provide the foundation for such a perspective, which requires a holistic approach to early marriage.

This means examining every implication of the practice, from its limitation upon personal freedom to its impact upon health and education. There is also a deliberate attempt to focus on unions that are recognized either in statutory or customary law as marriages, rather than informal or consensual unions. While boys are affected by early marriage, this is an issue that impacts upon girls in far larger numbers and with more intensity. In many societies, adolescence means an opening up of opportunity for boys, whereas for girls it often means a closing down of opportunity and personal freedom.

The experience for boys is, therefore, less likely to be as exploitative or physically harmful as it is for girls. The practice of marrying girls at a young age is most common in Sub-Saharan Africa and South Asia. However, in the Middle East, North Africa and other parts of Asia, marriage at or shortly after puberty is common among those living traditional lifestyles.

There are also specific parts of West and East Africa and of South Asia where marriages much earlier than puberty are not unusual, while marriages of girls between the ages of 16 and 18 are common in parts of Latin America and in pockets of Eastern Europe. One problem in assessing the prevalence of early marriages is that so many are unregistered and unofficial and are not therefore counted as part of any standard data collection system.

An exception is Bangladesh, where the Demographic and Health Survey (DHS) of 1996-97 reported that 5 per cent of 10- 14 year-olds were married.Small-scale studies and anecdotal information fill in the picture. They imply that marriage at a very young age is more widespread than country data suggest. National statistics often disguise significant rates of very early marriage in some regions and among some sub-populations. In the Indian state of Rajasthan, for example, a 1993 survey of 5,000 women revealed that 56 per cent had married before age 15, and of these, 17 per cent were married before they were 10.

A 1998 survey in Madhya Pradesh found that nearly 14 per cent of girls were married between the ages of 10 and 14. In Ethiopia and in parts of West Africa, marriage at seven or eight is not uncommon. In Kebbi State, Northern Nigeria, the average age of marriage for girls is just over 11 years, against a national average of 17. Plenty of marriage data exist for those aged 15-19, mostly in relation to reproduction or schooling. DHS data also allow some analysis of the proportion of women currently married who married below age 18.

Trends have been exhaustively examined courtesy of World Fertility Survey and DHS data. Analysts have detected two groups of countries: those where marriage age is rising, such as Kenya, Uganda, Zimbabwe and Senegal, and those where there is little change, including Cameroon, Cote d'Ivoire, Lesotho, Liberia and Mali.In several countries, over 40 per cent of young women have entered marriage or a quasi-married union by the time they reach the age of 18. By contrast, in only two countries are more than 10 per cent of boys under 19 married.

Early marriage is generally more prevalent in Central and West Africa - affecting 40 per cent and 49 per cent respectively of girls under 19 - compared to 27 per cent in East Africa and 20 per cent in North and Southern Africa. Many of these young brides are second or third wives in polygamous households. In some African countries, notably Botswana and Namibia, few girls marry in their teens.

However, cohabitation is relatively common. While the trend towards later marriage is clear for the continent as a whole, there are some countries, such as Lesotho and Mozambique,where the trend has been in the other direction. There are also cases where the stress of conflict or HIV/AIDS seems to be contributing to early marriage.

In Asia, marriage patterns are much more diverse. The extreme cases are Afghanistan and Bangladesh, where 54 per cent and 51 per cent of girls respectively are married by age 18. In Nepal, where the average age at first marriage is 19 years,7 per cent of girls are married before they are 10 years old and 40 per cent by the time they are 15. In China, the proportion of early marriages fell by 35 per cent in the 1970s, but rose from 13 per cent in 1979 to 18 per cent in 1987.

In many Asian countries, such as Vietnam and Indonesia, there are vast differences among regions, states or islands; some in line with ethnographic patterns. Meanwhile some countries have managed to raise the age of marriage significantly. In Sri Lanka, for example, the average age at first marriage is 25, compared to 19 in neighbouring India.

In Middle East and North Africa, early marriage is less common in this region than in South Asia or Sub-Saharan Africa. Data are scarce, but we know that 55 per cent of women under 20 in the United Arab Emirates are married, while in Sudan the figure is 42 per cent.In a number of countries, averages may again disguise major disparities. A Ministry of Health field study in Upper (southern) Egypt in the late 1980s discovered that 44 per cent of rural women married in the previous five years had been under the legal age of 16 at the time.

In Caribbean and Latin American region, UNICEF reports that 11.5 per cent of girls aged 15-19 are married. These figures also mask diversity, with much higher ages in the Caribbean, and lower ages in countries such as

Paraguay, Mexico and Guatemala.Marriage age among rural indigenous peoples is typically much lower than that of the urbanized population, in keeping with traditional patterns. In the Dominican Republic, the proportion of early marriages actually rose during the early 1990s from 30 per cent to 38 per cent.

In industrialized countries, few women marry before age 18; only 4 per cent do so in the USA and 1 per cent in Germany, for example.But in some parts of Central and Eastern Europe, early marriage survives; notably among the Roma peopleand in Macedonia where 27 per cent of the women who married in 1994 were aged between 15 and 19.In most of Eastern Europe and the CIS,average age at marriage is in the low to mid-20s, implying some proportion in the teens.

Throughout Oceania, the average age of marriage for women is over 20. However, in Kiribati, Marshall Islands, Papua New Guinea and Solomon Islands, at least 18 per cent of women are married between 15 and 19.Globally, it is important to note that early marriage, and early childbearing, have been more or less abandoned by the wealthiest sections of society, even in poor and highly traditional countries.

Virtually everywhere, poor women in rural areas tend to marry younger than those in urban areas, and educational levels also play a critical role. Customs surrounding marriage, including the desirable age and the way in which a spouse is selected, depend on a society's view of the family - its role, structure, pattern of life, and the individual and collective responsibilities of its members. The idea and function of 'family' varies across the world and is in a state of constant evolution.

In Western Europe and North America, marriages have historically taken place later in life. Average age at marriage for 16 century women in Europe (other than among a small landowning elite) was 24 years (26 for men), rising to 27 by the 18century. At that time, the family was the unit of economic production, as it is in many agrarian societies today. But households were usually separate, not combined; the newly-weds needed needed a place of their own and had generally saved some resources to start family life.

Later marriage in Europe has had an important impact on attitudes to consent. Because women and men marry as adults with experience of life, it is alien to accept unquestioningly a parental choice of spouse. The free consent of both partners to a marriage has been legally requisite since Roman times. This consent, and the relative independence it gives to marriage partners, is absent from unions where the girl is absorbed into the household of her in-laws and takes on the role of the mother-in-law's protégé and helper.

One important difference between marriage customs in many developing world societies and those in the industrialized world is that in the former, these customs tend to support high fertility even where overall fertility levels are falling. During the 1970s, concern about population growth, and perplexity about the widespread rejection of contraceptive technology by most couples in developing countries, led to efforts by social demographers to understand the reasons for what they saw as 'odd' behaviour.

These demographic studies extended into a historical examination of marriage and childbearing in Western Europe. The basic difference in family patterns identified was between the traditional 'familist' system and the modern 'individualist' systems. The traditional system is characterized by extended families, communal households, plural mating, authoritarian exercise of power by the paterfamilias, young age at marriage, spouses chosen by elders, absorption of the newly-wed into an existing household, no non-household role or identity for women.

In the 'individualist' system, which is the norm in industrialized countries, the opposites generally apply. In the familist model, fertility is deliberately maximized by marrying girls immediately after puberty. The family is the unit of economic production and is the only source of wealth, social status and security for its members. New children (especially boys) are needed to run the household and maintain the family's status. The need to maximize reproduction is reinforced where infant mortality is high.

Poverty is one of the major factors underpinning early marriage. Where poverty is acute, a young girl may be regarded as an economic burden and her marriage to a much older - sometimes even elderly - man, a practice common in some Middle Eastern and South Asian societies, is a family survival strategy, and may even be seen as in her interests.

In traditional societies in Sub-Saharan Africa, the bride's family may receive cattle from the groom, or the groom's family, as the brideprice for their daughter. A recent study of five very poor villages in Egypt found young girls being married off to much older men from oil-rich Middle Eastern countries via brokers.In Bangladesh, poverty-stricken parents are persuaded to part with daughters through promises of marriage, or by false marriages, which are used to lure the girls into prostitution abroad.

In Nigeria, which is currently facing economic difficulties and political instability, age at marriage has barely risen, and in the north of the country the average age has fallen since 1990.In West Africa as a whole, a recent UNICEF study shows that economic hardship is encouraging a rise in early marriage, even among some population groups that do not normally practise it. Men are postponing marriage because of lack of resources, and parents have become anxious about the danger of their daughters becoming pregnant outside marriage.

Thus any early opportunity for marriage may be seized upon. There are also reports from HIV/AIDS researchers in Eastern Africa that marriage is seen as one option for orphaned girls by caregivers who find it hard to provide for them. Some countries in the grip of on-going civil conflict show acute symptoms of child-related social stress: increasing child slavery and trafficking, rising numbers of children on the streets, very young prostitutes and labourers, and high levels of child neglect and abandonment. Evidence suggests that in such situations, early marriage is on the rise.

Families in refugee camps in Burundi, for example, protect their honour by marrying their daughters off as early as possible. Reports from Iraq indicate that early marriage is rising there in response to poverty inflicted by the post-Gulf War sanctions,and in Afghanistan, war and militarization have led to an increased number of forced marriages of young girls. Other pressures can promote early marriage in societies under stress.

Fear of HIV infection, for example, has encouraged men in some African countries to seek young virgin - and therefore uninfected - partners. Wherever the incidence of rape, trafficking, domestic violence, sexual servitude and child abduction is rising, it seems reasonable to ask whether early marriage is also making a comeback. Early marriage is one way to ensure that a wife is 'protected', or placed firmly under male control; that she is submissive to her husband and works hard for her in-laws' household; that the children she bears are 'legitimate'; and that bonds of affection between couples do not undermine the family unit.

Parents may genuinely feel that their daughter will be better off and safer with a regular male guardian. In conflict-torn Northern Uganda for example, some families marry their young daughters to militia members in order to defend family honour or secure 'protection' for themselves and the girl. The same thing has happened to girls in Somalia in the course of that country's conflicts.One important impetus for marrying girls at an early age is that it helps prevent premarital sex.

Many societies prize virginity before marriage and this can manifest itself in a number of practices designed to 'protect' a girl from unsanctioned sexual activity. In effect, they amount to strict controls imposed upon the girl herself. She may, for exameple, be secluded from social interaction outside the family. She may be told what she can and cannot wear. In North-East Africa and parts of the Middle East in particular, control may also include the practice of female genital mutilation (FGM) - surgically restricting entry to the vagina (infibulation) or removing the clitoris (excision), to restrict sexual pleasure and temptation.

In some societies, parents withdraw their girls from school as soon as they begin to menstruate, fearing that exposure to male pupils or teachers puts them at risk. These practices are all intended to shield the girl from male sexual attention, but in the eyes of concerned parents, marriage is seen to offer the ultimate 'protection' measure. Early marriage deprives a girl of her adolescence. In many traditional societies, the idea of an adolescent period between puberty and adulthood is alien.

A girl who menstruates can bear a child, and is therefore 'a woman'. This sits awkwardly with the fact that the CRC covers everyone up to age 18 and regards childhood as a process of development - one that does not end with a definitive physical maturity marker. In some societies, the independent sense of self that a girl may develop during adolescence is seen as undesirable. While women may be revered in such societies, they are also required to be subservient to the wishes of fathers, husbands, and sons - for their own protective good.

It follows that if they are not, they deserve retribution; in Kenya for example, violence against disobedient wives is widely sanctioned.In many societies, a girl is raised to show the self-control and deference to men that will be expected of her throughout life. By the age of five, a girl in rural Pakistan has learnt to 'go outside' as little as possible, and adopt 'an attitude of care and service towards men'. Obviously, in Pakistan as elsewhere, the younger the bride, the more chance of conditioning her into the appropriate subservient behaviour.

The theory of 'demographic transition', which has governed population policies since the 1970s, assumes that societies eventually abandon the strategy of high fertility when mortality declines due to health improvements, and under the pressures of urbanization and modernization.The extended family begins to break up into nuclear components, and some couples leave for the towns. Individual wage labour replaces family-based production and instead of being an economic necessity, children become a 'cost'. Women may join the labour force, and receive an education beyond that needed for household management.

In these circumstances, marriage and childbearing may be postponed. Many developing countries are part way through the 'demographic transition': witness recent declines in fertility. Parts of any national population - better-educated and better-off urban dwellers - may adopt the norms of the industrialized world, including later marriage and child bearing. However, other groups may continue in the old patterns. Extended and nuclear families may exist side by side, even in the same generation.

Where average age of marriage appears to be rising, this may disguise the fact that very large sub-populations are still marrying very young. Old beliefs, customs and moral codes tend to persist during demographic transition, transition, while new circumstances make only gradual inroads into actual practice. The resilience of traditional practices and customs is illustrated by the situation of British girls from families of South Asian and Middle Eastern origin sent on a visit home', only to discover that they are to be forcibly married to a stranger.Since older women are more likely than men to be excluded from new ideas, they are often the last to abandon the ideas that framed their own lives.

Marriage patterns - alongside other aspects of family formation - are subject to acute 'development' pressures such as declining incomes from the land, rapid urbanization, population mobility, and the volatility of global markets, all of which are currently causing profound social upheaval and economic marginalization. The outcome for families is increasing fragmentation and the erosion of their extended structure. Families in the process of transition may, therefore, be caught between traditional and modern values. Men in search of work may join the individualist world in town; while the women they married in their teens, and their children, continue their traditional lives in the countryside. This pattern is particularly common in Sub-Saharan Africa.

Thus the impact of early marriage may be reinforced in the shorter term by the very process the world calls 'development'. In many countries, early marriage falls into what amounts to a sanctions limbo. It may be prohibited in the existing civil or common law, but be widely condoned by customary and religious laws and practice. This is common where marriages typically take place according to customary rites and remain unregistered. The situation is further complicated in countries where legislation was introduced by the colonizing power on the understanding that many customary practices would continue even if they were inconsistent with new laws. Some were even codified to make them legal.

In Beṇin, for example, Article 68 of the 1931 Coutumier du Dahomey' regulating customary marriage states that: "A marriage is not settled by the interested parties, but by their father, or in his absence by his older brother, or failing him, by the head of the family". In Suriname, the legal minimum age of marriage is 15 according to the Civil Code; but under the Asian

Marriage Act, which codifies practice for particular group, the minimum age for girls is 13. Although most countries have laws that regulate marriage, both in terms of minimum age and consent, these laws may not be applied and few prosecutions are ever brought against lawbreakers - parents, officiators or spouses.

Some laws do not prescribe sanctions; the only outcome of a case would be to declare the marriage invalid, leaving the wife without legal protection. Moreover, such laws usually do not apply to customary marriages. In some countries, the legal minimum age of marriage set for boys and girls is clearly aspirational. Thus, the minimum age in two countries with a high prevalence of HIV/AIDS - Uganda, where 50 per cent of girls aged 15-19 are married, and Zambia, where the figure is 27 per cent - has been set at 21 for both males and females.

In most cases where a minimum age is set, it is 18 or above for both males and females. In 15 countries, it is 16. A number of countries nonetheless allow marriages to take place at much younger ages with parental consent. In cases where there is a discrepancy between the minimum age of marriage for boys and girls, it is consistently lower for girls. However, at least 20 countries either do not have legislation to regulate marriage, or do not set any minimum age for either girls or boys.

There is considerable discrepancy between the legal age of marriage and the actual age of marriage for many girls. Indeed, in a number of countries, the average age at marriage is almost the same as, or even lower, than the legal age. In a few Afghanistan, Chad, Democratic Republic of Congo (DRC), Mozambique, Niger - the only reason that the average age is not lower than the legal age is because the latter is not set or is set very low. In DRC, for example, the average age at marriage is 16.6 and the legal minimum age is 15. The situation is exacerbated by the fact that birth registration is so irregular that age at marriage may not be known.

In addition, many marriages go unregistered; if there are problems in the marriage, the wife has no means of legal redress. Thus, the use of law as a means of regulating early marriage is in no way sufficient. This does not mean that legal reform should not be sought. The Indian Child Marriage Restraint Act, 1929 stemmed from a campaign that helped reposition women, family life, and childbearing within modern India.While the Act did not declare child marriages invalid, it helped pave the way for change. In 1978 it was strengthened to inhibit marriage of girls until the age of 18 and boys until age 21.

However, the number of prosecutions under the Act did not exceed 89 in any year between 1994 and 1998. Some governments have taken steps to unify their customary law and civil or common law, or have passed legislation designed to protect those in customary marriages: South Africa's Recognition of Customary Marriages Act of 1998 sets 18 as the minimum age for such unions and requires their registration. In keeping with the spirit of the CRC, an increasing number of laws fix the minimum age at 18 years - the standard also set by the 1990 African Charter on the Rights and Welfare of the Child and suggested by the CEDAW Committee in its general recommendation 21 and by the UN Special Rapporteur on Violence against Women.

This standard responds to the growing consensus that the period of adolescence needs special support and protection. The Inter-African Committee (IAC) on Traditional Practices Affecting the Health of Women and Children states that early marriage is: "Any marriage carried out below the age of 18 years, before the girl is physically, physiologically, and psychologically ready to shoulder the responsibilities of marriage and childbearing".

The more important practical issue is, therefore, whether or not the idea of consent is socially rated. Difficult questions arise around the age a child should be before he or she can 'consent' as a mature, cognisant and independent being to sexual relations or marriage, but where no clear consent has been given by one or other partner, the marriage is clearly forced.

In the case of marriages under the age of 10, consent - other than to dress up and play a game - is not a consideration. Toddlers married at Akha Teej ceremonies in Rajasthan cannot 'consent'. Nor is consent given in the cases of young girls from very poor homes in the Indian city of Hyderabad, Andhra Pradesh, sold as wives to rich men in the Middle East. In Gojam, Ethiopia, marriages may be imposed from birth, with the girl sent to her future husband's home at around the age of seven to begin her integration into her marriage family.

Here again, consent by the girl does not enter the picture. Similarly, in marriages at or around puberty - from roughly ages 10 to 14 - 'consent' cannot be said to have been given since, at such an early age, a child cannot be expected to understand the implications of accepting a lifetime partner. The question of marital consent becomes more difficult at age 15 or 16, by which stage a girl may have reached the legal age of sexual consent.

In the CEDAW Committee's recommendation that the minimum age for marriage of both men and women should be 18, it commented that, "When men and women marry, they assume important responsibilities. Consequently, marriage should not be permitted before they have attained full maturity and capacity to act. "The Committee also observed that, "Some countries provide for different ages for marriage for men and women. As such provisions assume incorrectly that women have a different rate of intellectual development from men, or that their stage of physical and intellectual development at marriage is immaterial, these provisions should be abolished."

It could be argued that even older children cannot be said to give informed consent to such a potentially damaging practice as early marriage. Beyond the issues of maturity and non-discrimination, any argument for a child's ability to consent to marriage is further undermined by the risk that marriage represents to his or her well-being. Many international bodiesconsider early marriage to be one of the "traditional practices prejudicial to the health of children" cited in article 24(3) of the Convention on the Rights of the Child.

In many countries a girl or boy may have reached the legal age of sexual consent at the age of 15 or 16, this should not be taken to mean that they are ready to enter marriage. A lack of legislative clarity over the different implications of consent to sexual activity and consent to marriage can result in strange anomalies.

In Maryland, USA, the state law defines statutory rape as sex with a child younger than 14 by someone four or more years older. However, another law allows children under 16 (with no minimum) to marry with proof of pregnancy and parental permission, and this provision is sometimes used - in one notorious case to allow a 29-year-old man to marry a 13-year-old girl. In 1997, the Committee on the Rights of the Child protested a similar situation in Algeria. Here, as in other countries such as Chad, Costa Rica, Lebanon, Libya, Romania and Uruguay, the law allows a perpetrator of rape, including statutory rape of a minor, to be excused of his crime if he marries his victim; a judge simply legitimizes the union.

This has also happened in California in cases of underage pregnancies where the man is willing to 'stand by' the girl. In effect, the state welfare agency supports what is seen as a viable partnership as an alternative to costly state care for mother and child. In a number of countries, it takes only the parents' consent to override the legal age of marriage - a judge is not required. In Colombia, the legal age is 18, but with parents' permission girls of 12 and boys of 14 can be married.

In the Dominican Republic there is no minimum age in exceptional circumstances and with parental consent.The UK Home Office Report into forced marriages of British girls of South Asian parentage distinguishes between 'forced' and 'arranged' marriages. In arranged marriages, the initiative is taken by the parents of the couple, but consent is required from both partners and either has the right to withdraw. However, the pressures from parents may be very high, and the younger the bride or groom the less real chance there is to exercise this right.

Both types of marriage indicate the degree to which many societies view marriage as a family affair in which the views of people other than the couple are given priority. Parents' views will override children's, and men's will override women's -even taking precedence over the law. In Pakistan, the Commission on the Status of Women reported in 1989: "Men are constantly fighting to retrieve their women because they have run away". There are reports of young wives being locked up by their husbands in India, and in Zimbabwe it is often forbidden for a young bride to visit her own family until she goes there to give birth to her first child.

In one tragic case in Nigeria, a 12-year-old girl unhappy with her new husband ran away so often that he cut off her legs to prevent her absconding. She subsequently died. The CRC Committee has focused on laws and customs in its observations to a number of countries. Its most common complaints are low minimum age for girls and disparate - therefore discriminatory - marriage ages for girls and boys.

Impact of Child Marriage on Society

Young girls may endure misery as a result of early marriage and the number of those who would seek help, if they thought it existed, is impossible to calculate. Until more is known about their situation there can be no reliable estimates of the scale of their predicament, or of the social damage that is carried forward in the upbringing they give to their own children. One thing is clear: the impact of early marriage on girls - and to a lesser extent on boys - is wide-ranging.

Within a rights perspective, three key concerns are the denial of childhood and adolescence, the curtailment of personal freedom and the lack of opportunity to develop a full sense of selfhood as well as the denial of psychosocial and emotional well-being, reproductive health and educational opportunity. Early marriage also has implications for the well-being of families, and for society as a whole. Where girls are uneducated and ill-prepared for their roles as mothers and contributors to society, there are costs to be borne at every level, from the individual household to the nation as a whole.

The loss of adolescence, the forced sexual relations, and the denial of freedom and personal development attendant on early marriage have profound psychosocial and emotional consequences. The impact can be subtle and insidious and the damage hard to assess. It includes such intangible factors as the effect of a girl's loss of mobility and her confinement to the home and to household roles. Obviously there is a marked lack of data in these areas, and social researchers have failed to examine the impacts of early marriage in this context.

Most girls who are unhappy in an imposed marriage are very isolated. They have nobody to talk to as they are surrounded by people who endorse their situation. In Ethiopia, Inter-African Committee researchers were struck by the lack of interest from elders in the traumas suffered by young girls as a result of early marriages, premature sex and childbearing. These traumas were regarded as an "unavoidable part of life". Girls who run home to their parents may be beaten and sent back to their husbands. Distress is generally endured in silence.

Indian researchers on child marriage in Rajasthan and Madhya Pradesh state that girl spouses suffer more than boys: "Inadequate socialization, discontinuation of education, great physiological and emotional damage due to repeated pregnancies devastates these girls." If the husband dies, even before consummation, the girl is treated as a widow and given in nata to a widower in the family. Officially she is then his wife, but in fact under the practice of nata she becomes the common property of all the men in the family.

The child bride who is widowed very young can suffer additional discrimination. Widows suffer loss of status and they, along with their children, are often denied property rights, and a range of other human rights. In parts of Africa, a widow is remarried to a brother-in-law, a custom known as levirate, originally intended, in part, to provide economic and social support. If the widow resists, she may be cast out by the family. Child widows with little education and no means of earning are especially powerless.

At a 1994 Conference in Bangalore, India, participants told of being married at five and six years old, widowed a few years later, and rejected by their in-laws and their own families. These widows are, quite simply, left with no resources and nowhere to go. The notion of good reproductive health covers all aspects of the reproduction process - including a satisfying and safe experience of sexual relations, the capability to reproduce, and the freedom to decide if and when to bear a child.

The right not to engage in sexual relations and the right to exercise control over reproduction may both be violated by early marriage. In the case of girls married before puberty, the normal understanding between families is that there will be no sexual intercourse until first menstruation. In Gojam, Ethiopia, husband and wife may grow up playing together in the house of his parents. In this case, the mother-in-law must protect the girl from any advances by her son. This is also true in West African countries. However, this protection may fail, especially where the husband is much older than the girl.

Cases of forced intercourse by much older and physically fully developed husbands with wives as young as eight have been reported.For the vast majority of under-educated rural adolescent girls in the developing world, marriage remains the likely context for sexual intercourse. And while an unmarried teenage girl may find it difficult to resist unwanted sexual advances, her married sister may find it impossible.

Researchers have tended to focus on adolescent sexuality outside marriage, or have made no distinction between married and unmarried adolescents. This means that there are only limited data about sexual experience among married adolescents; the assumption prevails that sex within marriage is a priori consensual.

A 1997 study among women in Calcutta found that half had been married at or below the age of 15, and that this group were highly vulnerable to sexual violence in marriage. In 80 per cent of cases where these young wives informed their husbands of their unwillingness to endure sexual violence, they were ignored. Pain and trauma are enhanced where girls have undergone some form of FGM, especially where this has been undertaken recently, and especially in the case of infibulation which is designed to make penetration difficult.

Problems may be exacerbated after childbirth. In many societies, and in many millions of individual cases, women have no choice but to resume sexual relations within two or three days of childbirth, even if there has been vaginal cutting during delivery, and regardless of the pain it causes. Access to contraception and reproductive health advice Very few girls in early marriages in developing countries have access to contraception; nor would delayed pregnancy necessarily be acceptable to many husbands and in-laws.

Indeed, in many societies, childbearing soon after marriage is integral to a woman's social status. In Yemen, 11 per cent of wives aged 15-29 stated that they did not use contraception because of their husbands' opposition.In almost all Asian countries the family exerts strong pressure on the newly-married couple to begin childbearing quickly. In Cameroon, Mali and Nigeria, the modern contraceptive usage rates among married 15-19 year olds are only 1.5, 2.4 and 0.6 per cent respectively.

The girls' right to have any say over when and if they should become pregnant is unacknowledged, and their chances of early pregnancy are high. Analysis of DHS data indicates that the first birth usually occurs within 14-26 months of marriage, although it may be slightly longer where age of marriage is very low, as in Bangladesh. Teenage girls are also more susceptible than more mature women to sexually transmitted infections (STIs), including HIV. This is the result of both biological factors, such as hormonal fluctuations and the permeability of vaginal tissue, and social factors, such as skewed power relations between women and men that make it difficult for girls and young women to negotiate safe sex.

STIs can lead to infertility, and in the case of HIV, the outcome is premature mortality and risks of transmission to the foetus. In a recent study in Rwanda, 25 per cent of girls who became pregnant at 17 or younger were infected with HIV, although many reported having sex only with their husbands. According to the study, the younger the age at sexual intercourse published in 1990, one-third of young adults between ages 16 and 24 did not know the duration of a normal pregnancy. Less than 5 per cent had discussed reproductive health with their parents.

There are still a number of countries where reproductive health services are barred to adolescents, or require them to have reached a certain age.This excludes many married adolescents in countries such as Zambia or Bangladesh where age limits are in force - another of the anomalies surrounding early marriage. The risks of early pregnancy and childbirth are well documented: increased risk of dying, increased risk of premature labour, complications during delivery, low birth-weight, and a higher chance that the newborn will not survive.

Pregnancy-related deaths are the leading cause of mortality for 15-19 year-old girls (married and unmarried) worldwide. Mothers in this age group face a 20 to 200 per cent greater chance of dying in pregnancy than women aged 20 to 24. Those under age 15 are five times as likely to die as women in their twenties. The main causes are haemorrhage, sepsis, preeclampsia/ eclampsia and obstructed labour. Unsafe abortion is the other major risk for teenage women - most of those affected are unmarried.

Some specific local studies show worse outcomes for the very young mother: in Zaria, Nigeria, maternal mortality among women younger than 16 was found to be six times higher than for women aged 20-24, and similar findings have been reported from Cameroon and Ethiopia. For every woman who dies in childbirth, 30 more suffer injuries, infections and disabilities, which usually go untreated and some of which are lifelong. Part of this heavy toll has more to do with poor socio-economic status and lack of ante-natal and obstetric care than physical maturity alone.

However, physical immaturity is the key risk for the under 15s. High rates of Vesico-Vaginal Fistula (VVF) are clearly identified with marriage and childbearing in the 10-15 year-old age group; in one study in Niger, 88 per cent of women with fistula were in this age group at marriage. Mothers whose pelvis and birth canal are not fully developed often endure very prolonged labour.

Unless the mother receives emergency obstetric care, relentless pressure from the baby's skull can damage the birth canal, causing breakages in the wall, allowing uncontrollable leakage from the bladder into the vagina. The same problem may also occur in relation to the rectum, with leakage of faeces. Fistula conditions are permanent without surgical intervention to re-seal the tissues, such intervention may not be sought or may be hard to access. There is some evidence from Nigeria that FGM practices that damage the vagina may also increase the likelihood of VVF.

The prevalence of VVF/RVF is not fully known, but WHO estimates that there are two million women living with fistulas and an additional 50,000-100,000 new cases every year, many of which go untreated.A girl with the condition is usually ostracized as unclean, and is often divorced. In Nigeria, where the condition affects around 150,000 women, 80-90 per cent of wives with VVF are divorced by their husbands; in Niger VVF is the reason for 63.3 per cent of all divorces. Infant and early childhood care

The health problems linked to early marriage not only affect the pregnant mother and the foetus, but also continue after childbirth. Evidence shows that infant mortality among the children of very young mothers is higher - sometimes two times higher - than among those of older peers.A stronger likelihood of low birth-weight in the infant has been recorded among adolescent mothers than among older peers. This is mainly associated with poor maternal nutrition, reinforcing the point that adolescents are 'unready' for childbirth.

Low birth-weight babies are 5-30 times more likely to die than babies of normal weight. If a mother is under 18, her baby's chance of dying in the first year of life is 60 per cent higher than that of a baby born to a mother older than 19.A 1993 survey among women married young in Rajasthan found that 63 per cent of their children under four were severely malnourished. The immaturity and lack of education of a young mother undermines her capacity for nurture. Even children are able to work this out: it was one reason given by Nepali children for avoiding early marriage, as shown by Save the Children research.

Finally, early marriage extends a woman's potential childbearing capacity, which itself represents a risk to mothers. Not until the 'demographic transition' is relatively advanced, child survival adequately assured, and education valued, do families see the births of many children as a drain on resources rather than an asset. Until that time, women are under pressure to produce large numbers of children.

Population and family planning policies since the 1970s have tried to reduce large family size, focusing on the social, economic and environmental costs to countries that lack the resources to ensure a good quality of life for their rapidly growing populations. In this light, early marriage marriage can be said to have profound social and economic consequences for society as a whole. These consequences are reinforced by the fact that the children of young and illiterate mothers tend to face the same cycle of childhood deprivation and damage experienced by their mothers.

Early marriage inevitably denies children of school age their right to the education they need for their personal development, their preparation for adulthood, and their effective contribution to the future wellbeing of their family and society. Indeed, married girls who would like to continue schooling may be both practically and legally excluded from doing so. The interaction between the number of years of a girl's schooling and the postponement of marriage is firmly established by demographic and fertility studies.

On average, women with seven or more years of education marry four years later and have 2.2 fewer children than those with no education. However, the precise nature of the interaction between education and marriage is not always evident. The situation in Bangladesh, however, is clear - a girl will be withdrawn from school if a good marriage prospect arises. DHS data also show a clear link in some other countries, including Nepal, Kazakhstan and Indonesia.

Although attitudes towards the education of girls have begun to change even in traditional societies, many parents still believe that investment in a girl's education is wasted when she is simply going to be married and work in another household. The costs of the investment in education reinforce the impetus towards the girl's withdrawal from school. In rural areas, secondary education often means that a girl must leave home to live in a school dormitory. Parents fear that this may expose her to risks including premarital sex and pregnancy.

In Northern Nigeria, for example, girls are often kept out of school for this very reason. Even where girls can live at home while attending school, fears about their possible sexual activity, about sexual harassment, or about insecurity on the journey to and from school, discourage their attendance. The removal from school of a young girl to marry, or to work in her parents' or another household in preparation for married life, limits her opportunities to develop her intellect.

She also loses out on socializing, making friends outside her family circle, and many other useful skills. This reduces her chances of developing her own independent identity. Indeed, in the old patriarchal view this is an important reason for taking her away. The most important implication of this loss is that the girl grows up with no sense of the right to assert her own point of view and little experience in articulating one.

Lack of self-esteem or of a sense of ownership of her own body expose a woman to unwanted pregnancy and make her vulnerable to HIV infection. A typically submissive wife in, for example, Eastern Africa is not in a position to refuse sex to her husband, even if he has other sexual partners and she suspects that he may be infected with HIV. A woman has the right to refuse sex in any circumstances, but few young brides will ever gain enough self-confidence or self-esteem during the course of their marriage to assert such a right.

Lack of schooling also means that those girls and women who must work to earn a living have no qualifications or skills. Illiterate women who are abandoned, widowed or divorced, or who are victims of growing urban poverty, are forced into commercialized versions of their work as wives: cleaning, cooking, child-minding. They may even enter the commercial sex trade. In many Latin American countries (and elsewhere), there is a strong link between very poor, women-headed households in urban areas and menial occupations an association that will only diminish when educational levels are raised.

But work itself can have a positive impact on delaying marriage. A study in Penang Island, Malaysia, found that those women who worked before marriage tended to marry almost 2.5 years later than those who had never worked at all. Where work and education opportunities have opened up for women, this has had the effect of encouraging parents' support for their daughters' education.

Increased enrolment of girls in school and higher levels of educational completion have been conclusively shown to produce improvements in family well-being, increased use of contraception, reduced infant mortality and economic advantages for society. Marriage age is part of a wider picture of interaction between economic advance and increased participation of women in education.

The UK working group on forced marriage found that many of the victims of this practice suffered from prolonged domestic violence, but felt unable to leave the marriage because of economic pressures, lack of family support and other social circumstances. Many cases of selfharm and suicide among British women of South Asian origin were thought to be linked to forced marriage.

If a woman did feel able to challenge the situation, it often took her years to do so. If this is happening in a society where forced marriage is not the norm, it is safe to assume that such a challenge is far less likely from a girl in an environment where early and forced marriages are commonplace. Most available information on violent abuse is anecdotal, consisting of interviews with girls who have suffered trauma as a result of their marriages.

Some girls in brutal marriages become desperate enough to run away.Those who do so, and those who choose a marriage partner against the wishes of their parents, may be punished, or even killed by their family. These girls run the risk of the socalled 'honour killings' that occur in Bangladesh, Egypt, Jordan, Lebanon, Pakistan, Turkey and elsewhere.Early marriage is often linked to wife abandonment, as shown by its association with divorce and separation. Violent behaviour towards a wife, including coercive sex, plays a major role in marital breakdown.

In Java, it has been found that girls who marry early are three times more likely to be divorced than those married later. A study in Calcutta found that sexual violence in marriage is associated with a greater likelihood of separation than physical violence alone. Divorce or abandonment often plunges a woman into poverty, as she usually assumes sole responsibility for dependent children. If she married young, is under-educated and has few income-generating skills, her poverty may be acute.

Studies of young mothers in Latin America and the Caribbean found that they are more likely to be disadvantaged later in life; in Mexico they are six times more likely to be living in poverty than those who postponed childbearing. Thus early marriage contributes to the 'feminization of poverty' and its resulting impact on children.

Preventing Child Marriage

A range of policy and programmatic actions are needed to reduce early marriage and its impact. Actions to fulfil or restore the rights of those already married should go hand in hand with preventive actions aimed at wider society. In either case, the aim should be to inform parents and young people currently complicit in the practice of early marriage so that they are aware of its true implications and empowered to resist it. The role of government and civil society institutions is to develop and implement suitable systems to prevent or discourage the practice.

While the main actors helping those directly affected will operate at household and community level, the involvement of national and international policy-makers and rights advocates is essential in order to change the policy and programme climate. Over the entire action spectrum, a wide variety of actors must be engaged, including teenagers themselves, adult women and men, community leaders, politicians, policy-makers, academics, researchers, lawyers, the media, and national and international non-governmental and intergovernmental bodies. While prevention measures are essential, efforts must be made to ensure that all of the following interventions are available to married, as well as unmarried girls.

This is primarily intended to maintain sexual and reproductive health, starting by ensuring that both girls and boys learn about sex, reproduction and the related risks at an early age. Information should replace 'ignorance plus early marriage' as the child sexual protection strategy. Proposals that adolescents - male and female - should be given sex education and have access to reproductive health services, have often been greeted with resistance. In a number of African and Asian cultures, there is reticence about, or an actual taboo on, the discussion of sex. This feeds fears that sex education will encourage early sexual relations and pregnancy.

The key to girls' progress is education and learning. Persuading parents to keep their daughters in school and ensuring that they receive a basic education, as is their right, is important for a number of personal and family, as well as wider social and economic, reasons including postponement of marriage. Both Sri Lanka and the state of Kerala in neighbouring India have relatively high age of first marriage. They also have something else in common that has contributed to this phenomenon: both have given high priority to education for women as well as men.

This has changed the way men and women perceive their roles and potential, and has led to greater support for the rights of women than is found in many other parts of this region. Where girls have lost out on formal education, non-formal programmes can help them catch up on the intellectual and personal growth offered by schooling. Such programmes can have a direct impact on early marriage: a programme from the 1990s among the people of the Samburu district in Kenya led to a fall in early marriage and helped women assert themselves.While there has been a recent drive to increase participation of girls in basic education, the more significant gender gap is at the secondary level.

Throughout the developing world, with the exception of Latin America and the Philippines, boys have higher rates of secondary school enrolment. The decline of girls' enrolment and attendance after age 12-13 is most marked in sub-Saharan Africa. In Tanzania, for example, enrolment of girls and boys is equal at age 12-13 but by the age of 16-17 girls' attendance is only 71 per cent of boys'. Attempts to close gender gaps in education have included approaches to make schools more girl-friendly. These include building schools close to communities so that parents are less worried about their daughters' safety; employing more female teachers; improving the relevance of the curriculum and the quality of teaching; flexible schedules to allow girls to meet domestic responsibilities; in-school childcare facilities; penalties for male teachers who seduce girl students; and separate sanitary facilities for boys and girls.

Other strategies to increase girls' schooling include cash incentives for parents to keep their daughters in school; the expansion of non-formal education for girls who have left school; the involvement of communities in running schools; and conducting communication campaigns on the importance of girls' education. Where such efforts are made, resistance to girls' education can crumble surprisingly easily, even in highly traditional environments.

2

Impact of Abuse and Neglect

Children are usually not recognized as subjects of human rights and adults can place arbitrary limits on children's fundamental freedoms. Teachers and principals, for example, have broad discretionary powers and can restrict students' freedoms with little, if any, accountability. There are few redress mechanisms available to children. Most of the restrictions that children face on a daily basis are not entrenched in law but are part of school policies or are rules of the family.

In these situations, children's fundamental freedoms are very dependent on the good will of adults. In Canada, as in all countries of the world, some children are particularly vulnerable. Aboriginal children, children with disabilities, abused and neglected children and refugee children were found to be particularly at risk.

Aboriginal Canadians have a disability rate that is more than twice the national average. Aboriginal children are at a greater risk of school failure than other Canadian children. A disproportionate number of Aboriginal children are victims of abuse and neglect in comparison to non-Aboriginal children. The suicide rate among Aboriginal youth is about five times the national rate. Many aboriginal children live in poverty.

An estimated 535,000 children and youth under age 20 have some form of disability. Children with disabilities have varying opportunities to live "full and decent lives" and the supports and services they need are not considered an entitlement but a privilege.

Many families of children with disabilities do not receive adequate assistance. Early identification and intervention services are not universally available and the right to appropriate education in the most enabling environment is not guaranteed. Abused and neglected children continue to fall through the cracks in our child welfare systems.

Inquests and inquiries into the deaths of children who were killed by their parents speak of inadequate risk assessments, insufficient training for social workers, a lack of service coordination and information sharing, a shortage of placement facilities, failed foster placements, a crisis orientation, and the lack of long-term planning for children who are in the care of the state.

Generally, Canada does not grant asylum to overseas refugees who might be expected to cause excessive demands on health or social services. Child refugees who arrive in Canada can be detained and there are no detention standards. The refugee determination system is slow and the long wait unduly prolongs uncertainty in the lives of children and their families. Family reunification is rarely dealt with in a positive and expeditious manner. The interests of children are not taken into account in decisions to deport their parents.

Article 19 requires countries to take broad measures to protect children from maltreatment, including violence, abuse and neglect. In Canada, provincial and territorial child welfare systems are responsible for child protection. Child welfare legislation recognizes that families are primarily responsible for the care, supervision and protection of their children but when a child is at risk, the government has the duty to intervene to protect the child.

Child protection services investigate cases of suspected abuse and neglect and, depending on the circumstances, can elect to provide support services to a family or remove the child from the family home. Removing a child from the family home is referred to as "taking a child into care." Canadian legislation allows parents, teachers and persons "standing in the place of a parent" to use corporal punishment against children, even though physical punishment has been strongly linked to physical abuse.

In fact, one Ontario study found problems with punishment or discipline to be a factor in 72 percent of substantiated physical abuse cases. Section 43 of the Criminal Code allows "reasonable force" to be used against children and this provision has been used to justify a child being punched in the face or pushed down a flight of stairs.

In Canada, children are the only category of persons who can be subject to physical assault without due process. Canada has no national statistics on the number of children who are reported to child protection authorities because provincial and territorial child welfare systems collect and report data in different ways.

The federal government is working with the provinces and territories to begin collecting and analyzing data on reported cases of child abuse and neglect. Recent inquests and child death reviews have publicized tragic failures of child welfare systems and hundreds of recommendations for improvement have been made over the past few years. As a result, some Canadian child protection systems are broadening the grounds for finding a child in need of protection and developing tools to systematically assess levels of risk.

Systems are also trying to improve case management and information sharing within and across jurisdictions. Other ongoing child welfare reforms include workload standards and better training for child protection workers and the education of professionals and the public about the obligation to report suspected child maltreatment. Most of these reforms require increased funding and there are indications that some jurisdictions are starting to restore budgets so that child welfare systems can better deal with their ever-increasing caseloads.

But investigating, treating and preventing child abuse and neglect are complex social issues requiring a broad community response. It remains to be seen whether the current round of child welfare reforms will result in better protection for children, real help for families in crisis and effective treatment for the victims of violence, abuse and neglect. There has long been a link of abuse and neglect with poverty, especially in cases involving neglect.

Canada has had little success in reducing child poverty and child welfare workers have few, if any, tools to help families deal with this serious and persistent problem. Poverty and despair provide a fertile soil for child abuse and neglect and the social problems suffered by families across the country tend to be even more concentrated in Aboriginal communities. The destruction of native social systems by the mainstream society has left many Aboriginal children vulnerable and many Aboriginal communities mistrustful of child welfare interventions.

Canada has made little progress in improving the outcomes for Aboriginal children. For example, an Ontario review found that Aboriginal children receive the lowest level of child welfare services. In Manitoba, Aboriginal children represent 10 percent of the province's child population but 67 percent of children in care. Canadian jurisdictions are working towards the transfer of child welfare services to Aboriginal agencies.

However, these Aboriginal agencies and communities are struggling with overwhelming demand and a limited supply of culturally appropriate early intervention and treatment services. Article 23 recognizes that children with disabilities have the right to enjoy full and decent lives. They are entitled to special care, assistance and effective services, including education, training, health care, rehabilitation, preparation for employment and recreation opportunities. This assistance is to be provided free of charge, whenever possible, considering the financial resources of the parents or others caring for the child.

In Canada, an estimated 535,000 children and youth under age 20 have some form of disability. Aboriginal Canadians have a disability rate that is more than twice the national average. Surveys indicate that learning disabilities are the most common long-term condition. Almost 46 percent of children younger than 15 years of age with a disability have a disability that limits or prevents participation in school, play or other pursuits; almost 18 percent use a technical aid, such as a hearing aid, medically prescribed footwear or a brace.

The number of children with disabilities continues to increase as medical advances significantly improve survival rates. There is insufficient funding for the early diagnosis of children with disabilities and appropriate programs and services, such as child care, early education and early intervention. These services are often treated as discretionary expenditures, rather than as rights, and are subject to elimination or cutbacks during times of fiscal restraint. While the Canada Health Act ensures free, universal health care, related expenses such as prescription drugs are not covered under the Act.

Rehabilitation supports and specialized equipment such as leg braces and hearing aids are only partially covered, if at all. There are often long waiting lists for health services that can lead to early diagnoses and appropriate therapeutic interventions. There are wide variations in the provision of services across Canada, often within provinces, and services may be subject to a means test.

There has been a shift in recent years away from institutional care to providing services in the community. This has led to a growing number of children with disabilities living at home with their families. These families may require professional home care, respite care, income supports, child care and enhanced parental leave.

Often, families do not receive adequate assistance and frequently find themselves financially, physically and emotionally exhausted by efforts to care for their children. All children in Canada aged five, six or seven (depending on the jurisdiction) to age 16 are required to attend school. For children with disabilities, however, the right to appropriate education in the most enabling environment is not guaranteed.

Children in Canada, including those with disabilities, do not have a right to early education (preschool). Although every province and territory has a stated commitment to integrated, inclusive education, this commitment is not clearly operationalized in most jurisdictions. Inclusion in regular classes appears to be more successful for students with physical disabilities than for those with multiple, developmental or emotional disabilities.

Although early education can enhance the physical, emotional and cognitive development of children, few preschool children with disabilities have access to free, suitable early education. Increased demand coupled with cutbacks to education budgets have resulted in inappropriate educational services for students with special needs. There are variations in the services available in communities and provinces, due to variations in regulations and budgets.

Particularly limited are support services (such as teaching assistants and consultative supports), training in inclusionary educational strategies and rehabilitation services (such as physiotherapy, occupational therapy and speech therapy). Public recreation and play activities are usually delivered by municipal governments and these programs are often inaccessible to children with special needs.

There are no accessibility standards for children's play spaces in Canada. A survey of youth with disabilities indicated that cost and lack of opportunities were the most common obstacles to their participation in leisure activities. Governments fund occupational training opportunities for youth with disabilities, but only 48 percent of working-age Canadians with disabilities are in the paid labour force, compared with 73 percent of persons without disabilities.

Discrimination against persons on the basis of disability is prohibited by federal and provincial legislation but people with disabilities, and children in particular, still experience prejudice. Young people with disabilities experience more abuse and violence than the non-disabled. In addition, many disability issues are examined from the adult perspective and the special needs of children are often overlooked.

For example, provincial building codes include accessibility standards but are not designed with children in mind. The few complaint mechanisms that are available to children and youth tend to be difficult to access. Negative assumptions about the quality of life enjoyed by persons with disabilities undermine respect for their fundamental rights.

Article 22 requires countries to take appropriate measures to ensure that a child who is seeking refugee status or who is considered a refugee under international or domestic law, whether unaccompanied or accompanied by an adult, receives appropriate protection and humanitarian assistance as determined by international human rights instruments, including the Convention on the Rights of the Child. Appropriate measures include tracing family members and family reunification.

Canada selects large numbers of refugees from overseas for resettlement in Canada, compared with other countries. Canadian authorities occasionally select unaccompanied children for resettlement. Refugees selected from overseas are judged according to estimations of their ability to be financially self-sufficient within a year and whether they would make excessive demands on health or social services.

When a child is accepted as an unaccompanied refugee, however, there is no expectation that the child will be self-supporting. Refugee status can be claimed in Canada at the border or from within the country. Children can also make their own claims in this way. Unlike overseas applicants, a refugee claimant within Canada does not need to be medically admissible, establish an ability to be self-supporting or have any settlement arrangements. Any claim with a minimum credible basis for refugee status must be heard by the Immigration and Refugee Board.

The Immigration Act does not detail specific procedures for dealing with the claims of children, except to designate an adult to represent the child in hearings. There are federal guidelines, however, for processing the claims of unaccompanied children and for eliciting evidence from all child claimants. The guidelines' general principle is the best interests of the child. Best interests are defined broadly and can vary according to the circumstances of each case and the child's age, gender, cultural background and past experiences.

It takes an average of 13 months to determine an inland refugee claim. This is an extraordinarily long period of time from a child's perspective. Canada has one of the highest acceptance rates for refugee claimants among industrialized countries, but this rate has decreased from 62 percent in 1994-95 to 41 percent in 1996-97. If the Refugee Board determines that the claimant is a Convention refugee, then the claimant may apply to become a permanent resident of Canada.

The Auditor General has found major variations in the acceptance rates of claimants from the same country. If the Refugee Board denies a claim, there is no appeal. When a decision is made to deport a parent, the best interests of their children do not have to be considered, even if the children were born in Canada or have lived in Canada for a long period of time. However, the Supreme Court of Canada recently questioned that practice.

It is believed that few children are detained by immigration officials but no information is available. Children can stay with a detained parent if the family wishes to stay together. However, there are no standards for the conditions in which children are held. The Canadian Charter of Rights and Freedoms applies to refugee claimants. Claimants are eligible for health care under provincial or territorial plans or through the federal interim program.

All children from age five, six or seven (depending on the jurisdiction) to age 16 are obligated to attend school although immigration lawyers have reported delays in the issuing of student authorization papers. Settlement services are primarily delivered by non-profit, non-governmental organizations in communities across the country. Many of these organizations receive federal funding. National standards for the quality and quantity of settlement services are needed.

Government-sponsored refugees are eligible for financial assistance to cover accommodation, clothing, household effects and living expenses for up to one year. Unsponsored refugees are eligible for assistance through provincial and territorial social assistance programs. Families cannot come to Canada and refugees cannot travel out of Canada until their claims have been accepted. This includes parents who left young children behind.

For refugees who arrive in Canada without identity papers, family reunification can take longer than seven years. Family reunification can also be delayed by the inability to pay the $975 charged for every adult refugee applying for permanent residence.

Role of Media

The media play a powerful role in children's lives, and every day the media are sending important messages to kids. Television shouldn't be a scapegoat for the problems we face, but it should be part of the solution. For these reasons, we were pleased to gather many of the country's top entertainment industry producers and executives, along with leading academics, advocates and children's experts, to explore a number of important issues:

— What role can and do the media play in helping children develop a sound sense of values to prepare them for the many difficult choices they need to make in the years ahead?

— What can be done to ameliorate the negative messages many children may currently be receiving through the media?

— What steps can be taken to promote tolerance and respect by improving the quality of portrayals of women and minorities on programming watched by children?

Children grow up learning some unusual lessons from TV: karate chops and trickery can get you what you want; most people stick with their own ethnic group; it's okay for superheroes to kill off their enemies; sex is far more common than abstinence; and it's funny, not bad, to disobey your parents. At a time when most Americans believe we are facing a "crisis in values" in this country, are these really the messages we want TV to send our children? Even most kids say no.

Television has become today's storyteller. The problem is, there are too few morals to its tales. Even kids sorely miss them—eight out of ten kids polled said television should teach them right from wrong. And they should know. By age 18, the average child will have watched 22,000 hours of TV - more time in front of the tube than in the classroom. Children Now's survey showed that two-thirds of kids live in households with three or more sets; over half have a TV in their bedroom and usually watch TV without their parents. When it tries, TV can teach values such as tolerance and kindness and still remain entertaining.

The need for TV to fill this role has never been greater. The splintering of families, the decline in organized religion, and the disarray of public schools have left many young people feeling less connected than ever. The anchor they really need, many argue, is a shared code of universal values. While some in the industry deny responsibility, others are beginning to embrace it.

All of the broadcast networks have special standards for children's programmes, but the problem is that most kids watch adult TV, including nighttime soaps heavy on sex and violence. In the 94-95 season, nine out of the top ten shows watched by kids 2 to 11 ran in prime time. So while executives acknowledge that kids need special standards, most shows kids watch don't meet them. This disconnect has yet to be addressed.

Network executives argue that if parents don't like what their kids are watching, all they have to do is turn off the television. What drives those TV shows is not good taste, or what's good for kids, it's popularity.

Studies show that girls who are frequent viewers have the most negative opinion of their gender. Even preschool girls suffer from TV's sex stereotyping. Action-packed shows geared to younger kids have the fewest girl characters -- one out of four -- with girls less aggressive and combative than boys, unless they are evil witches. And these shows can erode girls' self-confidence. One study of 3 to 10 year olds found that those who watched the most TV were most likely to want to be housewives and nurses. In another study, three to six year olds agreed that men have more ambition and that women are happier raising kids. Yet, on the rare occasion when TV has been used to break down sex stereotypes, it's been successful.

TV is still black and white when it comes to portraying minorities. The number of African Americans on TV has increased substantially, but prime time may be one of the most segregated places in America, with most shows cast in all black or all white. The networks and other programmers have made some significant changes. The number of African American roles -- as doctors, lawyers, judges, and police lieutenants — has risen dramatically. Children in the United States have a high media IQ — and they are deeply affected by how and where the news is presented. Indeed, a significant number of children say the news media makes them feel sad, angry or depressed.

The news media help shape kids' perceptions of the world, and the world's perception of kids. Children are widely exposed to the news media. Children see a negative image of themselves in the news. Negative news has a real impact on children. More than half of all kids reported feeling angry, sad or depressed after watching the news.

Children long for more positive news about themselves. Children believe the news media can help. They are well-connected to the news media. Children see a negative image of themselves in the news. They get negative feelings from the news. While the media gets pretty good marks in general for its coverage of world events, crime, the economy and AIDS, when the subject is closer to home for children the news media fares far less well.

Children think the news is missing their stories. Children express a general feeling that the media does not understand people their age. Society's troubles are the same for children. Violence, crime and drugs dominate the concerns of kids. Children generally do not believe crime is over-sensationalized in the news — they think the media covers what it should. African-American children are very critical of the way they feel their ethnic group is presented in the news.

By the time a child today graduates from high school, he or she will have spent more time in front of a television set than in a classroom. One of the things kids often see on television is a reflection of themselves: images of children, as interpreted by the entertainment industry. How children see people their age portrayed on television is important.

Television's images help shape how young people view themselves and their place in the world around them: TV can expand a child's aspirations, or it can limit her horizons; it can teach him what is important or unimportant; what is to be valued and what is to be shunted aside. The picture television paints of kids also affects overall public perceptions about children and the validity and importance we attach to their concerns.

It is for these reasons that we set out to explore how children are portrayed on entertainment television. Children shown on entertainment television are motivated most often by peer relationships and romance, and least often by school-related or religious issues. One study found that in almost twice as many instances, children on television are motivated by romance rather than school-related issues.

Entertainment television almost never shows children grappling with important issues. While many children in the real world are forced to deal with increasingly difficult family and societal problems, their entertainment-television counterparts are leading much simpler lives.

We don't usually think of television as an educator for our children. We think of their most formative experiences as coming from our families, schools, churches, community groups, andpersonal relationsbips formed with parents, relatives, siblings, friends, classmates, and others. But our children are growing up in an age of media-TV, movies, video games, and now, computers and the Internet.

One journalist said that TV has become "the loudest voice in many American households." According to a recent book, teenagers are becoming "screen-agers, receiving most of their information from TV and computer screens. Most children spend more time with media than in school and much more time with media than in meaningful conversation with their parents. Recent research demonstrates how the mediaform powerful influences on our children's development--on their behaviours, attitudes, language, and values, from their earliest ages.

American children watch an average of 3 and 1/2 hours of TV each day, or 24 hours per week. Toddlers start watching TV at the age of two and, in some cases, as young as 18 months. By the time children graduate from high school, they have spent 18,000 hours in front of a TV set, and only 13,000 hours in a classroom.

There is a lot that is positive about TV, but heavy viewing of television places our children at risk of exposure to graphic violence, sexual portrayals, commercialism, racial and gender stereotyping, and vulgar language. An American child watching the average amount of TV will also see: 100,000 acts of TV violence, including 8,000 murders, by the time she reaches the 6th grade; and 20,000 TV commercials each year.

To many parents, these figures seem impossible. But they add up quickly: two TV murders and 60 commercials a day are easily seen in just a few hours of viewing. Busy parents are looking for ways to deal with this media onslaught and with their children's TV viewing habits. Armed with an awareness of TV's influence and a commitment to take TV seriously, many families are finding ways to use TV to promote family interaction and communicate important lessons.

How to Talk with Your Kids About TV

1. Start early in talking with your kids about the TV, movies and other media they use

For parents of preschoolers, get in the habit of talking about TV-about how much to watch and what to watch. Just as with other topics of sexuality, drugs, or violence, it's never too early to start talking with your children about TV, movies, and other media. Don't ignore what your children are watching, believing that "it is just TV," "it goes over their heads," or that TV can't possibly influence their knowledge, behaviors and attitudes.

When you see something on TV that you consider in appropriate, let your children know why. It is important that you discuss programs that glorify violence or send irresponsible messages about sexual behavior or reinforce gender and racial stereotypes. Many parents have walked into the TV room just in time to see their children watching sitcom characters joking about a "one night stand," or a drama about teenage pregnancy.

Children are often exposed to these storylines before parents are ready to raise these subjects with them. Parents, feeling awkward, often switch the channel or cover their children's eyes. Consider how the sexual stories on TV may compete with your efforts to guide your child's sex education by showing confusing, mistaken, or damaging information. Think also about how storytines or situations on television can be used to enrich your conversations with your child.

Parents may want to use references to pregnancy or AIDS to deliver accurate information. Also take advantage of "socially responsible" storylines found in many TV programmes to stimulate a discussion with your child. Parents should strive to open the door for their children to ask questions about what they've seen on TV. And as adults, don't be afraid to initiate the conversation by asking questions like - "What did you think about what you saw in that show?" It could lead to an important conversation about sex, love, and relationships.

2. ***Put your family on a Family TV Diet.***

Think about TV consumption much in the same way as you approach making healthy meals for your children. The first step is to bring total TV consumption under control. Many American families-parents and children alike-are "overeating TV' for five, eight, and even 10 hours a day. The National PTA, the American Medical Association, and many other organizations advocate that a child's TV viewing be limited to two hours a day or less.

Some diet plans start by keeping a food journal, listing everything consumed in a day and a week. Similarly, start by keeping a TV Diary for all family members. List all TV shows watched by each family member for a week, add up the number of hours spent and programmes seen. Have a family conversation about which programmes were worthwhile and which could be dropped and how some TV time could be redirected towards other activities.

3. Talk with Your children about setting TV rules for the family

In bringing TV consumption under control, involve your children in setting the rules for doing so. just as you are guiding your children to assume more responsibility for decisions and behaviors in other areas of their lives, do the same with TV. Have them come up with some rules about TV viewing that they can agree to. There are many different types of rules: no TV until after homework or the dishes are done.

Only programs agreed-upon in advance can be watched. Two hours of TV a day. One hour of TV a night during school nights and two hours on weekends. Establish rules that work for your family's schedule and values and the ages and stages of your children.

4. In the Family TV Diet, create balanced TV meals witb your children

Look for "main TV dishes" with nutritious content, positive messages and role models, and educational programmes. It may be all right to have a TV snack or dessert-a programme watched for entertainment or relaxation alone, but such shows should come after the main course and not dominate the diet. Talk with your child and compare the messages and characters of a variety of different programmes.

Ask them, "What do you learn from that programme?" "Why do you like to watch that character?" If a programme is "just fun," that's a tip-off that it should be in the dessert category and not the main course! Select shows that communicate values worth watching. Look for programmes that support school assignments, in language, arts, science, or history.

5. Find "family exercises" to accompany your Family TV Diet

Exercise is the key to a successful diet. Your Family TV Diet will be most successful when it is accompanied by family activities. Use TV programmes as springboards for further activities and discussions. Follow viewing with conversations with your child about a programmes content, whether the topic is TV violence or sexual activity.

Consult the booklet, "Talking with Kids About Tough Issues," for tips on how to talk with your children about these sensitive topics, using what you watched together as the starting point. Make a trip to the public library to find books to continue the conversation. Help your child weave "a web of leaming" between positive TV programmes, related books, conversations, and activities. Many quality shows have their own Internet web sites, which can be accessed from schools and libraries.

6. Help your child "see through TV"

The goal of media literacy curricula in schools is to foster critical viewing skills in young viewers. TV programmes, from dramas to comedies to news programmes, are highly manufactured products, with points of view, biases and innumerable decisions made by producers and writers on what to portray and what to leave out. Tell your child that, "TV violence is very different from violence in real life. We rarely see the pain of a real gunshot. TV violence often goes unpunished." Show them how TV ads rely on celebrities to sell products and special effects to make food look more appetizing.

7 Make it a point to watch prgrams witb your children whenever possible

Whether your children are in the preschool years are teenagers, find programmes you can watch together. The Family TV Hour, like the family rneal, should not become a casualty of life in the 90s. By taking the time to watch programmes together, you are sending the message to your children that you care about the TV shows they watch. You are modeling "conscious viewing" for your children.

8. Look for special programmes that help young people deal with "hot button" topics such as drugs, alcohol, sex and peer presure

Check TV highlights in newspapers and magazines. Check your public library branch and video store for educational videos for parents and children on these topics.

9. Be aware of fast-breakiug news stories with violent or sexual content

In recent years, American children have been exposed to the crash of TWA flight 800, the Oklahoma City bombing, and the Polly Klaas murder through repeated coverage on TV and in other media. It is likely that your child will be exposed to these stories via media outside of the home, through radios in school or in a friend's car, in newspaper headlines or from casual conversations.

Rather than ignoring these news stories, parents should use them as an opportunity to comfort their children and discuss fears and anxieties. Reassure your children that, "bad things do happen, but we're safe and I'll always protect you." And as Fred Rogers also recommends to parents, when a disaster occurs, "Show them all the people who are helping."

In this fantasy world, networks are greedy giants destroying innocent young minds with sex and violence. Children's advocates are pencil-necked geeks with no sense of the real world or the bottom line. Luckily, participants at the most recent Children. Advertisers struggle to meet two often contradictory mandates: selling products through popular shows and remaining popular with parents. This tradeoff has become even more difficult in recent years, as the level of violence and sex on TV — as well as public sensitivity to its impact on children — escalates in a competitive ratings war.

For most advertisers, numbers and mood are not the only raison d'etre. Corporate responsibility and image count, too. That's why some advertisers have company codes, guidelines that specify the avoidance of programmes with excessive violence or sex, negative stereotypes of minorities and glorifications of drugs and alcohol. (Few company codes, however, require their media buyers to also consider the impact of programmes on children.)

Most companies also prescreen individual episodes. But such measures don't always work. For one thing, many advertisers purchase "scatter" buys of advertising, rather than slots in particular programs, so that they don't always have the opportunity to prescreen shows. For another, the wording of company codes is often vague and open to different interpretations. Finally, codes are applied haphazardly.

Without advertisers and networks backing good programs and making them profitable, the marketplace simply doesn't work for kids—which is why advocates are pushing for regulations requiring three hours of educational television a week. In turn, networks and advertisers gloomily predict the required programmes will lead to dwindling revenues and audiences.

Computers, video games and other interactive media will gobble up even more of the market if television doesn't provide more challenging fare. In this environment, advertisers face some tough choices—and some great opportunities. Most kids had plenty of good things to say about the media as well, and both their concerns and their praise should be heeded by those in the entertainment industry whose work these kids are watching.

Children are widely exposed to the media. Children believe that kids their age are influenced by the entertainment media. The vast majority of children believe that television should help teach kids right from wrong. Girls are more likely to agree that television should help teach kids right from wrong, and that there is too much sex before marriage on television.

Children think that people on entertainment television—especially kids—do not deal with the same problems real people face. Children say television and movies do an average job addressing the issues they think are most important. Television is sending kids mixed messages about the moral condition of society. What young people see on television makes them think people are mostly dishonest, care more about money than about people, are selfish and talk back to their parents.

On the other hand, kids also report that what they see on television makes them think people take responsibility for their actions and have generally good morals. Kids think television does a pretty good job offering positive portrayals of girls and ethnic minorities.

Family Child Care

As a caregiver for small children, it is important to be aware of fire and life safety issues. Young children are very vulnerable. The information contained in this booklet will help you provide a safe environment for children in your Family Child Care Setting. As a provider of Family Child Care, you must ensure that the children you care for are safe. Although fire departments do not have a mandate to conduct fire inspections for Family Child Care, most of these departments have personnel who are qualified to conduct Fire Safety Assessments.

A Fire Safety Assessment of a Family Child Care Facility can be arranged in any area of the province. Some assessors may charge a fee for this service. To help ensure the safety of children in your Family Child Care setting, you must have a portable fire extinguisher. The fire extinguisher you buy should have a rating of 2A:10B:C or higher marked clearly on it.

A portable fire extinguisher can save lives and reduce property damage by putting out a small fire. However, portable fire extinguishers cannot do everything. They cannot fight large or rapidly spreading fires. They are useful for extinguishing small contained fires such as stove-top or oven fires, or a fire in a wastebasket. Use them only against fires caught in their early stages. They will not be effective against a large or established fire. Remember - Get children out first and make sure they are supervised by an adult.

Fire extinguishers should be mounted on a wall where they are easy to see. Put it up high, out of the reach of children, but make sure that it is easy for adults to reach. The most important place to have a fire extinguisher is in the kitchen. It is also a good idea to have an extinguisher in any room with a fireplace or open-flame heater.

Keep a portable fire extinguisher in your car if you transport children. Check all fire extinguishers at least once a month. If pressure has dropped below the acceptable level indicated on the unit, replace or recharge the extinguisher.

After ensuring that the children in your care are safe and are supervised by a responsible adult, begin fighting the fire from a safe distance. Do not expose yourself to extreme heat by standing too close to the flames. Avoid direct exposure to smoke as much as possible. Do not try to fight a fire if you cannot see clearly or if your escape route is in danger. Leave as quickly as possible.

Smoke alarms should be tested monthly by a responsible adult. Test your smoke alarm when there are no children present. Drift smoke from a just extinguished candle under the smoke alarm. The alarm should sound within 20 seconds. Smoke can be fanned away to stop the alarm. Mark your calendar to remind you of the next test.

Dust and dirt can build up and can lead to a false alarm or cause the alarm to malfunction. Clean the smoke alarms in your home every six months. you should remove the cover, carefully wipe it inside and out with a damp cloth, and gently vaccuum the interior of the alarm.

Change the batteries in your smoke alarm every year or as needed. Pick a day you're sure to remember (like your birthday) and mark it on your calendar. Never remove the battery for other uses. This would defeat the purpose of your smoke alarm. Humidity from a bathroom or steam or grease from a kitchen can affect the sensitivity of the detecting mechanism's and cause a false alarm. first, move it to another location. If the problem persists, buy a new smoke alarm with a "silencer button" that can be depressed to temporarily silence the unit during a false alarm.

You should not use candles or anything else with an open flame while children are on the premises. Do not smoke when you are looking after children. If there are matches, lighters, cigarettes, or ashtrays in you home, you must keep them securely stored out of children's reach at all times.

If you choose to use birthday candles or sparklers for special occasions, treat these items with respect. They are potential fire hazards. Do not let children light or handle matches or sparklers. Dispose of candles and sparklers appropriately. Sparklers are very hot after use.

Install the portable fire extinguisher on a wall close to an exit (eg door) where it is easy for an adult to reach. Fire extinguishers should be placed close to an exit so that fire cannot block your escape route. One of the nicest ways to decorate a room can be with posters or pictures that the children in your family day centre have made. Unfortunately, paper products sometimes catch fire, so they should not cover too much wall space. Limit are work made of materials such as paper, cardboard, and non-flame retardant cloth. Never put flammable art work or decorations on doors.

Liquids such as paint thinner, oil based paint, lacquer, gasoline and propane catch fire easily and are fire hazards. They must be stored in a locked area. It is best to store them in a garage or shed - not inside your home. All flammable and combustible liquids (liquids which easily catch fire and burn/explode) should be stored in container approved by Underwriters Laboratories of Canada (ULC) and stored in areas inaccessible to children. The letters ULC will be clearly stamped on approved containers.

If you have liquids such as paint thinner, oil-based paint, lacquer, gasoline or propane on your property, keep them in your locked storage area, garage or shed in their original containers. Do not repour these liquids into glass containers or plastic jars. This can create a fire hazard. Waste baskets and containers must be made of material which will not burn. Waste containers that are made of wicker or plastic, or covered with decorative cloth may be attractive, BUT they are also fire hazards. Use only waste baskets or waste receptacles which are made of metal or other non-combustible materials.

Your Family Child Care should have two easy-to-reach exits on each floor used by children. Make sure that the area in which children are cared for has two easy to reach exits such as a window or door. Windows should be low enough for children to escape from in the event of a fire. If there are locking devices on the window or door, they should be easy to open from the inside.

Small children sometimes try to put small items into electrical outlets. Ensure that safety plugs or protective covers are in place on all outlets. Toxic articles such as bleach and cleaning products must be kept out of children's reach in locked cupboards. Keep poisonous items such as household cleaners, dishwashing detergent, drain cleaners, bleach and laundry products, insecticides, prescription and non-prescription medications, vitamins, skin preparations, cosmetics and nail polish in their original containers out of children's reach.

Heating appliances such as wood, electrical or gas fired stoves must be protected with a permanently mounted and secured metal screen. Permanently mounted guards will help to ensure that children are not burned or injured by these hot appliances. Make sure that your chimneys are cleaned at least once a year to prevent build-up of combustible material and a possible chimney fire.

Buy a battery operated smoke alarm and install it yourself, or have a qualified electrician hard-wire one into your home. Make sure that the alarm is 110V ULC listed or Canadian Standard Association (CSA) approved. If you are unsure which model to buy, ask the sales person for assistance in finding or ordering the correct model. You must have a separate smoke detector for each floor of the building.

Practise fire drills each month while you are looking after children in your Family Child Care. A fire safety plan must be prepared and posted in an easy to see place on each floor. Children should learn the fire safety plan, and should practise fire drills monthly. Ensure that children wear sturdy shoes at all times. During fire drills or during a fire, children may need to go outdoors in cold weather.

Young children will be better prepared for an emergency if they have been taught basic principles of fire safety. The program has developed eight fire safety rules for preschool children. Following are the eight fire safety behaviours for preschool children:

1. Stay away from hot things that can hurt.

Suggested activities:

— Teach children to identify hot things that can hurt through a variety of activities.

— Using children's safety scissors, cut out pictures of hot things from old magazines. Paste pictures in a fire safety notebook or make a collage.

— Show children items which may become hot, such as irons, stoves, pots, and heaters.

— Using hot chocolate, show children to look for steam. If there is steam, wait until the drink has cooled off before you drink it.

— Teach children to turn on the cold water tap first, and then the hot tap, to reduce the danger of hot water burns.

2. Tell a grown-up when you find matches or lighters.

Suggested activities:

— Read children's stories which illustrate the danger of matches, lighters, and cigarettes.

— Talk about the danger of fires from cigarettes, matches and lighters in starting house and forest fires.

3. Stop, drop and roll if your clothes catch on fire.

Suggested activities:

— Practice "stop, drop, and roll" through safety drills. Teach children to cover their faces.

4. Cool a burn.

Suggested activities:

— Have children pretend that they have a small burn. Teach them to run cold water over the burn.

— Teach children that they should not put ointment or butter on a burn.

5. Crawl low under smoke.

Suggested activities:

— Teach children that smoke gives off dangerous gases.

— Practise crawling low to the floor. Crawl toward an outside exit.

6. Know the sound of a smoke alarm.

Suggested activities:

— Show children where the smoke alarms in your Family Child Care are located. Discuss smoke alarms in children's homes. Where are they located? Do the children know what they sound like?

— Press the test button of your smoke alarm so that the children can hear its sound.

— Have children practise your fire escape plan when your press the test button of your smoke alarm.

7. Practise an escape plan.

Suggest activities:

— Photocopy the escape plan for your Family Child Care. Have children practise the escape plan together.

— Arrange a place to meet outside after escaping. Have children practise meeting there.

— Send a copy of the escape plan home with children.

8. Recognize the fire fighter as a helper.

Suggested activities:

— Invite a fire fighter from your local fire department to to talk to children about fire safety.

— Visit your local fire department.

— Participate in your National Fire Prevention Week activities.

3

Child Abuse Reporting and Guidelines

Discipline is something adults do with and for children, rather than to children to stop them from behaving in undesirable ways. Guiding children's behaviour is intended to help children become self-disciplined as they learn appropriate and acceptable behaviour patterns. These methods of guiding behaviour are continuous. Discipline or guiding children's behaviour is done while appropriate behaviour is occurring, as well as before, during, and after socially unacceptable behaviour is displayed.

While there are a wide variety of theories and approaches related to guiding children's behaviour, the goal remains constant - to assist children in developing respect, self-control, self-confidence and sensitivity in their interactions with others. A. Gedrose says, "Self-discipline requires an understanding of oneself and an awareness of the ways in which one can cope with difficulties, frustrations, and disappointments. Self-discipline affords a person the inclination to concentrate on a task as long as is necessary to learn, perfect, or complete it."

Self-discipline methods are not humiliating to children, or to adults. Self-discipline is based on mutual respect and cooperation. Children's behaviour is influenced by their overall development, their environment, and the adults who care for them. By nature, children differ in terms of their activity level, distractability, and sensitivity. Parents and caregivers who accept and understand these differences in children's styles will be in a better position to offer effective and appropriate guidance for them.

When adults recognize that growth entails both experimenting and making mistakes, and that difficulties are a normal, expected part of children's development, they tend to be more accepting and patient with socially unacceptable behaviour. It is important to have reasonable expectations which are consistent with each child's developmental abilities. When adults have an understanding of appropriate developmental issues for children, they are more effective in dealing with them.

Caregivers who take the time to offer developmentally appropriate verbal explanations and guidance help children gain confidence, competence, and social problem-solving skills. Expectations for behaviour vary greatly from family to family, and from culture to culture. Some may place a higher value on compliance, dependence, and respect for elders, while others may give priority to risk-taking, assertiveness, and independence.

Knowledge about a child's background and respect for different value systems will help caregivers respond sensitively to varying child-rearing approaches. In summary, adults who appreciate these principles of child development will develop attitudes and practices which are based on realistic expectations of children's needs and abilities.

The environment refers to all that surrounds a child. This includes both physical and social elements.

— *Things:* When toys and materials are in good supply, familiar and developmentally-appropriate, children are encouraged to focus and become involved in productive learning experiences. Caregivers who are knowledgeable about the ways in which environments influence behaviour can plan their settings accordingly. With groups of infants and toddlers, providing duplicates of favorite toys is essential.

— *Space:* The way in which space is used can either encourage or discourage desired behaviour. Where space is sufficient, children can play and work in a relaxed setting. It is important that sufficient space is available for the program of activities. Where areas are specifically designated for adults or children, and/or for individuals or groups, conflict is minimized. In short, space which is aesthetically pleasing, planned, and organized contributes to an environment which promotes good mental health and diminishes the potential for problems.

— *People - (Adults and Children):* Adults who are committed to nurturing and guiding young children create an atmosphere which fosters trust, security, and comfort. An adult's verbal and physical communications skills are critical in modelling the behaviour they wish children to learn. When children are in an environment that encourages caring and cooperative relationships, they learn to relate with each other in positive ways.

— *Time / Program Schedule*: Schedules, routines, and transitions serve as a framework from which children gain trust, security, and order. While these can be flexible to some degree, they must provide children with clear guidelines about what is expected.

Meeting children's needs throughout the day requires that time be appropriately balanced between active and restful periods, individual and group activities, and child initiated/adult initiated content.

The following strategies are prevention oriented. They "set the stage" for a positive atmosphere and maximize opportunities for desirable behaviour.

1. *Establish Clear, Consistent, and Simple Limits*: Limits are statements of what behaviour is appropriate. They ensure children know what is expected. Limits should be clearly related to the safety and protection of self, others, and the environment. They should be few in number, consistently enforced, and within the child's ability to understand.
2. *Offer Straightforward Explanations for Limits*: When children understand the reasons or rationale for limits, they are more likely to comply and abide by them. Furthermore, teaching children the "why" of a limit helps them internalize and learn the rules of social living.
3. *State Limits in a Positive Way, Rather Than in a Negative Way*: Phrasing limits in a positive way focuses on what to do, rather than what not to do. When parents and caregivers offer these positive statements, they reinforce for children what is appropriate, serve as desirable models of communication for children to imitate, and decrease the likelihood for children to respond with defensiveness or resistance.

4. *Focus on the Behaviour, Rather Than on the Child*: Messages which focus on "You always . . ." or "You never . . ." may be perceived by a child as attacking and critical. They tend to produce feelings of guilt and shame and can ultimately result in lowering a child's self-esteem. When caregivers focus on a child's behaviour, rather than on a child's character, they preserve a child's integrity and offer positive guidance for learning.

5. *State What is Expected, Rather Than Pose Questions*: In matters of routines, limits, and expected behaviours, it is important to state, rather than to ask. Posing questions implies that the child has a choice. While there are many opportunities for children to make choices, offer these options only when they are appropriate. When there is not a choice, make a clear statement of what is expected.

6. *Provide Choices*: Providing choices is also a valid prevention strategy for young children which often avoids power struggles.

7. *Allow Time for Children to Respond to Expectations*: Children react more favourably when they are offered cues and warnings. This helps them to anticipate or prepare for change. Instead of demanding immediate results, parents and caregivers should be prepared to give children time to respond.

8. *Reinforce Appropriate Behaviour, With Both Words and Gestures*: When children are doing well, it is important to acknowledge this through words or gestures. Positive reinforcement helps children build self-confidence and encourages them to repeat desired behaviours. In using this strategy, adults should again take care to focus on the specific behaviour, rather than on the child.

9. *Ignore Minor Incidents*: Adults who work with young children need to develop tolerance for a certain amount of noise, clutter, and attention-seeking behaviour. As long as children's activities are not infringing on the rights of others, it is often best to "take a breath," rather than to speak.

10. *Encourage Children to Use You as a Resource*: Children feel a greater sense of comfort and trust when they know that the caregiver or parent is there to protect, guide, and help them. When children learn that the adult is willing to listen and respond in a fair and supportive manner, their security and control increases.

11. *Be Alert:* When adults observe children in their activities, they are in a better position to anticipate potential difficulties and step in to prevent problems.

12. *Proximity*: Often it is necessary to stay close by when younger children are still learning to play together.

While the preceding strategies will help to create a positive climate and minimize behaviour problems, there will inevitably be occurrences of inappropriate behaviour. At these times, adults will need to intervene. The following intervention strategies, or a combination of these strategies, will help ensure that guidance is supportive, rather than punitive.

Gain a Child's Attention in a Respectful Way

Apart from situations where physical danger is imminent, adults should approach children individually, state their name, get down to the child's eye level, and use a calm, controlled voice.

Use Proximity and Touch

In situations where children may be losing self-control, the closeness of an adult can often help calm them. Simply moving close to a child, moving between two children or putting an arm around a child can serve as effective guidance and intervention. This may be a helpful strategy when dealing with biting, hitting, pinching, kicking, or thrashing.

Remind

To clarify and reinforce limits, simple reminders are helpful to young children. In general, toddlers and preschoolers have a short attention span and can become easily distracted when engaged in activities. Caregivers must be prepared to remind often.

Acknowledge Feelings Before Setting Limits

In order that children perceive adult guidance as supportive, it is important for them to know that their feelings are recognized and understood. When limits are preceded by an acknowledgement of feelings, children will be less likely to respond in a negative way.

Redirect or Divert When Appropriate

This can be an effective strategy with children whose attention span and verbal abilities are limited. With upset toddlers or very young preschoolers, offering a substitute toy or engaging them in some other activity may quickly resolve problems or conflicts. As children mature, however, this strategy is less desirable, since it "sidesteps" children's involvement in problem solving and does not help them learn alternate approaches to situations.

Redirecting or diverting involves changing the circumstances that are causing unwanted behaviour. When adults redirect children's activity, they assume responsibility for solving a problem which children have been unable to resolve through other guidance strategies. As much as possible, children should be redirected towards activities that are in line with their needs.

Model Problem-Solving Skills

When children face discouraging or frustrating situations, it is natural for them to lose control. As parents and caregivers anticipate this, they can offer verbal and/or physical assistance which models problem solving. The following steps could be used in such situations:

(a) A starting point in providing coping skills is to acknowledge the problem.

(b) Following a statement of the problem, it may be appropriate to pose helpful questions.

(c) If further guidance is necessary, state a solution or physically demonstrate.

(d) When a situation has been resolved, it is helpful to summarize for older children.

The intent of modelling a problem-solving approach is to provide resources for overcoming obstacles to success. Whether the problem relates to working with materials or interacting with others, following the steps of problem solving helps children learn the process involved. As children become more familiar and experienced with this process, they can be encouraged to generate suggestions or alternatives of their own.

Offer Appropriate Choices

When clarifying expectations or reinforcing limits, caregivers can offer a simple choice. The choice should be posed in a non-threat-ening and non-punitive way.

Use Natural and Logical Consequences

A statement of natural consequences simply clarifies the inevitable or unavoidable outcome of a behaviour.

Limit the Use of Equipment

Redirecting often goes hand in hand with removing a piece of equipment from a child's play options. This strategy should be used sparingly and only when other strategies have proven unsuccessful.

Provide Opportunities for Children to Make Amends

Rather than demand a superficial apology, adults should offer genuine opportunities for children to restore relationships after an incident of hurt or harm. While children may not be immediately ready to "take" these opportunites, they should be suggested nonetheless. Ultimately, the goal of this strategy is to help children learn that making amends requires time and goodwill, rather than revenge.

Following are the challenging behaviours:

1. *Redirection*

This can be an effective strategy for all ages of children. With upset toddlers or preschoolers, offering a substitute toy or engaging them in some other activity may quickly resolve problems or conflicts. As children mature, this strategy enables them to recognize their own emotions and behaviours and to redirect themselves away from an over stimulating situation, activity or location before inappropriate behaviours occur or escalate. When children are guided to develop impulse control and redirect themselves to an area that helps them to "feel better"; they are able to interact cooperatively again in shared settings. Self directed environments should be anywhere that a child can begin to "feel good" again.

2. *Holding*

No matter what age of children you work with, holding should only be used for safety reasons and a behaviour plan needs to be in place. Where a child's loss of control and the ability to reason causes him or her to become a safety hazard to him/herself or others, a caregiver may assist the child in re-establishing control through this technique as a last resort. The intent of this strategy is to soothe the child and to keep them and others safe until self-control is regained. A calm and controlled attitude of the adult is critical in ensuring that this strategy is supportive, not punitive.

3. *Time Away*

Time away can show children that being redirected from an over stimulating environment to a more calming area allows them to manage their own behaviours before inappropriate behaviours occur or escalate. The intent of time away is to provide children with opportunities to develop self direction and to become aware of when they are becoming anxious or agitated. Unpredictable behaviours occur when children feel powerless and out of control. When children have determined where they would like to spend time to "feel better" and to regain control of their emotional and physical state, invite them to determine when they are ready to participate in activities with the group again - time in. Children learn self control when they feel encouraged, when they feel they belong and feel valued, and when they feel they have power in their lives. Some examples of environments where children can feel better are:

(a) A pillow corner with books, stuffies and music head sets

(b) A container filled with foam chips and surrounded with books and gentle sounds of nature (i.e. head sets of whale sounds, wind storms, etc.)

(c) A loft above a play centre with pillows, blankets, books and music.

When parents assault or molest their children, it is conventionally thought of as child abuse and, therefore, a child welfare problem. However, these acts are also crimes, and a substantial portion of child abuse cases are investigated and adjudicated by the criminal justice system. Some cases are referred to law enforcement agencies by child welfare investigators, while others are reported directly to law enforcement by victims, families, and other concerned individuals.

Unfortunately, the law enforcement perspective on child abuse is greatly neglected. Most publicly available statistics on the problem come from child welfare agencies and describe child welfare system activities alone. Even such a basic fact as the percentage of cases that are reported to law enforcement agencies is not tallied by the US, National Child Abuse and Neglect Data System (NCANDS), the main national system that measures and tracks child maltreatment.

Until recently, no law enforcement data were available to provide researchers with a criminal justice system perspective on child abuse equivalent to the child welfare system perspective provided by NCANDS. However, the National Incident-Based Reporting System (NIBRS) for law enforcement agencies is being implemented to capture much more detailed information about crime and its victims.

NIBRS will allow researchers to analyse incidents coming to the attention of police that involve child victims and parent or other caretaker perpetrators-incidents that are generally thought of as child abuse. Child abuse can come to the attention of police in a variety of ways: from victims and their families, from concerned community members, from professionals such as teachers and doctors, and from other authorities such as child welfare agencies.

Professionals in all States, and even ordinary citizens in some States, are mandated to report child abuse to responsible authorities. In some States, police are considered to be the responsible authority for reporting purposes, and in many States, statutes now require child welfare authorities to share all child maltreatment reports with law enforcement.

Child welfare investigations substantiate or confirm about one-third of all child maltreatment reports. In some States, these investigations are conducted jointly by child welfare and police; in a few jurisdictions, responsibility for investigation lies with law enforcement only. Thus the police have become increasingly involved in child abuse cases, but their role in the reporting and investigation of child abuse can vary quite a bit from jurisdiction to jurisdiction.

The large number of child abuse cases reported to law enforcement agencies suggests that more attention should be paid to how law enforcement agencies investigate these crimes and arrest and prosecute the offenders. How law enforcement handles cases of parental physical assault against children needs to be examined, particularly in light of recent policy debates over the arrest and prosecution of offenders who have committed other forms of domestic violence.

NIBRS collects a wide range of information on victims, offenders, and circumstances for a variety of offences. Generally, the term "child maltreatment" thought of as referring to offences and threats to a child's well-being that are committed or caused by parents and other caretakers. Although for child welfare purposes the definition of caretakers can vary somewhat from State to State, the term typically includes parents, other responsible adult family members, and, in some cases but not always, professional caretakers such as teachers, recreation leaders, and baby-sitters.

Unfortunately, NIBRS does not have a specific caretaker category, but it does specify parent and step-parent perpetrators, who constitute the vast majority of child maltreatment offenders. To these two groups, the authors added grandparents, other adult family members (but not in-laws), babysitters, and parents' boyfriends or girlfriends.

There is no NIBRS category that allows the separation of professional caretakers, such as teachers or recreation workers, from the larger category of acquaintances. However, in State child maltreatment reports, the categories that include nonfamily caretakers such as teachers and other school staff account only 6 percent of perpetrators identified. Furthermore, babysitters-a group identified separately in NIBRS records-are included in this 6 percent. Several crimes coded by NIBRS clearly fall within the child maltreatment domain when committed by caretakers: simple assault, aggravated assault, and sex offences.

In NIBRS, sex offences include both forcible sexual assaults, which are considered violent crimes and make up the great majority of sex crimes, and nonforcible sex offences such as statutory rape and non-forcible incest. These acts clearly correspond to child physical and sexual abuse. Unfortunately, no NIBRS code designates acts of neglect.

NIBRS collects information only on a standardized set of offenses that fall specifically within the domain of law enforcement. Neglect accounts for a large proportion of child maltreatment cases, but it is not often considered criminal in nature and frequently may not be reported to law enforcement. The same is true for psychological abuse.

Another offence reported in NIBRS and categorized as a violent crime is kidnapping, which, when committed by a caretaker, is clearly a child welfare offence. However, little is known about how kidnapping is reported or classified in the child welfare system's child maltreatment data.

Therefore, NIBRS data used in this analysis concern the violent crimes of assault, sexual assault, and kidnapping, plus nonforcible sex offenses, committed against juveniles under age 18 by parents, step-parents, grandparents, babysitters, other adult family members, and parents' boyfriends or girlfriends. Together, these crimes are categorized as "offenses by parents and other caretakers."

Analysis of NIBRS data on incidents known to police reveals that parents and other caretakers are responsible for nearly one in five of all violent crimes (plus nonforcible sex offenses) committed against juveniles. Strangers are responsible for only half as many of these police-known crimes. The largest category of those known to police who commit offenses against juveniles comprises noncaretaker acquaintances, both juveniles and adults, and the smallest category consists of noncaretaker family members, mostly juveniles.

The parent and other caretaker proportion for some offenses is quite a bit higher than for others. Parents and other care-takers commit 26 percent of sexual assaults of juveniles and 49 percent of kidnapings of juveniles, compared with 16 percent and 18 percent for aggravated and simple assaults, respectively. Also, as might be expected, offenses by parents and other caretakers play a particularly large role in the victimization of younger children, who do not have many persons other than caretakers in their lives.

Data on incidents known to police show that more than half of the crimes against children age 2 and younger are committed by parents and other caretakers; for juveniles age 12 and older, the role of parent and other caretaker offenders dwindles to less than 20 percent of all offenders. The high percentage of young children victimized by caretakers should not be misinterpreted. The majority of caretaker offenses in NIBRS are not actually committed against younger children.

Males are considerably more likely than females to be perpetrators. This gender difference holds true even among baby-sitter offenders, although males are much less likely than females to be babysitters. Biological fathers account for two-fifths of all offenders, and stepfathers and parents' boyfriends account for nearly one-fifth.

A somewhat larger number of girls than boys are victims of parent and other caretaker offenses. This is largely accounted for by the disproportionate number of female sexual assault victims. Victim gender is fairly evenly distributed for simple assaults, aggravated assaults, and kidnapings. In the category of sex offenses by parents and other caretakers, the percentage of victims who are female rises with age across the span of childhood.

In the category of nonsexual caretaker offenses (physical assaults and kidnapping), the percentage of victims who are female also rises at adolescence, perhaps because boys grow big and strong enough to deter parental assaults or because parental conflicts with girls (particularly concerning sexual behaviour) are intensified during adolescence.

Other Domestic Violences

Spouse abuse is one factor that may bring parent and other caretaker offenses against children directly to the attention of police. Officers responding to a home where domestic violence is occurring may discover an assault against a child as well. Multiple victims are coded by NIBRS, which means that incident data can include both spousal and child victims.

For incidents known to police, 3 percent of spouse and other intimate partner assaults also include a child abuse victim, while 13 percent of child abuse victimizations include a spouse or other intimate partner assault. Thus, response to spousal violence may be one way in which child abuse by a parent is discovered by the police. In some cases, more than one child is victimized by the same parent or caretaker.

NIBRS data on parent and other caretaker assaults show that 7 percent of physical assaults and 10 percent of sexual assaults involved more than one child. Multiple-victim assaults were more likely to involve younger than older children. Seventy percent of juvenile victims in multiple-victim assaults were under 12 years of age, compared with 42 percent in single-victim assaults.

Most offenses by parents and other caretakers do not involve weapons. Only 1 percent of episodes involved a firearm and only 2 percent involved a knife-rates of weapon use that are less than half those for other perpetrators against children. Severe injury is also relatively infrequent in offenses by parents and other caretakers reported to police.

NIBRS data indicate major physical injury (such as severe lacerations, broken bones, and unconsciousness) to only 3 percent of the juvenile victims and minor physical injury (such as bruises or scratches) to another 42 percent. The impression has been that, compared with other types of juvenile victimization, offenses by parents and other caretakers require a higher threshold of injury to bring them to the attention of police.

In fact, however, NIBRS data show that the level of injury in offenses by parents and other caretakers reported to police is about the same as that in offences committed against juveniles by other perpetrators. Major injuries are more common for younger children (6 percent for victims age 5 and younger versus 3 percent for children age 6 and older), which may reflect the greater physical vulnerability of younger children.

Law enforcement data confirm certain features of the child abuse problem that are known from child welfare sources. However, they also reveal some discrepancies. Law enforcement data validate child welfare data showing that parents are the most common caretaker abusers, that male caretakers are responsible for most sexual abuse, and that although girls are disproportionately victims of sexual abuse, the proportions of boys and girls who suffer physical abuse are about equal.

NIBRS data also confirm that there is substantially more physical abuse than sexual abuse of juveniles. Despite what might be inferred from the predominance of sexual abuse reports in the news, the majority of the parent and other caretaker offenses reported to police involve physical assaults, not sexual offenses, at a ratio of 2.9 to 1. The comparable ratio in the child welfare system national child maltreatment data for 1997 is 2.2 to 1.

Some earlier research had suggested that physical abuse was less likely than sexual abuse to be regarded as criminal and that child welfare sources infrequently passed on incidents of physical abuse to police. The more recent NIBRS data documenting more physical than sexual abuse suggest that this was not true or is no longer true and that physical abuse by parents and other caretakers is being regarded as sufficiently criminal to be referred to police. Whether physical abuse is prosecuted as aggressively as sexual abuse is another matter.

Despite some similarities, other comparisons of NIBRS and child welfare system data suggest that the two systems may not be dealing with identical populations. For example, although the age distribution of sexual abuse victims looks quite similar in the two systems, the distribution for physical abuse victims is different-the child welfare system has many more younger children than NIBRS.

Forty-two percent of the physical abuse cases in the child welfare system data involved victims who were age 7 and younger, compared with only 24 percent in NIBRS. This difference in the two systems regarding the distribution of victim ages is consistent with a difference in data regarding perpetrator gender: females constitute 51 percent of the physical abusers in child welfare data, but only 32 percent in NIBRS data.

Together, these discrepancies suggest that caretaker assaults against younger children and by females may be viewed by potential reporters as less criminal or as matters in which police have less expertise. Thus, these assaults may be less likely to be referred to police even by child welfare agencies.

It will be easier to know how NIBRS and child welfare system data correspond when complete data are available for entire States. Currently, only three States-Idaho, Iowa, and South Carolina-have both statewide child abuse data and close to 100 percent law enforcement agency participation in NIBRS. In both Idaho and Iowa, child welfare agency protocols dictate that law enforcement agencies must be notified of all maltreatment known to child welfare; nevertheless, police reports of caretaker assaults are only a fraction of the substantiated abuse recorded by child welfare authorities.

In Idaho, the NIBRS tally of physical assaults is only one-third as large as the number of physical assaults substantiated by child welfare; in Iowa, NIBRS records only one-fifth the number of substantiated cases. Possible factors that may explain this discrepancy include incomplete NIBRS data collection or broad child welfare definitions of child abuse that include noncriminal acts. However, the data are consistent with the possibility that a great deal of criminal child abuse is not reported to or recorded by law enforcement in some States.

The situation in South Carolina suggests a different story. In that State, sexual assault cases in NIBRS data are equal in number to sexual abuse cases in child welfare data, but physical assault cases in NIBRS data actually exceed the number reported in child welfare data. In South Carolina, it is possible that child abuse reports are readily passed on to law enforcement but that the threshold for substantiating physical abuse in the child welfare system may be higher than the threshold for recording a crime in NIBRS.

Up until now, in the absence of national law enforcement data, the only national statistics on violence specifically against children have been abuse data collected by child welfare agencies. An expanding NIBRS will eventually supply national data representing a law enforcement point of view on crimes committed against all juveniles and will provide a new and potentially contrasting perspective on the problem of violence against children.

For example, based on information from 43 States, child welfare data for 1997 documented nearly 300,000 substantiated cases of child physical and sexual abuse, yielding an estimate of 350,000 cases nationwide. These numbers, however, primarily capture incidents of violence committed against juveniles by parents and other caretakers and exclude assaults by noncaretaker perpetrators, which are outside the domain of the child welfare system.

The fact that a large number of physical assaults by parents and other caretakers are referred to police every year is an important, if generally unrecognized, reality for the justice system that also raises questions about how these cases are being handled. Most of the research on how the justice system manages juvenile victims of caretaker offenses focuses on sex crimes.

Many justice system reforms and innovations have been developed to deal with these sexual abuse cases, including the establishment of multidisciplinary teams and children's advocacy centres. There is little indication in this literature that the majority of parent and other caretaker assaults that enter the justice system involve physical rather than sexual assault. Policy-makers in this domain have had to balance competing needs: to reinforce clear norms against domestic violence, to sanction offenders, to protect victims who have ongoing relationships with perpetrators, to empower and respect victims whose interests differ from those of the justice system, and to use limited justice resources efficiently.

These needs all have parallels in dealing with physical assaults against children. Reforms are currently under way that will also increase the salience of criminal justice issues in the child abuse domain. For example, some States (e.g., Florida) are expanding the role of law enforcement in the investigation of child abuse, giving to sheriffs and police functions that were previously handled by child welfare authorities. In addition, children's advocacy centres and multidisciplinary response teams are being implemented across the country, further involving the criminal justice system in child abuse investigations.

4

Child Maltreatment

Infant mortality is an important measure of a nation's health and a worldwide indicator of health status and social well-being. As of 1995, the U.S. infant mortality rates ranked 25th among industrialized nations. In the past decade, critical measures of increased risk of infant death, such as new cases of low birth weight (LBW) and very low birth weight (VLBW), actually have increased in the United States. In addition, the disparity in infant mortality rates between whites and specific racial and ethnic groups persists. Although the overall infant mortality rate has reached record low levels, the rate for African Americans remains twice that of whites.

In 1997, 28,045 infants died before their first birthday, for an overall rate of 7.2 deaths per 1,000 live births. This rate has declined steadily over the past 20 years; in 1975, the infant mortality rate was over 15 per 1,000 live births. In 1997, two-thirds of all infant deaths took place during the first 28 days of life (the neonatal period). The overall neonatal mortality rate in 1997 was 4.8 per 1,000 live births. The remaining one-third of infant deaths took place during the postneonatal period from an infant's 29th day of life until the first birthday.

The U.S. postneonatal mortality rate in 1997 was 2.4 deaths per 1,000 live births. Four causes account for more than half of all infant deaths: birth defects, disorders relating to short gestation and unspecified LBW, sudden infant death syndrome (SIDS), and respiratory distress syndrome. The leading causes of neonatal death in 1997 were birth defects, disorders related to short gestation and LBW, respiratory distress syndrome, and maternal complications of pregnancy. After the first month of life, SIDS is the leading cause of infant death, accounting for about one-third of all deaths during this period.

Maternal age also is a risk factor for infant death. Mortality rates are highest among infants born to young teenagers and to mothers aged 44 years and older. The death of fetuses before birth is another important indicator of perinatal health. In 1996, nearly 7 fetal deaths were reported for every 1,000 live births and fetal deaths combined, representing a slight decline from the fetal mortality rate of 7.6 per 1,000 in 1987. Fetal death sometimes is associated with pregnancies complicated by such risk factors as problems with amniotic fluid levels and maternal blood disorders.

Early, comprehensive, and risk-appropriate care to manage such conditions has contributed to reductions in fetal mortality rates. Short gestation and LBW are among the leading causes of neonatal death, accounting for 20 percent of neonatal deaths. In 1998, a total of 11.6 percent of births were preterm, and 7.6 percent were LBW. Included in these statistics were VLBW infants weighing less than 1,500 grams (3.3 pounds). The rate of VLBW births was 1.4 percent in 1998. The VLBW rate has increased slightly since 1990 among whites and other population groups including African Americans, Puerto Ricans, and American Indians.

LBW is associated with long-term disabilities, such as cerebral palsy, autism, mental retardation, vision and hearing impairments, and other developmental disabilities. Despite the low proportion of pregnancies resulting in LBW babies, expenditures for the care of LBW infants total more than half of the costs incurred for all newborns. In 1988, the cost of a normal, healthy delivery averaged $1,900, whereas hospital costs for LBW infants averaged $6,200. The general category of LBW infants includes both those born too early and those who are born at full term but who are too small, a condition known as intrauterine growth retardation (IUGR).

Maternal characteristics that are risk factors associated with IUGR include maternal LBW, prior LBW birth history, low prepregnancy weight, cigarette smoking, multiple births, and low pregnancy weight gain. Cigarette smoking is the greatest known risk factor. VLBW usually is associated with preterm birth. Relatively little is known about risk factors for preterm birth, but the primary risk factors are prior preterm birth and spontaneous abortion, low prepregnancy weight, and cigarette smoking.

These risk factors account for only one-third of all preterm births. The use of alcohol, tobacco, and illegal substances during pregnancy is a major risk factor for LBW and other poor infant outcomes. Alcohol use is linked to fetal death, LBW, growth abnormalities, mental retardation, and fetal alcohol syndrome (FAS). Overall rates of alcohol use during pregnancy have increased during the 1990s, and the proportion of pregnant women using alcohol at higher and more hazardous levels has increased substantially.

Smoking during pregnancy is linked to LBW, preterm delivery, SIDS, and respiratory problems in newborns. In addition to the human cost of these conditions, the economic cost of services to substance-exposed infants is great: health expenditures related to FAS are estimated to be from $75 million to $9.7 billion each year. Over $500 million a year is spent on medical expenses for infants exposed to cocaine in utero. Smoking-attributable costs of complicated births in 1995 were estimated at $1.4 billion and $2.0 billion (15 percent for all complicated births, based on smoking prevalence during pregnancy of 27 percent).

Finally, breastfeeding is an important contributor to overall infant health because human breast milk presents the most complete form of nutrition for infants; therefore, the American Academy of Pediatrics recommends that infants be breastfed for approximately the first 6 months of life. Breastfeeding rates have increased over the years, particularly in early infancy. However, breastfeeding rates among women of all races decrease substantially by 5 to 6 months postpartum. The 1998 rates at 5 to 6 months were only 31 percent among white women, 19 percent among African American women, and 28 percent among Hispanic women.

Also important to child health are the prevention and treatment of disabilities in children. Twelve percent of all children under age 18 years have a disability. In 1994, 10.6 percent of all children aged 5 to 17 years had limitations in learning ability, 6 percent had limitations in communication, 1.3 percent had limitations in mobility, and 0.9 percent had limitations in personal care.

The burden of childhood disability is compounded because affected children live with their disabling conditions many more years than do persons acquiring disability later in life. In 1992, asthma and mental retardation were the most common disabling conditions, accounting for 40 percent of all activity limitations. Other major disabling conditions in childhood include speech impairment, hearing impairment, cerebral palsy, epilepsy, and leg impairment.

The objectives in this focus area cover the broad array of childhood conditions and genetic disorders. Examples of preventable birth defects are spina bifida and other neural tube defects (NTDs). The occurrence of these disorders could be reduced by more than half if women consumed adequate folic acid before and during pregnancy. All States require newborns to be screened for genetic conditions, such as phenyl-ketonuria (PKU) and hypothyroidism; the majority of States also require screening for sickle cell disease.

Although not necessarily preventable, these conditions are susceptible to intervention after delivery. For example, nutritional interventions in infancy can prevent mental retardation in children with PKU, penicillin can prevent infection in children with sickle cell disease, and hormone replacement can prevent mental retardation in children with hypothyroidism. Thus, adequate screening of newborns is the first step toward prevention of illness, disability, and death.

In addition to infant deaths and health conditions, the effect of pregnancy and childbirth on women is an important indicator of women's health. In 1997, a total of 327 maternal deaths were reported by vital statistics. While this number is small, maternal death remains significant because a high proportion of these deaths are preventable and because of the impact of women's premature death on families. The maternal mortality ratio among African American women consistently has been three to four times that of white women.

Ectopic pregnancy is an important cause of pregnancy-related illness and disability in the United States and the leading cause of maternal death in the first trimester. The risk of ectopic pregnancy increases with age; women of all races aged 35 to 44 years are at more than three times the risk of ectopic pregnancy than are women aged 15 to 24 years. Preeclampsia and eclampsia also are important causes of maternal death.

Other causes of maternal death are hemorrhage, embolism, infection, and anaesthesia-related complications. The rates of many of these indicators have shown improvement over the past decade. The rate of infant mortality declined more than 27 percent between 1987 and 1997. The rate of fetal mortality declined 8 percent between 1987 and 1995. Other indicators show less progress. The LBW rate increased 10 percent between 1987 and 1998. The rate of FAS has risen steeply, especially among African Americans.

In addition, the maternal mortality rate has not declined since 1982, nor has the disparity between African American and white women. Despite these unfavourable trends, evidence is encouraging about increases in women's use of health practices that can help their own health and that of their infants. The percentage of pregnant women who start prenatal care early increased 9.2 percent between 1987 and 1998. The percentage of mothers who breast-feed their newborns also went up 18.5 percent between 1988 and 1998, with greater gains among African American and Hispanic women.

Other maternal health practices have shown less improvement: in 1992-94, the proportion of women of child-bearing age reporting consumption of the recommended level of folic acid (400 micrograms) was 21 percent. Many of these conditions and risk factors disproportionately affect certain racial and ethnic groups. The disparities between white and nonwhite groups in infant death, maternal death, and LBW are wide and, in many cases, are growing.

The 1997 infant mortality rate among African American infants was 2.3 times that of white infants. Although infant mortality rates have declined within both racial groups, the proportional discrepancy between African Americans and whites remains largely unchanged. The rate of maternal mortality among African Americans is 20.3 per 100,000 live births, nearly four times the white rate of 5.1 per 100,000. African American women continue to be three to four times more likely than white women to die of pregnancy and its complications.

The maternal death differential between African Americans and whites is highest for pregnancies that did not end in live birth (ectopic pregnancy, spontaneous and induced abortions, and gestational trophoblastic disease). Rates of LBW for white women have risen from 5.7 percent of births in 1990 to 6.5 percent in 1998. Among African Americans, the LBW rate has declined slightly in the 1990s but remains twice as high as that of whites-13 percent in 1998.

African Americans also are more likely to have other risk factors, such as young maternal age, high birth order, less education, and inadequate prenatal care. Puerto Ricans also are especially likely to have LBW infants. American Indians or Alaska Natives and African Americans account for a disproportionate share of FAS deaths. In 1990, the rates of FAS among American Indians or Alaska Natives and African Americans were 5.2 and 1.4 per 1,000 live births, respectively, compared with 0.4 per 1,000 among the population as a whole. African American and Hispanic women also are less likely than whites to enter prenatal care early.

For both African American and white women, the proportion entering prenatal care in the first trimester rises with maternal age until the late thirties, then begins to decline. For example, in 1998, 57 percent of African American women under age 18 years began care early, compared with 66 percent of white women of the same age. Among women aged 18 to 24 years, 68 percent of African Americans received care in their first trimester, compared to 76 percent of white women. Among women aged 25 to 39 years, 79 percent of African American women entered care early, compared with 89 percent of white women.

Women in certain racial and ethnic groups also are less likely than white women to breast-feed their infants. In the early postpartum period, 45 percent of African American mothers and 66 percent of Hispanic mothers breastfed in 1998, compared with 68 percent of white women. These differences persist at 5 to 6 months postpartum, when 19 percent of African American women, 28 percent of Hispanic women, and 31 percent of white women breastfed.

Many of the risk factors mentioned can be mitigated or prevented with good pre-conception and prenatal care.

First, preconception screening and counseling offer an opportunity to identify and mitigate maternal risk factors before pregnancy begins. Examples include daily folic acid consumption (a protective factor) and alcohol use (a risk factor). During preconceptional counseling, healthcare providers also can refer women for medical and psychosocial or support services for any risk factors identified.

Counseling needs to be culturally appropriate and linguistically competent. Prenatal visits offer an opportunity to provide information about the adverse effects of substance use, including alcohol and tobacco during pregnancy, and serve as a vehicle for referrals to treatment services. The use of timely, high-quality prenatal care can help to prevent poor birth outcomes and improve maternal health by identifying women who are at particularly high risk and taking steps to mitigate risks, such as the risk of high blood pressure or other maternal complications.

Interventions targeted at prevention and cessation of substance use during pregnancy may be helpful in further reducing the rate of preterm delivery and low birth weight. Further promotion of folic acid intake can help to reduce the rate of NTDs. Other actions taken after birth can significantly improve infants' health and chances of survival. Breastfeeding has been shown to reduce rates of infection in infants and to improve long-term maternal health.

Infant death is a critical indicator of the health of a population. It reflects the overall state of maternal health as well as the quality and accessibility of primary health care available to pregnant women and infants. Despite steady declines in the 1980s and 1990s, the rate of infant mortality in the United States remains among the highest in the industrialized world. Moreover, the rate of decline in infant mortality has slowed since the 1970s, when major advances in neonatal care contributed to steep reductions in the neonatal mortality rate.

However, the rapid decline in this rate slowed during the 1980s. In the early 1990s, the introduction of synthetic surfactant contributed to declines in neonatal mortality rates through decreased new cases of intraventricular hemorrhage and decreased severity of respiratory disease in preterm, very small infants. The health of infants depends in large part on their health in utero. A fetus with severe defects or growth problems may not be delivered alive.

Because only live births are counted in infant mortality rates, perinatal and fetal mortality rates provide a more complete picture of perinatal health than does the infant mortality rate alone. Fetal death often is associated with maternal complications of pregnancy, such as problems with amniotic fluid levels and blood disorders. Rates of fetal mortality are 35 percent greater than average in women who use tobacco during pregnancy and 77 percent higher in women who use alcohol.

Fetal mortality rates also are high when birth defects, such as anencephalus, renal agenesis, and hydrocephalus, are present. The baseline fetal mortality rate of 6.8 per 1,000 represents only a 6.7 percent reduction since 1990, an average rate of decline of 1.3 percent per year. The fetal mortality rate among African Americans was 12.7 per 1,000 in 1995, 1.8 times that of the population as a whole. Moreover, this gap has widened since 1990.

The rate among African Americans declined by only 4.5 percent over this period, a decline of less than 1 percent per year. Targeting prenatal risk screening and intervention to high-risk groups, particularly African American women, is critical to reducing this gap. The perinatal mortality rate includes both deaths of live-born infants through the first 7 days of life and fetal deaths after 28 weeks of gestation. This rate is a useful overall measure of perinatal health and the quality of health care provided to pregnant women and newborns. The rate of perinatal mortality has declined by 40 percent since 1980.

The gap between African Americans and whites has increased, however, with the rate among African Americans now more than twice that of whites. The infant mortality rate is made up of two components: neonatal mortality and postneonatal mortality. The leading causes of neonatal death include birth defects, disorders related to short gestation and LBW, and pregnancy complications. Of these, the most likely to be preventable are those related to preterm birth and LBW, which represent approximately 20 percent of neonatal deaths.

Postneonatal death reflects events experienced in infancy, including SIDS, birth defects, injuries, and homicide. Birth defects, many of which are unlikely to be preventable given current scientific knowledge, account for approximately 17 percent of postneonatal deaths; the remainder are likely to stem from preventable causes. SIDS is the leading cause of postneonatal death among all racial and ethnic groups, representing nearly one-third of all cases of postneonatal death.

Moreover, the rate of SIDS among African Americans is 1.4 per 1,000 live births, twice that of whites. Therefore, a reduction in the rate of death from SIDS, particularly among African Americans, would contribute greatly to reducing the overall infant mortality rate and particularly to closing the racial gap in postneonatal death. The 2010 target should be achievable with continued education.

Rates of death from birth defects can be reduced either by preventing the occurrence of the defect itself or by providing the necessary care to prevent death. In the case of NTDs, the birth defects themselves can be prevented. Death from birth defects that are not so easily prevented, such as heart problems, can be reduced with access to appropriate medical care. A particular issue in the reduction of infant death is the reduction of disparities among select populations, particularly as defined by race and ethnicity, maternal age, and infant birth weight.

The gap between whites and African Americans in infant death is large and has not diminished since 1990. The deaths of children after infancy also present a public health concern and an opportunity for prevention. In 1997, 13,562 children aged 1 to 14 years died, representing a death rate of 25.1 per 100,000 children in that age group. The leading cause of death for children of all ages is injury, which accounts for 13.1 deaths per 100,000 preschool children and 8.7 deaths per 100,000 school-aged children.

Among children aged 1 to 4 years, the leading injury-related causes of death are motor vehicle crashes, drownings, and fires and burns. Among those aged 5 to 14 years, the leading causes of death include motor vehicle crashes and firearms. These deaths are, for the most part, preventable. Other leading causes of death among children that are less likely to be preventable include birth defects, malignant neoplasms, and diseases of the heart.

The deaths of young adolescents, older adolescents, and young adults are more likely to be due to external causes than to congenital diseases. There were 4,261 deaths among adolescents aged 10 to 14 years in 1998, for a mortality rate of 22.1 per 100,000. The leading cause of death for adolescents in this age group was motor vehicle crashes at 5.4 deaths per 100,000 or 24.3 percent of the total mortality. Other unintentional injuries (such as falls, drownings, and poisonings) caused 3.5 deaths per 100,000 (15.9 percent); homicides caused 1.5 deaths per 100,000 (6.8 percent); suicides caused 1.6 deaths per 100,000 (7.4 percent); and AIDS caused 0.1 deaths per 100,000 (0.6 percent). Fifty-five percent of the total deaths in this age group, therefore, can be attributed to unnecessary (that is, preventable) causes.

Other causes of death for this age group that are less amenable to prevention strategies given current scientific knowledge include malignant neoplasms, which caused 2.7 deaths per 100,000 (12.3 percent); birth defects, which caused 0.9 deaths per 100,000 (4.1 percent); diseases of the heart, which caused 0.9 deaths per 100,000 (4.0 percent); and a combination of other causes, which caused 5.5 deaths per 100,000 (25 percent). There were 13,788 deaths in 1998 among adolescents aged 15 to 19 years, for a death rate of 70.6 per 100,000.

The leading cause of death for adolescents in this age group was motor vehicle crashes at 28.4 deaths per 100,000 or 37.4 percent of total deaths. Other unintentional injuries (such as falls, drownings, and poisonings) caused 7.3 deaths per 100,000 (10.4 percent);

homicides caused 11.8 deaths per 100,000 (16.8 percent); suicides caused 8.9 deaths per 100,000 (12.6 percent); and AIDS caused 0.1 deaths per 100,000 (0.2 percent).

Consequently, a majority (77 percent) of the total deaths in this age group can be attributed to unnecessary (that is, preventable) causes. The remaining 23 percent of deaths among adolescents aged 15 to 19 years resulted mostly from malignant neoplasms, which caused 3.7 deaths per 100,000 (5.2 percent); diseases of the heart, which caused 2.1 deaths per 100,000 (3.0 percent); birth defects, which caused 1.1 deaths per 100,000 (1.6 percent); and a combination of other causes, which caused 9.1 deaths per 100,000 (12.9 percent).

Prenatal care includes three major components: risk assessment, treatment for medical conditions or risk reduction, and education. Each component can contribute to reductions in perinatal illness, disability, and death by identifying and mitigating potential risks and helping women to address behavioural factors, such as smoking and alcohol use, that contribute to poor outcomes.

Prenatal care is more likely to be effective if women begin receiving care early in pregnancy. Since 1990, the proportion of infants whose mothers entered prenatal care in the first trimester increased 8.8 percent, from 76 percent to 83 percent. Among African Americans, this proportion grew 19 percent and among Hispanics, 22 percent. Thus, increases in early entry into prenatal care have been concentrated in those populations whose perinatal illness and disability rates and mortality rates are highest and who are most likely to have low incomes.

These increases are likely due, in part, to increased access to Medicaid coverage for pregnancy-related services and improved outreach by Medicaid programs.

In addition, the likelihood of early entry into prenatal care rises with age. The risk of poor birth outcomes is greatest among the youngest mothers (aged 15 years and under).

Clearly, therefore, continued work is needed to educate women, particularly young women, about the need to begin prenatal care early in pregnancy. Prenatal care should begin early and continue throughout pregnancy, according to accepted standards of periodicity. For example, the American College of Obstetricians and Gynecologists recommends that women receive at least 13 prenatal visits during a full-term pregnancy.

Therefore, assessment of the adequacy of the care pregnant women receive must include monitoring not only the month of initiation of prenatal care but also the adequacy of the care they receive throughout pregnancy. The Adequacy of Prenatal Care Utilization Index (APNCU) measures two dimensions of care: the adequacy of initiation of care and the adequacy of the use of prenatal services once care has begun (by comparing actual use to the recommended number of visits based on the month of initiation of care and the length of the pregnancy).

These dimensions are combined to classify each woman's prenatal care history as inadequate, intermediate, adequate, or adequate-plus. The baseline rates presented above include all women who received either adequate or adequate-plus care. Overall, nearly three-quarters of women receive adequate prenatal care. However, this proportion varies across racial and ethnic groups.

The likelihood of receipt of adequate prenatal care rises with maternal age, with fewer than half of pregnant women aged 15 years and under receiving adequate care. Prevention of unwanted pregnancy in adolescents and education of women about the need for early, continuous prenatal care are essential. Increase the proportion of pregnant women who attend a series of prepared childbirth classes.

As part of comprehensive prenatal care, a formal series of prepared childbirth classes conducted by a certified childbirth educator is recommended for all women by the Expert Panel on the Content of Prenatal Care. These classes can help reduce women's pain and anxiety as they approach childbirth, making delivery a more pleasant experience and preparing women for what they will face as they give birth. A full series of sessions is recommended for women who have never attended.

A refresher series of one or two classes is recommended for women who attended during a previous pregnancy. At a minimum, the childbirth classes should include information regarding the physiology of labour and birth, exercises and self-help techniques for labour, the role of support persons, family roles and adjustments, and preferences for care during labour and birth. The classes also should include an opportunity for the mother and her partner to have questions answered about providers, prenatal care, and other relevant issues, as well as to receive information regarding birth settings and cesarean childbirth.

Attendance is recommended during the third trimester of pregnancy so that information learned will be used relatively soon after presentation. Classes should begin at the 31st or 32nd week and be completed no later than 38 weeks. The refresher class should be completed at any time between 36 and 38 weeks.

Data for population groups currently are not analyzed. Much research has demonstrated the benefits of delivering high-risk infants in settings that have the technological capacity to care for them. Specifically, research has shown that VLBW infants have lower death rates when they are delivered at level III hospitals, which are equipped to care for very small infants.

To ensure that high-risk pregnant women have access to appropriate levels of obstetric care, many States have implemented perinatal regionalization strategies and protocols for the transfer of high-risk women to level III facilities. Evidence, however, indicates that these systems may be eroding as health care networks and financing systems change. The proportion of VLBW infants who are delivered in the level III obstetric hospitals best equipped to provide appropriate neonatal care should be measured to monitor the continuing effectiveness of these systems.

During the 1980s, rates of cesarean births rose steadily, with a peak rate of 25 percent of deliveries reported in 1988. Since then, the rate has been slowly decreasing, with the majority of the decline attributable to a reduction in the rates of primary cesarean births. In 1989, the rate of vaginal births among women who had a previous cesarean birth was 19 percent; in 1995 it increased to 28 percent. The improvements are likely to be attributable to use of such strategies as clearer guidelines for trials of labour and labour management, continual labour support, and focused attention on physician practice patterns.

Expert opinion called for use of risk-adjusted rates of cesarean births (that is, rates standardized by patient characteristics) to monitor progress over time. (The targets presented here apply to the population as a whole and are not intended to be used as practice outcome objectives for individual physicians or institutions, as the medical needs of the patients in each practice will vary.) In addition to monitoring rates of cesarean births, the outcomes of these deliveries should be watched closely to assure that changes in the mode of delivery do not put women or their infants at risk.

LBW is the risk factor most closely associated with neonatal death; thus, improvements in infant birth weight can contribute substantially to reductions in the infant mortality rate. Of all infants born at low birth weight, the smallest (those weighing less than 1,500 grams) are at highest risk of dying in their first year.

However, some researchers have proposed that further improvement in the survival of VLBW infants is nearly impossible, and reduction in the underlying rate of VLBW births is the only avenue toward reduction of neonatal mortality rates. Another important issue is the long-term effects of LBW on affected infants who survive their first year, as these infants are more likely to experience long-term developmental and neurologic disabilities than are infants of normal birth weight.

Recent increases in LBW are due largely to preterm delivery related to increases in multiple gestation. Smoking accounts for 20 to 30 percent of all LBW births in the United States. The effect of smoking on LBW rates appears to be attributable to intrauterine growth retardation rather than to preterm delivery. VLBW is primarily associated with preterm birth, which may be associated with the use of illicit drugs during pregnancy.

Approximately two-thirds of LBW infants and 98 percent of VLBW infants are born preterm. In addition, preterm birth is the leading cause of those neonatal deaths not associated with birth defects. Survival rates of infants have been shown to increase as gestational age advances, even among very preterm infants. Therefore, reduction in preterm delivery holds the greatest promise for overall reduction in infant illness, disability, and death.

Because the specific causes of preterm delivery are unclear, research is needed before tailored interventions can be developed. Preterm birth is associated with a number of modifiable risk factors, including the use of alcohol, tobacco, or other drugs during pregnancy and low prepregnancy weight or low weight gain during pregnancy.

Other important risk factors for preterm birth are vaginal infections and domestic violence. Rates of preterm delivery in the United States increased over the last three decades of the 20th century. Between 1989 and 1996, this increase was due largely to an increase in multiple gestation. The gap between African American and white infants persists as well, for reasons that are largely unexplained and that have been shown to be independent of other known risk factors. Risk factors that African American women may disproportionately experience include short inter-pregnancy intervals and exposure to psychosocial stress.

Increase the proportion of mothers who achieve a recommended weight gain during their pregnancies. Maternal weight gain is susceptible to intervention and represents an avenue for prevention of poor birth outcomes. The Institute of Medicine's 1990 guidelines for weight gain in pregnancy recommend a graduated level of weight gain based on a woman's prepregnancy body mass index (BMI). In 1988, approximately three-quarters of married women who delivered at full term gained the recommended weight during pregnancy.

The American Academy of Pediatrics has recommended that healthy full-term infants be put down to sleep on their backs. The National Institute of Child Health and Human Development and the Maternal and Child Health Bureau instituted the "Back to Sleep" campaign in 1994 to educate parents and physicians about this recommendation. While the percentage of infants put to sleep on their stomachs dropped dramatically between 1992 and 1997, much of the improvement was in the percentage of infants put to sleep on their sides. Although not as dangerous as the stomach, from the side position infants may roll onto their stomachs.

Therefore, the objective focuses on increasing the percentage of infants who are put down to sleep on their backs. Specific developmental disabilities will be monitored among school-aged children since not all occurrences are manifested or recognized until those ages. Interventions to reduce the occurrence of some intrauterine infections and increased access to genetic counseling should reduce prenatal causes of developmental disabilities.

The early identification and prophylactic treatment of sickle cell disease are expected to reduce the occurrence of postnatal cerebrovascular complications, which are known postnatal causes of cerebral palsy and mental retardation. Increased safety belt use and other measures to prevent unintentional childhood injury, interventions to prevent child abuse, Haemophilus influenzae immunization, and increased access to medical care to reduce meningitis also will reduce the occurrences of developmental disabilities due to postnatal causes.

The Metropolitan Atlanta Developmental Disabilities Surveillance Program (MADDSP) is the only high-quality surveillance system that monitors the number of cases of mental retardation and other developmental disabilities. MADDSP is a regional data source from a principally urban area, and therefore MADDSP findings cannot be generalized to the Nation; in particular, MADDSP findings may not be representative of rural regions. Efforts are under way to use MADDSP methods to build similar data systems in other regions of the country. NTDs, including spina bifida, occur when the fetal neural tube fails to close fully, interrupting development of the central nervous system.

Approximately 50 percent of pregnancies affected with NTDs may be prevented with adequate consumption of folic acid from 1 month before conception through the first 3 months of pregnancy. In 1992, the U.S. Public Health Service (PHS) recommended that all women of child-bearing age consume 400 micrograms of folic acid daily. For women who already have had an NTD-affected pregnancy, PHS recommends that women consult with a health care professional about taking a much larger amount of folic acid-4,000 micrograms (4.0 milligrams)-when planning a pregnancy.

In 1998, the Institute of Medicine further recommended that to reduce the risk of an NTD-affected pregnancy, all women capable of becoming pregnant should consume 400 micrograms of folic acid daily, from fortified foods or supplements or a combination of the two, in addition to consuming folate-rich foods, such as orange juice, green vegetables, and beans.

Most grain products (including enriched flour, breads, breakfast cereals, rice, and pasta) now are fortified with folic acid. However, the amount of folic acid that some segments of the reproductive-aged population might receive through their diet may not adequately meet the PHS recommendation of 400 micrograms daily. Thus, women capable of becoming pregnant need to review their dietary options, eat a diet that includes folate-rich foods, and target consumption of folic acid-fortified food as well as take a folic acid-containing supplement.

A range of effects, including spontaneous abortion, LBW, and preterm delivery, have been associated with prenatal use of licit and illicit drugs, including alcohol, tobacco, cocaine, and marijuana. As discussed above, tobacco is associated with LBW and spontaneous abortion. Heavy alcohol use is associated with FAS, and even moderate alcohol use has demonstrated effects on preterm delivery.

The use of cocaine during pregnancy is associated with premature birth and impaired fetal growth. In addition, women who use cocaine are at especially high risk of infectious diseases, including hepatitis B and HIV. Exposure to marijuana in utero may be associated with LBW, preterm birth, and neurobehavioural functioning. However, isolating the effects of marijuana use on newborns is difficult because users of the drug often use alcohol and tobacco as well.

Self-reported use of illicit drugs, such as cocaine and marijuana, is quite rare, with 98 percent of pregnant women reporting abstaining from these drugs. Rates of abstinence from harmful substances during pregnancy appear to be declining slowly. The use of alcohol during pregnancy, despite the established health risk, exemplifies this trend.

In 1996-97, 86 percent of pregnant women abstained from alcohol use, an increase of 9 percent from the 1988 baseline. Rates of frequent drinking (at least seven drinks per week or at least five drinks on any occasion in the past month) among pregnant women have begun to decline, with only 1.3 percent of pregnant women reporting recent binge drinking in 1996-97, compared to 2.9 percent in 1994-95.

Unintentional alcohol exposure is particularly likely to occur early in pregnancy, before a woman knows she is pregnant. In addition to the objectives presented here, objectives in Focus Area 26. Substance Abuse, address alcohol consumption among women of reproductive age and tobacco use by pregnant women. FAS is one of the leading preventable causes of mental retardation and a leading cause of birth defects, including growth deficiency and microcephaly. Affected children also are likely to show infantile irritability, poor coordination, hypotonia, and attention deficit/hyperactivity disorder.

The diagnosis of FAS is based on three criteria: prenatal or postnatal growth retardation or both, central nervous system impairment, and characteristic facial malformations. Abnormalities of other organs and systems, however, have been noted in combination with these characteristics. Estimates of the cases of FAS vary from 0.2 to 1.0 per 1,000 live births. In addition to FAS, studies have documented more subtle growth and neurodevelopmental deficits among children whose mothers drank alcohol during pregnancy.

Alcohol-related birth defects and alcohol-related neurodevelopmental disorders are thought to occur three to four times more often than diagnosed cases of FAS. Because of these lifelong effects, and because a safe level of alcohol consumption during pregnancy has not been identified, the American Academy of Pediatrics and the American College of Obstetricians and Gynecologists recommend that women who are pregnant or are planning a pregnancy abstain from the use of alcohol.

Despite broad agreement on the importance of FAS, consistent diagnosis of the syndrome at birth has been difficult to achieve. Thus, accurately estimating the number or proportion of infants affected by FAS is challenging for a number of reasons: the difficulty of evaluating an infant's central nervous system, lack of training among clinicians, inconsistent diagnostic criteria, clinicians' tendency to avoid associating their patients with the stigma of alcohol problems, and failures of mothers to report alcohol intake during gestation.

Breast milk is widely acknowledged to be the most complete form of nutrition for infants, with a range of benefits for infants' health, growth, immunity, and development. The benefits of breastfeeding include decreased new cases or severity of diarrhea, respiratory infections, and ear infections, among others, and reduced cost to the family. In addition, breastfeeding has been shown to improve maternal health, with demonstrated effects, including reduction in postpartum bleeding, earlier return to prepregnancy weight, reduced risk of premenopausal breast cancer, and reduced risk of osteoporosis, continuing long after the postpartum period.

In general, the American Academy of Pediatrics considers breastfeeding to be "the ideal method of feeding and nurturing infants. "Universal breastfeeding is not recommended in the United States. Women who use illicit drugs, who have active, untreated tuberculosis, or who test positive for HIV, as well as those who use certain prescribed drugs, should not breast-feed. In general, however, increasing the rate of breastfeeding, particularly among low-income and certain racial and ethnic populations less likely to begin breastfeeding in the hospital or to sustain it throughout the infant's first year, is an important public health goal.

Rates of breastfeeding are highest among college-educated women and women aged 35 years and older. The lowest rates of breastfeeding are found among those whose infants are at highest risk of poor health and development: those aged 21 years and under and those with low educational levels. However, many of these groups have shown the greatest increase in breastfeeding rates since 1989. Rates of breastfeeding among African American women during the postpartum period increased 65 percent, and rates of African American women breastfeeding at 6 months grew 81 percent between 1988 and 1997.

Breastfeeding rates among women aged 20 years and under at both periods also increased substantially, as did those among women with a grade-school education. While these improvements are encouraging, education of new mothers and their partners; education of health providers; changes in routine maternity ward practices; social support, including support from employers; and greater media portrayal of breastfeeding as the normal method of infant feeding are needed to increase breastfeeding rates among those at highest risk.

Significant illness, disability, and death are associated with sickle cell disease because of increased susceptibility to severe bacterial infections-meningitis, pneumonia, and septicemia-all major causes of death among children with the disorder. Life-threatening episodes of sepsis from pneumococcus and other organisms are well-recognized complications of sickle cell disease in children. The efficacy of daily oral penicillin prophylaxis in preventing infection among young children with sickle cell disease has been demonstrated.

Sepsis rates have been shown to be clearly improved by prophylactic therapy in the U.S. penicillin trial, but concerns about actual use of penicillin in large populations and about penicillin-resistant organisms necessitate continued monitoring of sepsis rates in large populations. Historically, services for children with special health care needs have been difficult for families to access and for providers to coordinate.

Families must navigate a variety of organizations and providers and often face geographic and financial barriers to care. Primary care providers in the community are not always comfortable providing care to children with complex needs, nor do they have time to co-ordinate the variety of resources families need. A lack of knowledge-of comprehensive needs and corresponding community-based resources and of payment mechanisms-presents a challenge for both families and providers.

Poor communication between families and providers and cross-cultural misunderstandings are additional concerns for both families and providers. Care for children with special health care needs should be provided and coordinated through a "medical home" that is accessible, family-centered, continuous, comprehensive, coordinated, compassionate, and culturally competent and linguistically appropriate.

Physicians and parents share responsibility for ensuring that children and their families have access to all the medical and nonmedical services needed to help them achieve their maximum potential. Family-centered care recognizes that the family is the principal care-giver and the center of strength and support for children. Family-centered services share unbiased and complete information with families on an ongoing basis.

Continuous care assures that the same primary pediatric health care professionals are available from infancy through adolescence and provide assistance with transitions (to home, school, and adult services). Coordinated care links families to support, educational, and community-based services, and information is centralized.

Compassionate caregivers express concern for the well-being of the child and family. Culturally appropriate and linguistically competent care recognizes, values, and respects the family's cultural background. Families continuously face the challenge of obtaining and coordinating the primary and special services their children require. Differing eligibility criteria, duplication and gaps in services, inflexible funding sources, and poor coordination among service sectors are some of the barriers consistently reported.

Many of these issues can be resolved only through the concerted effort of a system of services- the broad array of public and private entities serving children and families in the Nation's communities. These service systems should ensure access to a source of insurance for primary and specialty care and enabling services, an identified medical home, and care coordination. Families and their care professionals should participate in the design and implementation of these service systems.

A great deal of attention is now being paid to both violence against women and to the effects of such violence on their children. Hughes' study of children is a good example of this. Hughes mentions that 60% of the children accompanying battered women to a shelter were reported by their mothers to have also been physically abused.

The focus of Hughes' study was the psychological and behavioural problems associated with a child's witnessing violence in the home, not on the overlap between child maltreatment and woman battering. As a result, we have an estimate of the overlap in this shelter-based population but little more about how these forms of abuse are interconnected.

Researchers have come to study the overlap between child maltreatment and woman abuse mostly from two different directions. One strategy has been to identify evidence of woman battering in families where known cases of child maltreatment exist. These studies have most often examined existing records in cases of child abuse and looked for information indicating that a child's mother was also being abused.

For example, Hangen looked at the Massachusetts Department of Social Services' Child Protection case records for indications that an incident of adult domestic violence had occurred since the last case review. He examined computerized records for all active child protection cases in Massachusetts over a seven month period and found that the average incidence of adult victimization recorded in cases was 32.48% across all state child protection offices.

The statewide average overlap jumped to 48.2% when Hangen added cases where records indicated a service goal of protecting the child from adult domestic violence. In another study, Stark and Flitcraft used suspected cases of child abuse and neglect at a major hospital to then search for indications of victimization in the mother's medical records. They found that records of 45% of these children's mothers showed some evidence of being battered.

A second strategy has been to look for evidence of child abuse in the families where abuse of the mothers is known to exist. The percentages of overlap offered include only battered women with children present in the home, not all battered women. Some of these studies have drawn their data from interviews of women residing in battered women's shelters, others have advertised in the media to recruit families, and still others have located battered women who were using other social services.

In the same way, child protection records are likely to give a very different picture of overlapping abuse than reports by battered women in a shelter or using another social service. Few studies have used multiple sources that include data collected from both battered women and from child protection sources. One such study found that 46% of the battered women interviewed reported that at least one of their children had been maltreated; because some women reported that one, but not all of her children, had been abused, this totalled 34% of the children in the study.

Interestingly, when Petchers examined county child protection records she found that 62% of the children in her study had reports of child maltreatment. Petchers found that mothers' reports and those of the county were consistent in only 41% of the cases. Mothers reported many incidents of child maltreatment that were not recorded in county files and vice versa. Still other studies examine the overlap between forms of abuse in one's family of origin as recalled by adults many years later.

Studies that rely on only one source of information are likely to underestimate the overlap. One needs to consider carefully the source of information reported and likely reasons for under or over-reporting of violent incidents. In some studies mothers may be fearful of reporting child maltreatment unknown to official sources. In other studies county child protection agencies are unlikely to record all instances of child maltreatment, or adult recollections of childhood experiences may be highly edited.

Some study found that child abuse was less severe than woman battering in the families studied. They also found that the more dominant a husband is in a family's decision making, the more likely a child is to be abused. Finally, the larger the number of children in a family the more likely there is to be child abuse in the home.

Rosenbaum and O'Leary reported that men who batter their wives were much more likely than others to have grown up in homes where adult domestic violence was occurring. Similarly, Suh and Abel found that batterers who were abused as a child were more likely to abuse their own children. More recently, Straus and Gelles reported that women who were beaten were at least twice to abuse their children when compared to non-abused women.

Walker reported that while 53% of the batterers were reported to abuse their children, 28% of the women she interviewed also reported perpetrating abuse against their children. These studies suggest some type of link between woman battering and subsequent abuse of the child by the mother. An in-depth understanding of this link, however, remains very unclear and in need of study.

Only a few studies state the racial, ethnic or cultural composition of their samples. Even fewer examine differences in regard to racial, ethnic or cultural influences on the overlap between these forms of domestic violence. In short, there is a large overlap between child maltreatment and woman battering.

Child Abuse in Working Sector

Millions of children in India toil as virtual slaves, unable to escape the work that will leave them impoverished, illiterate, and often crippled by the time they reach adulthood. These are India's bonded child laborers. A majority of them are Dalits, so-called untouchables. Bound to their employers in exchange for a loan, they are unable to leave while in debt and earn so little they may never be free of it.

The Indian government knows about these children and has the mandate to free them. Instead, for reasons of apathy, caste bias, and corruption, many government officials deny that they exist at all. Somewhere between sixty to 115 million children are working in India, most in agriculture, others picking rags, making bricks, polishing gemstones, rolling beedi cigarettes, packaging firecrackers, working as domestics, and weaving silk saris and carpets.

In the last decade, efforts in some regions have driven bonded child labor out of factories and into households, which are partially exempt from the law, changing bonded child labor's manifestation but not its prevalence or intensity. In many areas, bonded child labor still flourishes openly.

Poverty contributes to bonded child labor, but it is not the only cause. A lack of access to credit and lack of a concerted social welfare scheme to safeguard against hunger and illness; inaccessible, low quality, and discriminatory schools; the lack of employment and living wages for adults; corruption and apathy among government officials; and historical economic relationships based on the hierarchy of caste are other key elements.

Moreover, bonded children are likely destined for poverty as adults, and likely to bond their own children in order to survive. Both Indian and international law prohibit the use of bonded child labor. As a party to international instruments such as the Convention on the Suppression of Slave Trade and Slavery; the Supplementary Convention on the Abolition of Slavery; the Slave Trade, and Institutions and Practices Similar to Slavery; the Forced Labour Convention; the International Covenant on Civil and Political Rights; the International Covenant on Economic, Social and Cultural Rights; and the Convention on the Rights of the Child, India is obliged to prohibit all forms of slavery, including debt bondage, child servitude, and forced labor, as well as affirmatively protect children from economic exploitation and hazardous work.

Bonded child labor is also specifically identified as among the "worst forms of child labour" by ILO Convention No. 182 concerning the Prohibition and Immediate Action for the Elimination of the Worst Forms of Child Labour, which India has not ratified. India must also take measures to realize its commitments under international law to provide free and compulsory primary education and available and accessible secondary education to every child.

Indian law has long prohibited bonded labor, and regulated and restricted child labor up to age fourteen. The practice of bonded child labor violates various provisions of Indian law, including the constitutional rights to life and liberty; the prohibition on trafficking, begar and other similar forms of forced labor; the prohibition on employment of children under age fourteen in factories, mines, or other hazardous occupations; and other constitutional protections for children.

Labor by children under age fourteen in industries deemed hazardous, including all aspects of the silk industry, is expressly forbidden. Boiling cocoons, hauling baskets of mulberry leaves, and embroidering saris, children are working at every stage of the silk industry. These children work twelve or more hours a day, six and a half or seven days a week, under conditions of physical and verbal abuse. They suffer injuries from fumes, machinery, sharp threads, boiling water,and dead worms.

Girls face particular abuses, including sexual abuse by employers. Mature cocoons are transformed into silk thread through a process of reeling and twisting. Children are cooking cocoons, picking out the dead worms, twisting the filaments into thread, and helping with odd jobs.

Reeling is the process in which dried cocoons are turned into hanks of multi-strand yarn. The first stage of the reeling process is called "cooking" -boiling the cocoons. The cocoon consists of a single long cluster of silk fibers held together by the water-soluble protein sericin. Boiling the cocoon dissolves the protein. Children stand over open basins of boiling water that are heated below by charcoal or fire, keeping the cocoons immersed in the water with a ladle and palpating the boiling cocoons with their hands to see if the sericin is dissolved and the fibers loosened enough to be unwound.

The children are required to reach into the boiling water to feel the cocoons with their hands, rather than with a spoon, on the theory that their hands can more accurately tell when the cocoons are ready to reel. After reeling, individual threads are twisted into strong, multiply silk thread. Twisting usually takes place in small factories with between fifty and a few hundred spindles. These factories use bonded child labor. Children stand for long hours loading the spindles, guiding the thread, and performing other tasks.

As with silk weaving, children reported seeing the books, but many were illiterate and relied on the employer to tell them what was written, rendering them even more vulnerable to exploitation. Children typically reported working ten to fourteen hours a day, with breaks to eat, six days a week. Children will work for even longer when the demand for thread increases; for example, before a festival when women purchase new saris, factories will sometimes operate twenty-four hours a day.

Most children working in reeling units are fired at about age fifteen or sixteen and replaced with their younger brothers or sisters; some will go to work in twisting units, but most must seek other work. Thus whatever skills they may have acquired in the silk unit do not help them in adulthood. Indeed, the injuries and illness suffered as child workers limits what work many can do as adults.

Children also suffer cuts to their hands from the threads and from the machines while winding and twisting the silk thread. Medical examinations in early 2000 of two hundred children ages six to fourteen working in reeling and twisting in Ramanagaram and Channapatna taluks of Bangalore Rural District found high rates of respiratory diseases and skin infections. Children also complained of cuts and other injuries from threads and machines; headaches; pain in the back, legs, neck, and abdomen; colds and bronchitis; hearing loss; and vision problems.

When children are injured or ill, they often must continue to work or lose the income, which forces them deeper into debt. Girl factory workers also suffer sexual abuse from their employers. Activists and investigators in Bangalore Rural District have told Human Rights Watch that sexual abuse by factory owners is so prevalent that factory girls are shunned as potential brides because everyone assumes that these girls have been "touched"-molested or raped -by their employers.

Bonded child labor is not "so rampant" in moriculture, or worm rearing, according to activists in Bangalore Rural District, a major silk worm producing area. In addition to the bondage itself, the hazards of children 's work in agriculture are well-documented and include pesticide poisoning, injury from dangerous tools, and dropping out of school.

As already noted, approximately 40,000 to 50,000 children work in bondage on silk handlooms in Kanchipuram. Until around age fourteen or fifteen, children are usually too small to operate the looms themselves. Instead, they assist weavers by sitting next to them at the loom, legs dangling in the pit, catching the shuttle and embroidering the border. Girls and women also wind the weft thread onto bobbins that are loaded onto the shuttle and woven through the warp threads. In Varanasi town, in nearby Dalit villages, and in Kanchipuram, we saw girls and boys working at the looms, assisting weavers and winding thread on bobbins.

In both Varanasi and Kanchipuram, even if they attended a night school, children reported working twelve to thirteen hours a day with breaks for breakfast and lunch. In Kanchipuram, children reported working seven days a week with two half-days off a month. Girls rarely become weavers, which limits how much they can earn. Researchers in eastern Uttar Pradesh, where most silk weavers are Muslim, have found that girls ' labor is nearly invisible.

In contrast, the children of a loom owner, who himself held other children in debt bondage, lived in markedly different circumstances. Sitting at crowded silk looms for long stretches of time exposes children to a variety of health problems. The rooms are often damp and poorly ventilated; children sit with their legs tucked under them or dangling down into the pit underneath the loom. The crowded work environment encourages the spread of contagious diseases, especially tuberculosis and digestive disorders.

Poor lighting and constant visual strain damages the eyesight. The fine silk threads cut the fingers, and the cuts are difficult to heal properly. A medical examination at a health camp for some eighty-five children released from bondage in Kanchipuram's silk looms in November 1997 found that all were malnourished, two had pulmonary tuberculosis, twenty-six had various skin infections, and many had vision, dental and hearing problems.

Researchers in Uttar Pradesh have found similar problems among children working on silk looms in that state. For example, a worker with a community health organization in Varanasi told Human Rights Watch that silk workers report breathing problems and pain in their shoulders and upper backs. Employer Abuse in Silk Weaving Many children reported that loom owners and weavers abused them verbally and physically.

Bonded labor in India is not just an economic issue but a social issue linked with caste. Allocation of labor on the basis of caste is one of the caste system 's fundamental tenets. Within the caste system, Dalits, or so-called untouchables, have been assigned tasks and occupations deemed ritually polluting for other caste communities. Most bonded laborers are low-caste, illiterate, and extremely poor, while the creditors/ employers are usually higher-caste, literate, comparatively wealthy, and relatively more powerful members of the community.

The traditional silk weaving caste is a lower caste, called a "backward caste," but in both Varanasi and Kanchipuram districts, Dalits have entered the weaving profession in significant numbers, often by being bonded as children. Muslims also dominate sari weaving in some areas, including in urban Varanasi. However, in Varanasi district, Dalits and lower castes have begun weaving in increasing numbers, in part because communal violence and attacks on Muslims have pushed them out of the profession.

Land is the prime asset in rural areas that determines an individual 's standard of living and social status. Lack of access to land makes Dalits economically vulnerable; their dependency is exploited by upper-and middle-caste landlords and allows for many abuses to go unpunished. Landless agricultural laborers throughout the country work for a few kilograms of rice or Rs. 15 to Rs. 35 a day, well below the minimum wage.

Many laborers owe debts to their employers or other moneylenders. Thus, although poverty plays a significant role, connection between caste and bondage goes far beyond poverty to what Professor Thorat has described as the "extra economic compulsion of caste". Extreme economic and political measures are meted out for transgression of caste norms. Bonded labor flourishes in this environment because people cannot complain.

When the families' economic assets are destroyed, the parents are more likely to need the children to work. There are many occurrences where Dalit children stay out of school for one to three months because, for example, of a riot in the village or reprisals against Dalits, and police take men away ....Children are stranded ...There is a decreased interest in going to school, and they need the income. Researchers at the National Labour Institute have confirmed these findings. Discrimination against Dalit children in school also encourages them to drop out and go to work.

Most of the government schools in which Dalit students are enrolled, where they exist at all, are deficient in basic infrastructure, classrooms, teachers, and teaching aids. Dalit students sit at the back of the class and are often treated badly by upper-caste teachers and staff. A majority of Dalit students are also enrolled in vernacular schools whose students suffer serious disadvantages in the job market as compared to those who learn in English-speaking schools.

India's national and state governments share responsibility for protecting bonded child laborers. Their most basic obligations are to prevent children from becoming bonded in the first place, to remove those who are from bondage, and to prevent them from becoming bonded again. On paper, the government has developed a wide array of laws and policies on bonded labor and child labor, which in theory should protect bonded children.

In practice, these are never implemented for most bonded children. Without effective enforcement of either bonded labor or child labor laws, children in bondage - the most vulnerable of all working children -are without recourse. In the mid-and late 1990s the Indian government, under scrutiny from local NGOs and international organizations, paid increased attention to child labor and, to a lesser extent, bonded labor.

Some argued that families need the children's income and that children would be pushed into more marginal and dangerous occupations. Others contended that law enforcement was irreparably ineffective and, therefore, not worth pursuing, even when they were themselves responsible for ensuring effective law enforcement. Rehabilitation programmes for both bonded and child labor remain promising but extremely limited.

Child labor and bonded labor are treated entirely separately in law and in government policy, although both regimes are based on punishing the employer and rehabilitating the worker. The child labor regime revolves around the distinction, enshrined in the Child Labour Act, 1986, that some work is hazardous to children and some is not. For children under fourteen, the law prohibits work deemed hazardous and regulates everything else; children employed illegally are to be withdrawn from work and, following a 1996 Supreme Court order, rehabilitated.

Employers who violate the law are to face fines and imprisonment. All aspects of the silk industry are considered hazardous to children under age fourteen. Children age fourteen and older are not protected by the child labor law. The bonded labor regime is based on the same tenets as those of hazardous child labor: finding, freeing, and rehabilitating the bonded worker, and punishing the employer.

The Bonded Labour System (Abolition) Act, 1976, which prohibits all forms of bonded labor for people of any age, establishes this framework. However, compared with the child labor law, the bonded labor law allows for a longer maximum prison sentence, protects children over as well as under fourteen years old, extinguishes the debt, and actually codifies the rehabilitation requirement. In addition, offenses under the bonded labor law, unlike the child labor law, are cognizable, meaning that a police officer may arrest without a warrant and initiate prosecution.

Despite these two sets of laws, there are no specific programs for bonded children, who fall at their intersection. In contrast with extensive rhetoric on child labor; the government continues to pay little attention to bonded labor. Although there are an estimated twenty to sixty-five million bonded laborers, adults and children, in India, the government identified only 1,795 bonded laborers from 2000 to 2002, according to its own records, and fined or jailed almost no employers.

High-level government officials adamantly deny that children are bonded at all, but fail to collect basic information, including age, on bonded laborers. An exception is the National Human Rights Commission (NHRC), which the Supreme Court ordered in 1997 to supervise the 1976 Bonded Labour System (Abolition) Act's implementation. The NHRC has been able to pressure some local officials into freeing and rehabilitating bonded children in some areas, primarily in Uttar Pradesh's carpet belt.

But its resources and power are limited. District, State, and National Responsibility for Bonded Labor States are responsible for enforcing the Bonded Labour System (Abolition) Act, 1976, and do so through their district magistrates, in some states called district collectors or deputy commissioners, who are directed to form bonded labor "vigilance committees."

States bear primary responsibility for withdrawing children from illegal work, for rehabilitating them, and for punishing employers. The Ministry of Labour is ultimately responsible for the states' compliance with the law and determines which industries are hazardous. The ministry also runs child labor elimination programs, consisting primarily of transitional schools for some 181,000 former child workers. Because sericulture and silk weaving are classified as hazardous, employing any children in these sectors up to age fourteen-bonded or not-is illegal under Indian law.

Rehabilitating child workers is critical to preventing them from immediately returning to work. It is generally conceived of as providing education to the child and employment or sources of credit to parents. Rehabilitation of child laborers became legally required in 1996, when the Supreme Court, finding continued use of child labor prohibited by the Child Labour (Prohibition and Regulation) Act, 1986, ordered state labor inspectors to identify children employed illegally, to fine employers Rs. 20,000 (U.S. $ 417) per child, and to deposit this money in a "Child Labour Rehabilitation-cum-Welfare Fund," the income on which must be used only for the child concerned.

Where the child is employed in a factory, mine, or other hazardous work, the Court requires the state to employ an adult family member in lieu of the child or, where this is not possible, to deposit an additional Rs. 5,000 (U.S. $ 104) into the fund on the condition that the child be withdrawn from work and sent to school. Parents should then receive the income on the Rs. 25,000 (U.S. $ 521) for as long as they continue to send the child to school.

There is no minimum age of employment. Children under age fourteen are protected by the Child Labour (Prohibition and Regulation) Act, 1986, which prohibits their work in hazardous occupations and regulates their work in non-hazardous occupations. In addition, the Factories Act, 1948, forbids the employment of children under age fourteen in all factories, and allows fourteen and fifteen-year-olds to work only with a certificate of fitness from a doctor. Otherwise, children age fourteen and older are not protected, although like all workers, they are covered by the Bonded Labour System (Abolition) Act, 1976.

The Indian Constitution in article 24 also prohibits the employment of children under age fourteen in factories, mines, and other hazardous occupations. This provision is considered one of India 's constitutionally-proclaimed fundamental rights. In addition, article 39 provides:

— (e) that the health and strength of workers, men and women, and the tender age of children are not abused and that citizens are not forced by economic necessity to enter avocations unsuited to their age or strength;

— (f) that children are given opportunities and facilities to develop in a healthy manner and in conditions of freedom and dignity and that childhood and youth are protected against exploitation and against moral and material abandonment.

A plethora of national laws regulate or prohibit various forms of child labor. The most significant is the Child Labour (Prohibition and Regulation) Act, 1986, which prohibits the employment of children under age fourteen in thirteen occupations and fifty-seven processes, including cloth printing, dying, and weaving and, as of 1999, sericulture processing and zari (gold thread) making, the act also regulates the working conditions of children in legal occupations.

Thus, children in occupations not designated as hazardous, such as mulberry cultivation and other agricultural work, are limited in the number of hours and days per week they may work. The law does not apply to children working for their immediate families (parents or siblings) or in schools that the government has established, financed, or recognized.

The Court charged the inspectors with ensuring that the children identified received free, compulsory education until age fourteen and charged the Ministry of Labour with monitoring the decision's implementation. The Court also called on the act's penal provisions to be used, and instructed states to conduct surveys to determine the extent of child labor in their territories.

Education is a fundamental right under Indian law. The Supreme Court held in 1993 that education up to age fourteen had become a fundamental right; in December 2002, the 93rd Constitutional Amendment became law, adding to the list of fundamental rights a state obligation to provide free and compulsory education to all children ages six to fourteen.

The amendment narrows the constitution's directive principle on education to early childhood care and education through age six, and adds to the list of citizens 'fundamental duties parents' and guardians' obligation to provide their children ages six to fourteen with opportunities for education. Activists have strongly objected to the exclusion of children up to age five and over age fourteen from the amendment and to the obligation placed on parents.

Guidelines of Maltreatment

For years, in fact, most communities have treated the abuse of a woman and the maltreatment of a child in the same family as separate phenomena having little to do with each other. Now, however, communities are asked to confront a new and compelling set of facts:

1) adult domestic violence and child maltreatment often occur together and

2) new responses are required of everyone, if violence within families is to stop.

To date, community institutions and families have been offered few resources and tools to resolve the complex issues raised by overlapping domestic violence and child maltreatment in a family.

As communities work to improve their responses to families experiencing domestic violence and child maltreatment, Effective Intervention offers a framework for developing interventions and measuring progress. Effective Intervention focuses on three primary systems: the child protection system, the network of community-based domestic violence programs, and the juvenile or other trial courts which have jurisdiction over child maltreatment cases.

Many other systems-including law enforcement, child welfare, faith institutions, schools, health care systems, extended families, and community-based agencies-contribute in important ways to the solutions outlined below, and many of the recommendations in Effective Intervention are relevant to these systems as well.

Community leaders should join together to establish responses to domestic violence and child maltreatment that provide meaningful help, supports, and services for families. Simultaneously, communities should hold violent perpetrators responsible for their behaviour and provide legal interventions and services to stop this violence.

This first principle is an overriding one from which flow most other principles and recommendations in the book. Three core values. To implement this guiding principle, interventions should be designed to create safety, enhance well-being, and provide stability for children and families.

Children in the care of their non-offending parents. To ensure stability and permanency, children should remain in the care of their non-offending parent (or parents), whenever possible. Making adult victims safer and stopping batterers' assaults are two important ways to do this. Community service system with many points of entry. To provide safety and stability for families, a community service system with many points of entry should be created.

This service system should be characterized by the provision of services in appropriate settings as soon as problems are identified; services providers trained to respond meaningfully and respectfully; services designed to minimize the need for victims to respond to multiple and changing service providers; and adequate resources to allow service providers to meet family needs and avoid out-of-home placements.

Community leaders should design interventions and responses that are appropriate to the diverse range of families experiencing domestic violence and child maltreatment. Families with less serious cases of child maltreatment and domestic violence should be able to gain access to help without the initiation of a child protection investigation or the substantiation of a finding of maltreatment.

Because domestic violence encompasses a wide range of behaviours-from the extremely dangerous to the less serious-families require a range of interventions, some of them voluntary and some mandated.

Collaboration for the safety, well-being, and stability of children and families. Every community should have a mechanism to close gaps in services, coordinate multiple interventions, and develop interagency agreements and protocols for providing basic services to families.

Existing coordination efforts should be expanded to include active involvement of domestic violence advocates, child protection workers, and community residents. Expansion and reallocation of resources to create safety, well-being, and stability. The services recommended in Effective Intervention require the expenditure of significant additional resources.

Some of these services include placing battered women's advocacy and support services within courts and child protection services, locating family support services in domestic violence agencies, and providing services for every victim of domestic violence and child maltreatment who needs or requests them. Respect and dignity for all people coming before agencies and courts. Agency leaders should make an ongoing commitment to fact-finding in order to determine whether children and families of diverse backgrounds are served fairly and capably by their agencies.

Agencies and juvenile courts should develop meaningful collaborative relationships with diverse communities in an effort to develop effective interventions in those communities. Commitment to building internal capacity to respond effectively to families experiencing domestic violence and child maltreatment. Every community should cross-train its service providers on identification, assessment, referral, and safety interventions.

Agencies and courts should build staff capacity to attend more competently to clients from diverse communities and income levels. Fact-finding and confidentiality. Agencies and courts should develop memos delineating the mandates of each system, their confidentiality requirements, and agreements for sharing information.

Child protection services and the juvenile courts should support the principle and policy goal of privileged communication protections for battered women. Development of information gathering and evaluation systems to determine the intended and unintended outcomes of collaborative efforts. Policy makers and programme developers should support evaluation and research studies that directly inform policy and programme decision-making.

Leadership in developing new services and publicly articulating the need for additional resources to promote family safety. Child protection services and community-based child welfare agencies should collaborate with others to assess the availability of resources in the community, develop new responses, and monitor the effectiveness of community programmes. Improvement in capacity to promote safety for all family members.

Child protection services should develop screening and assessment procedures, information systems, case monitoring protocols, and staff training to identify and respond to domestic violence and promote family safety. Development of service plans and referrals that focus on the safety, stability, and well-being of victims and hold domestic violence perpetrators accountable.

Agency policy should state clearly when children can remain safely with non-abusing parents; the assessment required to determine safety; and the safety planning, services, support, and monitoring that will be required in these cases. Child protection services should develop separate service plans for victims and perpetrators, and assess thoroughly the possible harm to a child resulting from being maltreated or witnessing domestic violence and develop service plans to address this harm.

Community agencies providing services to families in the child protection services caseload should screen every family member privately and confidentially for domestic violence and provide help to them, including safety planning and meeting basic human needs. By policy, they should allow workers adequate time to assist domestic violence victims.

Leadership to promote collaborations and develop new resources for adult and child safety and well-being. Domestic violence programs should collaborate with others to develop new joint service models for families, develop joint protocols to remove interagency policy and practice barriers and enhance family safety and well-being, and improve access to services.

Domestic violence organizations should develop a community dialogue about the prevention of family violence, and provide leadership to inform policymakers and funders about the economic, legal, emotional, and social supports that battered women and their children need to be safe and secure. Development of internal capacity to respond to the safety and support needs of families.

Domestic violence organizations should create supportive interventions for battered women who maltreat their children, and provide child-friendly environments for the families they serve. All domestic violence organizations, especially shelters and safe homes, should have well-trained, full-time children's advocates on staff to provide services or develop referral linkages.

They also should consider the needs of battered women with boys over the age of 12 who are often turned away and families with substance abuse and other mental health problems, as well as ways to provide community-based services to women who are referred to them voluntarily and involuntarily by child protection services and the juvenile court.

Interventions with perpetrators of domestic violence should be part of larger, coordinated networks of criminal justice responses and community services, address the safety and well-being of both child and adult victims, and hold perpetrators accountable for stopping violent and threatening behaviour.

Full participation in national and local efforts to improve juvenile courts. Juvenile courts must have sufficient judicial and staff resources to allow appropriate time and attention for each case, treat each case with the highest priority, adopt recognized best practices in administering the juvenile court, and collaborate with other courts that may be dealing with family members and others involved in the case, including criminal court, civil court, and domestic relations and family court.

Leadership to ensure that the goals of the juvenile court law are realized. The juvenile court should take a leadership role to ensure cooperation among all parts of the juvenile court system, identify needed resources to serve families experiencing domestic violence, and develop strategies to obtain these resources. Judges should collaborate with others to determine what resources must be made available in the community.

They also should have specific powers to enable them to ensure family safety and should use their judicial powers to see that adequate efforts to ensure safety for child and adult victims are provided. Where there is domestic violence in a child protection case, judges should make orders which keep the child and parent victim safe, keep the non-abusive parent and child together whenever possible, hold the perpetrator accountable, identify the service needs of all family members, and create clear, detailed visitation guidelines which focus upon safe exchanges and safe environments for visits.

Best practices for the management of cases involving child maltreatment and domestic violence. Petitioners in child protection proceedings should allege in petitions or pleadings any domestic violence which has caused harm to a child. The juvenile court should prioritize removing any abuser before removing a child from a battered mother, and work with child welfare and social service agencies to ensure that separate service plans for the perpetrator and the victim of domestic violence are developed.

5

Child Abuse Prevention

Today, society is challenge those who would prey upon youth - either by altering their minds with illegal substances or through physically or sexually assaulting their bodies. These scourges - drug abuse and child abuse- must be eliminated. There are many challenges that confront today's youth, and child abuse is one of these.

Child abuse is a fact in our society and a matter of great concern for most parents. Fortunately, child abuse is preventable and parents can help their children master prevention strategies. There are three underlying principles to effective youth protection strategies:

— The child needs to be able to recognise the situations that may result in abuse.

— The child needs to be able to assert the right to resist the abuser.

— The child needs to be able to tell an adult when he or she has encountered abuse and to feel confident that the adult will take actions to prevent further abuse.

Traditionally, children have been told of the risks associated with strangers. As we have come to learn, child abuse is committed most often by a person who is known to the child, often in a position of authority over the child and sadly by some parents or guardians. Therefore, if we teach only to be wary of strangers, we are not protecting our children as completely as we must.

The Protective Behaviours model encourages children to be aware of their body signals. Some instances might include when they are feeling threatened their stomach might feel sick, their palms become sweaty and so on. Interviews with child molesters document that when children resist advances made by the molester, the molester will usually abandon further attempts with that child.

A relatively low incidence of child molestation involves the use of physical force. Children need to be trained to "yell" when inappropriately approached by anyone - friend, relative, or stranger. Children need to be taught to tell their parent, teacher or other adult whenever they encounter questionable situations or attempted abuse.

Since adults do not always listen when a child talks to them, the child needs to be told to keep on telling until someone listens. Sometimes, a child may not be able to talk about what has happened, but will communicate in other ways. For example, the child may go out of the way to avoid being alone with a particular person, such as a baby-sitter. Sometimes children who have been sexually abused wear additional clothes and cannot bear to be touched even on so-called "neutral" areas such as the shoulder or hand.

This is a kind of communication to which parents need to be sensitive as it may be an indicator of abuse. If your child becomes a victim of abuse, your initial reaction can be very important in helping him or her through the ordeal. The following guidelines may help you:

— Don't panic or overreact to the information disclosed by your child.

— Don't criticise your child or claim that your child misunderstood what happened.

— Do respect your child's privacy and take your child to a place where the two of you can talk without interruptions or distractions.

— Do reassure your child that he or she is not to blame for what happened. Tell the child that you appreciate being told about it and that you will help make sure that it will not happen again.

— Do encourage your child to tell the proper authorities what happened but try to avoid repeated interviews, which can be very stressful for the child.

— Do consult your paediatrician or other child abuse authority about the need for counselling to assist your child.

Finally, if abuse happens to your child, do not blame yourself or your child. Individuals who victimise children are not readily identifiable; they come from all walks of life and all socio-economic levels. Often, they present a pleasant image - they are prominent citizens and are active in the community. The molester is skilled at manipulating children, often by giving excessive attention, gifts, and money. Most abuse occurs in situations in which the child knows and trusts the adult.

It is important that your child understands the right to react assertively when faced with a situation which he or she perceives as dangerous. When teaching your child self-protection skills, make it clear that although some of the basic strategies involved seem to contradict the sort of behaviour you normally expect of your child, these strategies apply to a situation that is not normal. When feeling threatened, your child must feel free to exercise the right to:

— Trust his or her instincts or feelings.

— Expect privacy.

— Say no to unwanted touching or affection.

— Say no to an adult's inappropriate demands and requests.

— Withhold information that could jeopardise his or her safety.

— Refuse gifts.

— Be rude or unhelpful if the situation warrants.

— Run, scream, and make a scene.

— Physically fight off unwanted advances.

— Ask for help.

It's important to remember these are protective strategies designed to give youth the power to protect themselves. When the child has responded to one of the situations ask them "When would it be safe to do that" or "Would doing that keep you safe?" What if you are home alone and the telephone rings; a voice on the other end asks if your parents are home. What could you do?

(a) Tell the caller your parents are busy and cannot come to the phone.

(b) Take a message and the phone number of the caller.

(c) If the message needs an immediate response, call your parent.

(d) Do not tell the caller you are home alone.

What if an older child hangs around your school and tries to give pills to younger students. What could you do?

(a) Tell your teacher.

(b) Tell your parent even if you told the teacher.

(c) Stay away from the person with the pills.

What if you are home alone (or with your brother or sister) and someone knocks on the door and asks to read the indoor electric meter. This person is not wearing a uniform. What could you do?

(a) Keep the front door or screen door locked.

(b) Do not open the door to anyone without permission from a parent.

(c) Tell the person to come back later when your parent can come to the door. Do not let the person know your parent is away.

(d) Use the telephone to call a neighbour and ask for assistance.

What if someone comes to you and says that your parent is sick and you must go with him or her. What could you do?

(a) If at school, go to the principal or your teacher for assistance and verification.

(b) If at home or somewhere else, call the emergency number parent's employer, neighbour, close relative - for assistance and verification.

(c) Do not go anywhere without verification from someone in authority who you have been told to trust.

What if you are in a public restroom and someone tries to touch you. What could you do?

(a) Yell "STOP THAT" as loudly as you can.

(b) Run out of the room as quickly as possible.

(c) Tell your parent, a police officer, security guard, or other adult (such as your teacher) what happened.

What if you are walking to school in the rain. A car stops and the driver asks if you want a ride. What could you do?

(a) Stay away from the car - you do not need to go close to the car to answer.

(b) Unless you have your parent's permission to ride with the person, say "No, thank you. "If the driver persists, say "No!"

(c) Tell your teacher when you get to school and tell your parent when you get home.

What if you are playing on the playground and an adult comes up to you and asks you to help find his or her lost puppy. What could you do?

(a) If you do not know the person, stay away and go directly home.

(b) Even if you know the person, do not help. Adults should ask other adults for help. Before you assist, you must get your parent's permission.

(c) Tell your parent what happened.

What if you are walking down the street and someone comes up to you and wants to take your picture. The person asks you to come to his or her house. What could you do?

(a) Stay away from the person and say in a loud voice "No, 1 don't want my picture taken!"

(b) Do not ever go into anyone else's house without your parent's permission.

(c) Tell your parent about the person.

What if an older child you know invites you to play a game, and to pretend that he or she is the doctor and you are the patient. This child tells you to take off your clothes so that the "doctor" can examine the "patient". What could you do?

(a) Keep your clothes on.

(b) If he or she persists, yell and get away.

(c) Tell your parent.

This exercise will help your child be prepared to avoid situations that could lead to abuse or molestation. The safety notebook can be a loose-leaf notebook or pages fastened together with staples for which your child has made an original cover which uses the fleur-de-lis or the salute. The safety notebook provides a place where your child can list emergency telephone numbers, including parents 'work numbers and a neighbour or friend's number to be contacted when parents are unavailable (Home Safety, Emergencies, etc.).

In addition, your child can list the safety rules that you have discussed together. Encourage your child to decorate each page with pictures and drawings that illustrate some of the rules. In the special notebook your child should trace their hand and in each finger outline write the name of a trusted adult. The thumb is reserved for a close family member.

He or she may also want to list other kinds of safety guidelines, such as rules for bicycle safety. When children (or young people) join the Scouting programme, they assume an obligation to be faithful to the principles of Scouting as embodied in the Joey Scout Promise, Joey Scout Law, Joey Scout Theme, Cub Scout Promise, Cub Scout Law, Cub Scout motto, Scout Promise, Scout Law, Scout motto.

The principles of Scouting do not require that children place themselves in potentially dangerous situations quite the contrary, we want children to "be prepared" and to "do their best" to avoid these situations.

Sometimes children enjoy creating a script for a play or skit that will dramatise their understanding of the safety rules. These may then be presented to other children as a service project. As a parent, you can guide the creation of the script so that the situations are based on reality and demonstrate successful avoidance of abuse. It is important that children can feel they can protect themselves.

The most important step a parent can take to protect his or her child from abuse is to establish an atmosphere of open communication in the home. A child must feel comfortable in bringing his or her parent any sensitive problems or relating experiences in which someone approached the child in an appropriate manner or in a way that made the child feel uncomfortable.

Studies have demonstrated that more than half of all incidents of child abuse are never reported because the victims are too afraid or too confused to report their experiences. It is important that your children be allowed to talk freely about their likes and dislikes, their friends, and their true feelings.

One way to create open communication is through family meetings at which safety issues can be addressed by the entire family. Self esteem strategies need to be included with the entire family. This activity should focus on positive good health. Encourage each family member to share a special compliment about another member. The aim of this activity is to get the family to experience feeling good about themselves and others in their support network.

The basic rules for child safety, it is important to stress that traditional cautions about "strangers" are not sufficient to protect our children. Child abusers are usually known to the child. Therefore, a more appropriate protection strategy is based upon teaching children to recognise situations or actions to be wary of. To teach following safety rules with your child.

— If you are in a public place and get separated from your parent (or authorised guardian), do not wander around looking for him or her. Go to a police officer, a checkout counter, the security office, or the lost-and-found area and quickly tell that you have been separated from your parent and need help.

— You should not get into a car or go anywhere with any person unless you have your parent's permission.

— If someone follows you on foot or in a car, stay away from him or her. You do not need to go near the car to talk to the person inside.

— Adults and older youths who are not in your family and who need help (such as finding an address or locating a lost pet) should not ask children for help; they should ask other adults.

— You should use the buddy system and never go anywhere alone. Always ask your parent's permission to go somewhere, especially into someone else's home

— Never hitchhike.

— Never ride with anyone unless you have your parent's permission. No one should ask you to keep a special secret that makes you feel uncomfortable. If this happens, tell your parent or teacher.

— If someone wants to take your picture, tell your parent or teacher. No one should touch you on the parts of your body covered by a bathing suit (unless it is your doctor while treating you or during a physical examination), nor should you touch anyone else in those areas. Your body is special and private.

— You have the right to say "No!" to someone who tries to take you somewhere, touches you, or makes you feel uncomfortable in any way.

These are some simple safety rules that can be approached in the same non-frightening manner in which you tell your child not to play with fire. They emphasise situations common to many child molestation cases.

Communicating with Kids

Communicating with kids - yours or someone else's -

isn't all that easy, particularly when the subject is something like drugs or child abuse. It's not easy, but neither is it impossible, especially if you keep these tips in mind:

— Establish rapport: Rapport comes from a record of friendly, honest, face-to-face adult/kid relations. Welcome their suggestions. Laugh at their jokes. Downplay the lectures. Stay flexible—but stay firm.

— Don't wait till there's a problem. Play and work and talk together as part of the normal, day-to-day routine. Then, when a problem hits, you can communicate.

— Whenever possible, join the group your kid joins—or at least work closely with it.

— Use peer pressure—the influence of kids on other kids—to help get your message across.

Drug Abuse Prevention

Every child is unique. If your son or daughter's problem doesn't seem to fit into one or more of these reasons, ask them why they drink, or take drugs without being accusing. Drinking and drug taking is a learned behaviour.

A child under the influence of alcohol or other drugs may have various symptoms, depending on the substance. But for all drugs, you are likely to observe slurred or incoherent speech, memory lapses, and indifference to hygiene and grooming.

Help a child build Confidency by:

— Help them to feel good about themselves - praise them when they do well and build up their confidence when they find the going tough.

— Encourage them to be responsible for their own actions - trust them.

— Try not to talk down to your children. Maybe they have seen you drinking alcohol - be honest with them about this.

— Listen to them - show that you care. Show them you under stand how they feel and what their real problem is in making decisions on how to behave.

— Spend time together - make your children feel an important part of the family.

— Provide leadership - if children are to learn to set limits on their own behaviour they need guidelines from you.

— Encourage healthy activities - such as relaxation and sport.

— Encourage them to say "no" to drug offers.

— Know the facts about drugs. Inventing dangers that don't exist won't help, but providing information on the real dangers of drug use will.

— Participation in community activities - talk to concerned people at your parents association, Scout Group, school, social clubs or church about drug education.

Talking with your children about Drugs. Telling scary stories about drugs often increases curiosity and can inspire "thrill-seeking". Forbidding the use of drugs may prompt your child to challenge your authority - and experiment. Try to keep discussions friendly and honest. There are no "winners" or "losers" in this sort of talk, but rather two people who respect and care for each other.

Your aim is to point out your concern for their well-being. Be prepared to discuss drugs whenever someone in the family is concerned about drugs or any sensitive issue. Your children might know more about some drugs than you do. Marching in without the facts, or going overboard about a drug when what they have heard tells them otherwise, might dent your credibility.

Discussion might bring out new information that needs to be considered by all concerned. Be prepared to discuss your own use of drugs. What do you get out of alcohol, a cup of coffee, smoking or taking a headache tablet? It helps your children make up their own minds if you can be open and honest about the choices you have made and about your feelings.

Your child will disregard your advice if you deny that alcohol and tobacco cause real harm. Moralising, lecturing, "pumping" for information or shutting off might make you feel better, but won't help. Your child is more likely to respect your experience and accept your advice in all areas, including drugs, if you listen and discuss.

If you suspect drug abuse:

Dont Panic

Try very hard not to panic. Over-reaction can actually promote drug use, because of all the attention the young person receives.

Get the facts

Try to find out from the child, other members of the family or friends, which drug is being taken (and how and how often). The child may have experimented with the drug and stopped after trying it (and you) out. Some young people also pretend to use drugs, or possess them, in order to gain attention.

Recognise problems

If your child is regularly using a drug to try to satisfy a need or to solve a problem at home, school or work, then they need your help.

Personal problems usually lie behind drug problems. Unusual and unexplained behaviour persisting for some time, such as:

— wild swings in mood, from being explosive to being depressed

— repeatedly staying out overnight, or very late

— the dropping of school activities, especially sport

— marks dropping, absenteeism increasing

— breaking off friendships for no reason

— could indicate a personal or drug problem.

Getting professional help

Don't cover up on a drug problem. There is nothing wrong with seeking professional help - that's why it's there! The sooner help is sought, the better. Discuss your concerns with your doctor, phone your drug information and counselling service. You can call just for a chat - nothing needs to be wrong for you to use this service.

A parent is always communicating - whether by words or actions, and for better or for worse, is always influencing the behaviour of their kids.

Listen!

1. Learn to listen! Listen with your eyes, your body and your heart! To be a good listener means hearing what your kids are saying from their perspective, not yours. Avoid interpreting. Avoid evaluating. Avoid judging.
2. Listening is a way of helping your kid by validating the importance of their thoughts, feelings, and opinions. Being a good listener is a way of making kids feel wanted, cared about.
3. Your listening is a way of helping kids to understand or know about themselves better.
4. Being a good listener is a way of increasing the probability of having a good mutual exchange with kids.
5. Avoid interrupting. Listen!
6. To keep them talking, use questions to help clarify meanings, to make sure you really understand their feelings.
7. Use open-ended questions, questions that begin with what, how, and could you. Avoid questions that can be answered by yes or no, and questions that begin with why.

8. Being a good listener may call for asking for clarification of their feelings, especially when they say you don't understand. Example - "Could you give me an example of what you mean by . . . " Then honestly try to understand. Avoid making assumptions.

Listen to yourself - how you sound as well as what you say. Actions and facial expressions often communicate rejection even while your words try to communicate acceptance.

Feelings!

1. We solve problems and work out differences with our kids best on the level of feelings - honest and respectful communication of feelings.
2. Listen to your kids' feelings. Try to understand them. You do not necessarily have to agree with them, but you need to respect them and discuss them.
3. Sharing talk time will improve understanding. Your not dominating a conversation will help kids feel better about themselves so they will want to talk again.
4. Develop a feeling of courtesy and respect in your voice. A pleasant, understanding voice will pay big dividends in parent child communications and make kids feel good about themselves and their family.

Attitudes!

Many outside influences compete with the parent in forming kids' attitudes about alcohol.

Television and the mass media are major influences on kids. The way they portray alcohol and other drugs through ads, commercials and programs does raise questions and issues that parents should discuss with their kids.

Because of the many hours kids spend watching television it becomes a primary source of information and attitudes for them.

Parents should control the types of programs and the amount of time young people spend viewing television.

Who is in control in your home, the parent or the TV?

Honesty:

Be honest about how it feels to be a parent. If your children see that you are being honest, they will most likely respond honestly.

Non Language Communication

— What am I saying with my eyes?

— What am I saying with my facial expressions?

— What am I saying by the tone of my voice?

— Is my total response sarcastic or friendly, positive or negative?

6

Current Trends in Child Abuse

Over the past two decades, the mental health treatment of child victims of sexual and physical abuse and their abusive parents has received much attention by both the clinical and research communities. Over the years, a large and rich clinical treatment literature has developed describing interventions that appear to be theoretically sound and have good clinical utility. Child abuse cases often are enormously complicated and frequently require considerable clinical innovation, judgment, and flexibility. Intervention for problems related to child abuse must be set within this larger mental health context regarding cultural, religious, and racial/ethnic groups.

Core individual and familial values and beliefs are directly relevant to the treatment of all cases of child abuse. Values and beliefs about issues pertinent to child abuse, such as sexuality, nudity, discipline practices, family boundaries, respect for elders, personal and familial privacy, family roles, acceptance of strangers, and help-seeking attitudes, are all influenced and often directly guided by a family's cultural, religious, and racial/ethnic identification.

Perceptions about the helpfulness and purpose of mental services often must also be addressed. Therefore, discerning, understanding, and accommodating to the root value and belief structure of every family they treat is a fundamental skill required of therapists working with victims of child abuse and their families.

Many studies investigating questions germane to the treatment of victims of child abuse and their families, such as abuse effects, abuse-related cognitions, and mediational models, as well as treatment outcome, have included substantial proportions of participants from varied cultural and ethnic groups. Surprisingly, the role of religious identification is rarely examined despite the importance of religion on core values and beliefs.

Treatment Protocol Classification System

A primary goal of this project was to establish a clear, criteria-based system for classifying interventions and treatments according to their theoretical, clinical, and empirical support. This system can be applied to judge the utility of other current treatments and treatments to be developed in the future. Therefore, the classification system is a tool that can be used by practitioners and others to make decisions about the appropriateness of certain treatments.

Consequently, treatments likely will change their classifications over time as more research is completed. Therefore, the treatment classification system is a tool that can be applied to a dynamic area where information is constantly increasing.

The classification system uses criteria regarding a treatment's theoretical soundness, clinical support, acceptance within the field, potential for harm, documentation, and empirical support to assign a summary classification score. A lower score indicates a greater level of support for the treatment protocol.

The treatment has a sound theoretical basis in generally accepted psychological principles. A substantial clinical-anecdotal literature exists indicating the treatment's value with abused children, their parents, and/or their families. The treatment is generally accepted in clinical practice as appropriate for use with abused children, their parents, and/or their families.

There is no clinical or empirical evidence or theoretical basis indicating that the treatment constitutes a substantial risk of harm to those receiving it, compared to its likely benefits. The treatment has a book, manual, or other available writings that specifies the components of the treatment protocol and describes how to administer it. At least two randomized, controlled treatment outcome studies (RCT) have found the treatment protocol to be superior to an appropriate comparison treatment, or no different or better than an already established treatment when used with abused children, their parents, and/or their families.

The treatment has a sound theoretical basis in generally accepted psychological principles. A substantial clinical-anecdotal literature exists indicating the treatment's value with abused children, their parents, and/or their families. The treatment is generally accepted in clinical practice as appropriate for use with abused children, their parents, and/or their families.

There is no clinical or empirical evidence or theoretical basis indicating that the treatment constitutes a substantial risk of harm to those receiving it, compared to its likely benefits. The treatment has a book, manual, or other available writings that specifies the components of the treatment protocol and describes how to administer it.

Supported and Acceptable Treatment

The treatment has a sound theoretical basis in generally accepted psychological principles. A substantial clinical-anecdotal literature exists indicating the treatment's value with abused children, their parents, and/or their families. The treatment is generally accepted in clinical practice as appropriate for use with abused children, their parents, and/or their families. There is no clinical or empirical evidence or theoretical basis indicating that the treatment constitutes a substantial risk of harm to those receiving it, compared to its likely benefits.

Promising and Acceptable Treatment

The treatment has a sound theoretical basis in generally accepted psychological principles. A substantial clinical-anecdotal literature exists indicating the treatment's value with abused children, their parents, and/or their families. The treatment is generally accepted in clinical practice as appropriate for use with abused children, their parents, and/or their families. There is no clinical or empirical evidence or theoretical basis indicating that the treatment constitutes a substantial risk of harm to those receiving it, compared to its likely benefits.

Innovative or Novel Treatment

The treatment may have a theoretical basis that is an innovative or novel, but reasonable, application of generally accepted psychological principles. A relatively small clinical literature exists to suggest the value of the treatment. The treatment is not widely used or generally accepted by practitioners working with abused children. There is no clinical or empirical evidence or theoretical basis suggesting that the treatment constitutes a substantial risk of harm to those receiving it, compared to its likely benefits.

Concerning Treatment

The theoretical basis for the treatment is unknown, a misapplication of psychological principles, or a novel, unique, and concerning application of psychological principles. Only a small and limited clinical literature exists suggesting the value of the treatment. There is a reasonable theoretical, clinical, or empirical basis suggesting that compared to its likely benefits, the treatment constitutes a risk of harm to those receiving it. The treatment has a manual or other writings that specifies the components and administration characteristics of the treatment that allows for implementation.

Child Abuse: An Assessment

A basic principle of all clinical practice is that assessment should precede the initiation of interventions. Based upon the results of the assessment, a treatment plan should be developed that is tailored to the problems and needs of individual family members and the family as a whole. The likelihood of successful outcome is enhanced substantially when effective interventions are matched correctly to specific problems discerned through appropriate assessment.

A mismatch of treatment to problem is at best a waste of scarce resources, and can prolong suffering, lead to deterioration in the client, or even endanger children. Most important, when proper assessment is not conducted or the treatment approach fails to target the problems identified, children do not receive the treatment they need for the problems they have.

Assessment is also an integral component of the ongoing treatment process. Periodic evaluation of previously identified problems, emergent problems, and treatment progress are necessary parts of therapy. Ongoing assessment results provide feedback about whether the target problems have resolved or if a different intensity or type of therapy is indicated. All of these generally accepted principles of assessment apply to cases of child abuse.

Child maltreatment cases have special characteristics that must be addressed in assessment. The most important of these is determining how safe the living environment is for the child victim. Since many abused children continue to live with the caregivers or siblings who have hurt them or in families where domestic violence occurs, this focus on safety is a priority.

Therefore, understanding the level of risk for harm in the child's environment and subsequent safety planning are the first steps in assessment in abuse cases.

Evaluation of risk identifies what structural and contextual interventions may be necessary (e.g., separation, professional supervision, chaperone program), as well as initial treatment targets (e.g., parental substance abuse, behaviour management skills, anger control).

It also forms the basis for clinical assessment and intervention. For example, even if children exhibit posttraumatic stress symptoms, it is difficult to proceed in therap'y while they are still in dangerous (and fear-producing) situations. Treatment of fear and anxiety symptoms likely will be fruitless or even harmful because it would be appropriate for a child to continue to be afraid and vigilant in such a situation. If treatment continues, children may be desensitized to real danger cues, placing them at greater risk in the future.

Therefore, evaluation of environmental and contextual risk and safety is a unique and critical part of the assessment process in abuse cases. Another special consideration in abuse cases is the stance of caregivers with regard to the charges of maltreatment. In many cases parents enter or bring their children to treatment because child protection authorities have intervened and recommended or required their attendance.

In some cases they may be seeking treatment only because they are court-ordered to do so. Parents may dispute the abuse allegations or minimize the harmful impact on their children. Assessment of parental perceptions and stage of readiness to change is a central ingredient of developing a meaningful treatment plan. Successful therapy outcome for maltreated children who live with their parents and for parental deficits requires some degree of cooperation with a treatment process.

Belief and support by a non-offending parent has been shown to contribute to the treatment of child distress in sexual abuse situations.

Identifying the nature and extent of the obstacles to parental engagement provides direction for the focus of treatment especially in the early stages of intervention. Maltreated children often have emotional or behavioral problems as a result of their abuse experiences or their abusive family environment. As noted above, substantial research has documented the types of problems and mental health disorders frequently experienced by abused children.

These common problems include fear, anxiety, posttraumatic stress symptoms, depression, sexual difficulties, poor self-esteem, stigmatization, difficulty with trust, cognitive distortions, difficulty with affective processing, aggression, disruptive behavior, peer socialization deficits, and other problems. Consequently, each of these problems that are commonly exhibited by abused children should be assessed carefully using the best assessment tools available.

The nature and severity of disturbance can vary substantially from child to child. In some cases, abused children will not exhibit any clinically significant distress at initial assessment. Abused children will be terribly disturbed and suffer from major mental health disorders, and still others will have moderate problems. The absence of detectable problems may be the result of active symptom suppression by the child, avoidance coping strategies, or simple resilience. At least some of these asymptomatic children will have a delayed onset of disturbance.

That is, they will develop abuse-related problems months or even years after the abuse has stopped. Therefore, assessment should consider risk factors for the development of future problems, as well as reported difficulties. The first task of assessment involves determining the direct effects of the abusive events, i.e., those problems that clearly stem squarely from the abusive behaviors experienced by the child and likely have no other significant etiology.

For example, probably the most abuse-specific outcome of physical or sexual abuse experiences is posttraumatic stress symptoms. About half of sexually abused and one third of physically abused children will meet diagnostic criteria for posttraumatic stress disorder (PTSD), and more will have at least some posttraumatic stress symptoms. Therefore, PTSD symptoms should be targets for evaluation. Screening for posttrauma symptoms requires that the experience be explicitly discussed so that re-experiencing and avoidance symptoms can be assessed.

Numbing and hyperarousal symptoms may not be identified without specific inquiry. Consequently, assessing for PTSD requires directly approaching the abuse experiences in the evaluation process. This axiom is true for other abuse-related fears and anxieties as well. Assessment of abused children should be abuse-informed, but not exclusively abuse-focused.

That is, the assessment should evaluate not only the potential problems that are the direct effects of abuse, but also pre-existing and concomitant difficulties as well. The abuse informed component of assessment should address cognitions as well as symptoms. Abuse-specific and abuse-related attributions are associated with increased distress and may lead to conditions such as depression, low self-esteem, and impaired socialization that are common in abused children.

For the most part, practitioners must rely on clinical interviews to determine whether children have maladaptive beliefs about their experiences. Some behavior problems are common among maltreated children, although they can have other etiologies. For example, sexual behavior problems are noted in about one-third of sexually abused children. Anger control problems and aggression are frequently observed in physically abused children.

These disruptive behaviors may be the result of intense negative emotions associated with maltreatment or learned responses to the experiences. However, they can also arise from causes other than abuse. Comprehensive assessment will include targets that are commonly exhibited by abused children, even though they may have other causes. In addition to the abuse focus of assessment, abused children also should be evaluated for the presence of emotional and behavioral problems that may or may not be the direct result of the abuse experiences, but none the less impair functioning.

Diagnostic interviews and standardized behavior checklists can be useful in assessing for these problems. At minimum, evaluators should screen for the presence of depression, anxiety disorders, and disruptive behavior disorders. It goes without saying that assessment of children should be developmentally informed.

One consequence of abuse and reactions to abuse is that the developmental trajectory of the child victim is derailed. What may begin as an abuse-specific symptom can lead to problems of functioning, which may produce negative socialization patterns, that can create risk for serious pathology. Or the pathway to disrupted development may be quite direct and will interfere with normal peer social relationships.

One assessment approach is to determine systematically the level of functional impairment or the degree to which children are having difficulties in role functioning at home, school, in the community and in their behavior with others. Parent/caregiver-child relationship quality is a critical part of any abuse case and should be a target of assessment.

Assessment and treatment must pay attention not only to the offender-victim portion of the relationship, but also the parent-child aspect, which may be more important to the child. Common areas of assessment are similar to targets of assessment in any family case and include parent-child communication, affectional connection, styles of conflict management, discipline practices, and levels of trust. A special point of assessment is insecure parent-child attachment. Insecure attachment often is associated with abuse experiences either as a precursor to abuse or a result.

This problem tends to significantly disrupt parent-child relationships, and is presumed to set the stage for lifelong problems in relating to others as children acquire working models for interpersonal relationships within their families. Assessment of attachment style in the clinical setting is generally based on the reports of children and parents about the quality of the relationship, as well as observations of parent/caregiver-child interactions. There are a number of ways to make crude classifications.

For example, one way to think about attachment style is children's valuations of self and others, with secure children evincing consistent positive views of self and others, while insecure children tend to have either negative perceptions of themselves, others or both. Parental responses to children can also be evaluated in terms of the degree to which they are responsive versus inconsistent, distant, or a source of danger.

Classifying children into one of the insecure attachment categories is less important clinically than assessing the nature and quality of parent-child relationships, and identifying problematic relationships that should be a treatment focus. While the importance of evaluating and addressing children's capacity to form and maintain successful relationships is not disputed, there are controversies about the determination of attachment problems in children.

Anecdotally, there is reason to be concerned that in some cases, application of the label or diagnosis may lead to very negative or even hopeless perceptions of these children. This is of special concern for children in foster care who may have options for permanency or adoption foreclosed because of the associated stigma. Assessment for attachment problems should clearly specify the basis for drawing conclusions and the nature of the disturbance in order to form a basis for treatment interventions.

Parental approaches to discipline should be an important focus evaluation in all cases, and should not be limited to cases referred for physical abuse. Inconsistent, ineffective, or coercive discipline practices create negative interactional patterns and child behavior problems. They may also lead to physical abuse in an escalating cycle of child misbehavior, parental frustration and loss of control that leads to abuse.

The practices of nonoffending as well as abusive parents should be assessed. Nonoffending parents may be contending with children's abuse related-symptoms or reactions to the family disruption at a time when they feel overwhelmed. Many cases of less serious physical abuse are the result of discipline gone too far. Exploration of how parents handle children's misbehavior will identify areas for inclusion in the treatment plan.

Family system characteristics, sibling relationships, extended family relationships, and couple/marital and sexual relationships between parents are also important areas of assessment and possible intervention. Several studies have found that abusive families tend to be more socially isolated, have more rigid patterns of interaction, value familial control over individual behavior, are more likely to have authoritarian interpersonal styles, and have significant levels of marital and sexual relationship dissatisfaction.

These family system and marital/couple factors often constitute a context for abuse to emerge and be maintained. Therefore, marital and family relationships and system characteristics are appropriate targets of clinical assessment and intervention. Assessment of Parents Screening for parental disorders or family characteristics that may impact children's adjustment and parental capacity to cooperate with treatment is an essential element of assessment.

Parental depression and substance abuse are specific disorders that, when present, will substantially undermine parents' abilities to provide assistance to their children in the aftermath of abuse and are associated with re-referral to child protection authorities. Fortunately, especially in the case of depression, effective treatments are available. When necessary, therapists treating abused children should refer parents to appropriate intervention programs or be able to provide the services as part of a comprehensive treatment plan.

Explaining the ways that these conditions interfere with helping children recover may be a helpful strategy to overcome parental resistance to a focus on their problems since most non-offending parents and some offending parents do have concern for their children's welfare. Level of parental distress regarding abuse of the child in sexual abuse cases has been shown to be an important determinant of children's emotional and behavioral status.

Therefore, the impact on the parent of learning about and coping with results of child maltreatment is important to address. In addition to children's emotional needs, there may be system interventions including investigations, legal proceedings, child placement, and disruption in living situations and arrangements that are a source of stress for the parents.

Problem solving and stress management strategies may be indicated to alleviate distress that interferes with parental capacity to respond to their children and participate in other interventions. Level of belief and support about the abuse experience has been found to correlate with children's adjustment in sexual abuse cases and are typically a focus of intervention. Whether these factors are important for physically abused children has not been the specific subject of investigation.

Treatments for physically abused children have not generally required that parents acknowledge the abusiveness of the behavior. In fact, some writers have recommended against an emphasis on labeling the behavior. This is probably because in most cases of physical abuse in treatment contexts, the children are living in the home with the abusive parent and both are participating in joint treatments. However, some assessment of parental views about what happened, and the wrongful or harmful nature of the behavior is likely to be relevant to treatment planning.

Offending parents or siblings, especially in the case of sexual abuse may suffer from a variety of deficits that require specific interventions. In the case of physical abuse, these may be assessed in terms of attitudes toward the use of violence and the repertoire of behavioural skills parents possess for responding to child misbehavior. In sexual abuse cases, degree of responsibility taken for the abuse, attitudes about the harmful consequences, skills deficits, and empathy are frequent targets for treatment.

In addition, certain pathologies, sexual deviance and antisocial or psychopathic characteristics are predictive of risk to reoffend. Standards for assessment methods for sexual offenders have been promulgated by the Association for the Treatment of Sexual Abusers and may involve the use of psychophysiological technologies such as the polygraph and penile plethysmography.

Sexual offender treatment is generally considered an area of specialty practice that requires highly specialized knowledge and training..Use of Standardized Measures Standardized assessment instruments can be very useful tools in the assessment of abused children and their families. As the term implies, they provide a standardized and structured approach to measuring problems commonly experienced by abused children, and can help provide a more precise assessment of target problems.

They also can be administered over time to assess treatment progress and aid in clinical decision-making. Several instruments have been developed specifically for measuring abuse-related problems and have been tested with abused children. They are designed to evaluate problems frequently experienced by these children and to be used specifically in cases of abuse. In addition, many general mental health measures that are used with all sorts of child populations have been used successfully with abused children.

All of these instruments can be clinically valuable when assessing abused children and their families. Standardized measures should be considered as part of any comprehensive clinical assessment process. A treatment plan should be based directly on the results of the assessment. It should coincide with problems and needs that have been identified for the children, their parents, and the family. Feedback and discussion of the results with family members are important ingredients of the assessment process. They can also aid in generating cooperation with the treatment plan and positive expectations for treatment.

The acceptability of a treatment plan may rest in part on the degree to which children and families perceive that there is respect for their particular circumstances, background, and values. Cultural and religious factors can be especially relevant. Family, religious, or cultural values that are supportive of corporal punishment may conflict with treatment approaches that eschew these methods. Families may prefer to seek treatment with providers or in settings where they believe there will be greater understanding or appreciation of their cultural identity and values and where they are more comfortable.

The practicality of treatment plans is also important. It is not helpful to present families with a long list of treatment recommendations that may overwhelm them and seem never ending. Plans that call for services that are unavailable, require many sessions per week, or are beyond the financial means of the family are not useful because it is unlikely they will be followed. Many families where child maltreatment has occurred are poor or struggling in the first place, and their financial circumstances may have been worsened by abuse-related systems interventions.

Maltreating families often lack organizational skills, tend to be socially isolated, and may not have much experience with using resources outside the family. Triage, constructing a plan with a reasonable number of recommended interventions, identification of specific settings that offer the needed services, flexibility in scheduling appointments, and advocacy to secure concrete assistance with transportation and child care may be necessary to implement a treatment plan.

In short, assessment is the cornerstone of the treatment process. Without accurate, comprehensive, and sophisticated assessment, followed by reasonable treatment planning, interventions are likely to be misguided and ultimately ineffective. Assessment in abuse cases should focus on, but not be limited to, problems known to be common among abused children.

The special issues surrounding abuse cases such as risk assessment, safety planning, and the complicated familial and parent-child relationship issues that exist should be a part of the assessment process. Assessment should result in an accurate portrayal of the functioning of the abused child and their family within their cultural context. Treatment planning should target these problems in a realistic way and apply the best treatments available to the revealed problems.

They target abuse consequences in children, problems of parents or parent/child relationships significantly associated with maltreatment, or abusive behaviours of parents. These approaches do not constitute an exhaustive or comprehensive list of treatments that may be necessary or useful in child abuse cases. For example, pharmacological interventions are not included although they may be helpful adjunctive treatments for children or parents. Many parents will have substance abuse disorders or major depressive disorder, both of which are risk factors for reabuse.

There are well-established interventions for depression and substance abuse that are not covered in these guidelines. In many cases children or parents will suffer from comorbid psychiatric conditions (e.g., ADHD, conduct disorder, oppositional defiant disorder, personality disorders) or live in environmental circumstances (e.g., poverty, inadequate housing) that may need to be a focus of intervention but are not specific to child abuse.

The selected interventions are designed to reflect the array of abuse specific interventions typically used or considered in cases of child maltreatment. In some cases particular programme models were chosen because they represent exemplary programmes of the type and have been the subject of evaluation or research (e.g., therapeutic childcare and intensive family intervention).

The various parenting interventions are presented because parenting classes or interventions are routinely recommended or ordered in child maltreatment cases. Although it is likely that most of the usual community-based parenting programmes are not as intensive or empirically grounded as the programmes described in this document, treatments focused on parenting practices are a central component of the treatment response to abuse situations.

Most of the remainder of the interventions were specifically developed to treat abuse-related conditions. Treatments are divided into three sections:

— Child-Focused Interventions

— Parent, Parent-Child, and Family Focused Interventions

— Offender Focused Interventions

In many cases children and families will benefit by more than one protocol, including treatments that are not included here. In a particular case, different practitioners may deliver different treatments to provide a comprehensive treatment approach to families. However, it is assumed that the abuse-related problems and the needs of the abused children will be the clinical priority and the primary focus of treatment. Whenever possible it is desirable that non-offending parents participate in children's therapy.

Some treatment approaches include components designed to strengthen the parent-child relationship. In other situations, it may be incorporated into an abuse-focused treatment program as a separate component. Treatment that is specifically directed at the parent's abusive behaviour may or may not be relevant to treatment planning for the abused children depending on the clinical presentation and family structural context.

In cases of less serious physical abuse, children will often remain living with the abusing parent, and treatment that includes a focus on the parent-child relationship and parental disciplinary practices is essential. In other cases, children will be separated from abusing or non-protective parents. Treatment for the parents will be required if the child is to be returned to the home. However, the parents may not be available or cooperative with treatment recommendations. In these cases, children should still be assessed and treated for abuse consequences, regardless of whether the parents are involved.

Cognitive-Behavioral and Dynamic Play Therapy

These two group treatment approaches were designed for children ages 6 to 12 and their caregivers who exhibit sexual behaviour beyond normal child sexuality and that causes problems in .their functioning. One approach is based on the principles of cognitive behavioural therapy, and the other is based on dynamic play therapy. They are designed to reduce the occurrence of inappropriate and/ or aggressive sexual behavior in children. Children who have been maltreated sometimes develop sexual behaviour problems.

Two theoretically different approaches to group treatment have been developed and tested. The two approaches, cognitive-behavioural therapy and dynamic play therapy, are frequently used for behaviour problems in children, have evidence for effectiveness, and can be used in a wide range of mental health settings. The principles of cognitive-behavior therapy and its use with children have been well described in the literature.

The behavioral component is straightforwardly concerned with human behaviour and broadly based on the principles of learning theory. The cognitive aspect emphasizes the complex cognitions involved in information processing in human beings, such as beliefs, attributions, decision-making processes, and their influence on behavior. The cognitive-behavioural approach used in this program relies on behaviour modification principles for group management and incorporates strategies directed at cognitive rules, decision making, impulse control, and education. It is highly structured and uses a teaching-learning model.

The rationale for the use of dynamic play therapy is that children with sexual behavior problems may be experiencing intense negative emotions stemming from sexual, physical and/or emotional abuse, neglect, and/or other trauma. Inappropriate processing and expression of these feelings may result in sexual behaviour. Play therapy assumes that play is the child's natural medium for expression and is a vehicle for emotional processing and behavior change.

The spontaneous interactions combined with the controlled conditions in a play therapy setting provide a means for achieving goals that therapists have identified as critical in working with children with sexual behavior problems. These goals include helping children gain insight into their own behaviour;

— increasing children's ability to observe and appreciate other people's feelings, needs, and rights;

— helping children understand their needs and values, and to develop their own goals and internal resources;

— increasing children's ability to meet their needs in socially appropriate ways; and

— increasing children's connectedness to positive others and building internal strengths that support future growth.

The dynamic play therapy approach used in this programme incorporates aspects of client-centered and psychodynamic play therapies. The client-centered aspects help instill self-efficacy and self-worth in the participants. The psychodynamic aspects help ensure productive interactions between group members and increased self-understanding or insight.

Both approaches have been found equally effective in reducing children's sexual behavior problems at the two-year follow-up. The treatments consist of twelve once weekly sessions. Caregiver participation in collateral group treatment that includes education regarding age-appropriate sexual behavior in children, assisting children with applying the Sexual Behaviour Rules and Turtle Technique, child behaviour management techniques, and rules for supervision.

— Dynamic Play Therapy

— Reflection to increase child's self understanding (insight).

— Acceptance to convey positive regard for the child and improve the child's self-esteem.

— Interpretation to assist children in identifying and expressing feelings.

— Facilitating group interaction to improve peer relationships.

— Caregiver participation in collateral group treatment that uses acceptance, reflection, and interpretation to process problems presented by the caregivers; encourages interaction among the parents; and uses the group process/interaction as the modality of change.

Cognitive Processing Therapy (CPT)

Cognitive Processing Therapy (CPT) is a brief, structured, cognitive-behavioral treatment designed to treat posttraumatic stress disorder (PTSD) and associated features such as depression. CPT is a therapy consisting of exposure to the traumatic memory, training in cognitive restructuring, and modules on topics that are most likely to be affected by rape and other interpersonal trauma.

Exposure-based and cognitive therapies are often used to treat trauma victims. CPT combines both approaches with the cognitive components tailored for rape victims, although treatment strategies can be modified for other traumatic experiences. CPT has been developed to help trauma victims (1) understand how thoughts and emotions are interconnected, (2) accept and integrate the traumatic experience as an event that actually occurred and cannot be ignored or discarded, (3) experience fully the range of emotions attached to the event, (4) analyze and confront maladaptive beliefs, and

(5) explore how prior experiences and beliefs both affected reactions and were affected by the trauma.

The goals of CPT are twofold. One goal is exposure to the traumatic memory. Although exposure is important because it helps to activate the client's fear-structure, it does not provide direct corrective information regarding misattributions or maladaptive beliefs. Therefore, a cognitive component is added to address these issues. The cognitive component is based on the theory that traumatic experiences are often problematic because the new information often does not fit into existing schemas.

Without a way to understand and categorize the experience, the strong emotions associated with traumatic experiences are left unprocessed. In addition, when individuals encounter new information that is inconsistent with preexisting beliefs or schemas, one of two things can occur: assimilation or accommodation. Assimilation involves distortion of new information so that such information is consistent with schemas, while accommodation involves altering schemas because of the new discrepant information.

Over-accommodation occurs when schemas are changed at an extreme level as a result of the traumatic experience. Assimilation and over-accommodation are problematic because they often lead to self-blame, guilt, manufactured emotions such as embarrassment or shame, or dysfunctional cognitions. One goal of CPT is to help clients move from using these strategies to using accommodation while processing cognitions related to the traumatic experience. Outcome studies support CPT as a treatment for PTSD and PTSD-related depression.

CPT produces symptomatic relief within 12 treatment sessions. Following are the Treatment components:

— Information and education regarding symptoms of PTSD, information processing theory.

— Explore meaning of event, client writes impact statement of Identification of thoughts and feelings, Antecedents-Behaviour-Consequences sheets.

— Discussion of self-blame and labeling of event.

Eye Movement Desensitization and Reprocessing (EMDR)

EMDR is a multi-component therapeutic procedure for traumatic memories and for post-traumatic stress disorder (PTSD) that purports to restart and facilitate blocked processing of the traumatic memory, promote more adaptive cognitions regarding the trauma, and to install alternate positive cognitions, coping strategies, and adaptive behaviours.

EMDR theory is grounded in adaptive cognitive network theories of learning and emotion and in Piagetian views of learning in which assimilation and accommodation are seen as key processes in the adaptive efforts of human beings. Shapiro has proposed an "accelerated information processing" model to account for traumatic memories and for their resolution through EMDR which draws on these traditions. The model is based on a number of key propositions. First, traumatic memories are not fully assimilated into the broader cognitive network which demarcates a person's experience; that is they remain partially associatively isolated from the person's larger life experience.

Because such memories are not fully assimilated within the person's pre-existing cognitive schemas, they exert a disequilibrating influence on subsequent information processing. Second, traumatization interferes with psychological and biological processes that normally promote assimilation and accommodation of memories. Trauma memories contain a number of semantic and affective distortions reflecting this partial dissociation from the broader semantic-cognitive network.

Storage in this unaccommodated form can impact other processing negatively, leading to distortions in perception, feeling, and response. Third, EMDR theory proposes that there exists within people an intrinsic self-healing mechanism that is activated by the EMDR procedure. The activation serves to dynamically restart the integration of trauma memories and their assimilation into a normalized form. This inherent information processing mechanism is hypothesized to account for extremely rapid treatment related changes.

Fourth, EMDR theory extends other information processing theories of PTSD by specifically describing the importance of self-representations in the encoding of trauma memories. Fifth, EMDR theory emphasizes the importance of systematic skill-building to compensate for the trauma's interference with the acquisition of appropriate competencies.

While some have proposed that EMDR's effects are accounted for by its exposure component, traditional theories of exposure do not account for the efficacy of the brief duration of the exposure in EMDR. Additional research on EMDR's mode of action is needed. Evaluation of child readiness, barriers to treatment, dysfunctional behaviours, symptoms, and illness characteristics.

Development of a treatment plan that addresses trauma-specific memories as well as present reminders of the traumatic event and identifies remedial skills needed for the patient's future use.

Resilient Peer Training Intervention

This is a school-based intervention for young abused children that is based on an ecological model and uses competent peers and parent helpers to increase children's social competence. Resilient Peer Training (RPT) intervention is a preschool, classroom-based intervention developed for maltreated children at higher than average risk for maladaptive social functioning. RPT is designed to enhance the development of social competencies for vulnerable children by capitalizing on the strengths of resilient peers and the natural support provided by teachers and parent volunteers in a therapeutic pre-school or Head Start classroom environment.

A number of studies have been conducted to evaluate the effectiveness of the RPT intervention for social isolated, low-income preschool children, who have been maltreated. These randomized field tests supported the effectiveness of the RPT intervention. Socially withdrawn maltreated children showed a significant increase in positive interactive peer play behaviour and a decrease in solitary play behavior as a result of the RPT Intervention.

Treatment gains in observed social interactions were validated by teacher and parent ratings of social functioning. Children who received RPT were found to exhibit significantly higher self-control and interpersonal skills and interactive play. Treatment children also showed significantly fewer incidences of behavior problems than children in the control condition.

Therapeutic Child Development Programme

This treatment is a milieu based intervention for maltreated preschool children that seeks to reduce risk factors and enhance protective factors by providing children with positive nurturing interactions with adults and a consistent, safe, monitored environment. The therapeutic child development approach is based on research by expert child practitioners and scientists showing that early life experiences and brain development affect later-life functioning.

Early maltreatment can alter or stunt brain development and often occurs in the context of disrupted attachment. Because the most active and critical time of brain development occurs during the first 33 months, and because emotional behaviour and impulse control require practice and develop in the context of an attachment relationship to a caregiver, the programme treats children at the earliest period of development - birth to five years.

This type of programme is usually recommended when there are significant concerns about parental capacity to respond appropriately to their young children or where the children are exhibiting substantial developmental lags and an intensive exposure to an alternative environment is considered necessary. It is designed to develop empathy and emotional attachment to others, to learn to control and balance feelings, especially those that can be destructive, to develop capacity for cognitive processes, such as problem solving, and to learn the interactive skills necessary to form other secure relationships.

A central mechanism for creating protective factors is providing emotionally attuned primary caregivers that create a growth-promoting environment and help children form emotional attachments to caregivers. Children attend a milieu-based programme during the day and parents are provided with some educational and supportive services. In a long-term follow-up, treated children were significantly less aggressive, had fewer internalizing behaviour problems, were less frequently arrested for violent and non-violent crimes, and were less often identified as violent by caregivers.

Trauma-focused Play Therapy

This treatment is a psychotherapeutic intervention that uses play as a mechanism for allowing abused children to use symbols (toys) to externalize their internal world, project their thoughts and feelings, and process potentially overwhelming emotional and cognitive material from a safe distance. Play has been chronicled as a vehicle to help children with tasks such as mastery, problem-solving and conflict resolution, communication, affective expression, cognitive stretching, developmental strides, and relational issues.

Therapeutic play is used by trained professionals as a tool for assisting children with a range of psychosocial problems. Therapeutic play can therefore be considered the child's natural way of experiencing gradual exposure, a cognitive-behavioural strategy for addressing anxiety or fear. Through post-traumatic play, traumatized children expose themselves to the story, scenario, or behavioural sequence they may fear, avoid or misunderstand. Through this external reconstruction they are able to contain and manage otherwise overwhelming and fragmented affect and cognition.

Trauma-focused play often gives way to affective discharge, cognitive evaluation, and frees up psychic or emotional energy that is bound by traumatic memories. The trauma-focused play therapist witnesses the child's reality, provides unconditional acceptance of the child's feelings, thoughts, and reactions, challenges cognitive distortions and promotes empowerment and resiliency.

Behavioural Parent Training Interventions

Behavioural parent training encompasses several treatment protocols that target behaviour-disordered children and their families. They typically use a short-term behavioural intervention and usually involve teaching parents skills based upon behaviour theory designed to increase child compliance, decrease child disruptive behaviour, and minimize coercive interactions between parent and child at home and in other settings.

Maltreated children often display disruptive behaviours that may be the result of maltreatment or stem from disordered family interactions Child behaviour problems may contribute to risk for maltreatment as well. Treatments designed to change parenting practices are, therefore, considered risk reduction strategies as well as responses to the children's behaviour problems.

These interventions differ from didactic "parenting" classes in that they are based on established principles of behaviour change and involve teaching skills in addition to conveying information. A number of different approaches have been developed and tested.

Corrective Attachment Therapy

Corrective Attachment Therapy is a unique synthesis of many different techniques which are employed to facilitate the development of attachment between child and parent. These are rooted in an understanding of neurobiological factors, the function of memory, the effects of trauma, grief and loss, and the critical importance of attachment to the healthy development of a child. Treatment occurs within the context of a safe, nurturing, and respectful environment.

This treatment is based on the premise that children who have not developed an attachment to a primary caregiver during the first 2-3 years of life are arrested in their development, as indicated by lack of trust, inability to give and receive genuine affection, lack of reciprocity in relationships, lack of cause and effect thinking, lack of remorse after hurting others, as well as manipulative, aggressive and destructive behaviour.

The treatment presupposes that these children do not benefit from traditional talk or play therapy that relies on mutual trust, internal conflict, and emotional honesty and that they have their greatest difficulty in family settings, where respect and reciprocal interactions are expected. Finally, there is the belief that these children, left untreated, become over-represented in the prison and criminal justice population, domestic violence situations, homeless and mental health populations.

Treatment Components:

— Contracting
— Cognitive restructuring
— Role modeling
— Behavioural shaping
— EMDR
— Emotional cathartic therapy
— Psycho-educational therapy

Family Focused, Child Centered Treatment Interventions

Focused Treatment Interventions (FTI) is a protocol of sequential treatment interventions focused on increasing child safety, reducing risk and clarifying responsibility in child maltreatment cases. FTI is designed for use in a coordinated multidisciplinary community system of care. The goals of FTI are to identify and reduce barriers to child safety and protection following the disclosure or discovery of maltreatment and to prevent future abuse. FTI is based on guiding principles from the empirical literature on the impact of child maltreatment, child protection state and federal mandates and supports the overarching goal of family reunification with preconditions of child safety and personal responsibility for behavior.

A uniform and comprehensive forensic and clinical assessment in response to suspected maltreatment involving the non-offending caregiver and child victim provides a baseline of history and experience of the child and family. The guiding principles of FTI support beliefs that the safety of the child is paramount; that family strengthening and reunification are the desired outcomes of community interventions; the safety of the child is a precondition to family reunification; adults are accountable for any abusive and /or neglectful behaviours toward their children; acknowledgment of responsibility for protection and safety is required from the adult caregivers; family strengths and resources in support of safety and protection are the primary focus of interventions; barriers to future safety and protection must be identified and overcome in support of family reunification; necessary community resources are key to supporting the family in overcoming any identified barriers to safety and protection of the child; contact between child victims and adults who have not been treated and who do not acknowledge responsibility for their abusive or neglectful or nonprotective behavior is not in the child's best interest; a uniform assessment that focuses on identification of family strengths, risk factors for child safety, and the impact of abuse or neglect guides the focused interventions in support of family reunification; the overarching goal of focused interventions is reducing child safety risk and rapid, safe preservation of the child with family members or safe rapid reunification of the child with a protective caregiver; and when the goal of family reunification is not possible, early permanency planning is in the best interest of the child.

This model focuses on specific factors that created risk to the child and family and identifies the required behavioural outcome to reduce that risk. Rather than providing a menu of services that require participation to be considered successful, the FTI focuses on identifying risk factors and required behavioural change, and uses input from the caregiver regarding what will be needed to make the required change. For example, when alcohol use is identified as a barrier to child safety/protection, the FTI directs a specific change in alcohol use behaviour.

The caregiver is involved in what will be required to stop using alcohol in support of the safety and protection of their child. Not using alcohol or not being incapacitated by alcohol is the observable behaviour for success vs. participation in an evaluation or alcohol programme for a given length of time. If the caregiver does not acknowledge alcohol use as a problem or exhibits no motivation to stop using alcohol, the focused intervention would be on overcoming barriers to motivation vs. forced participation.

This system of interventions focuses the responsibility for change on the caregiver (client) and places the responsibility for providing the resources to support that change on the system. This clarifies roles and responsibilities between the "community system" and the family system and is consistent with the most recent federal mandate and provides documentation regarding reasonable effort.

Family Resolution Therapy (FRT)

Family Resolution Therapy (FRT) is a protocol of procedures designed to help families where sexual or physical abuse has occurred to develop a long-term resolution for family relationships. It is concerned with the latter stages of the treatment process with abusing families and deals with constructing safe, functional, and stable family structures and processes that will continue well after professional intervention with the family is completed.

Resolution outcomes may range from full family reunification to termination of all parent-child contact. FRT seeks to maintain an appropriate level of safety for children while enabling children to maintain the benefits of continuing parent-child relationships where possible.

FRT is based upon several assumptions drawn from the principles of family systems theory-based family therapy, family and child development, social learning theory, and theories of relapse prevention. First, FRT assumes that the growth and development of children is best promoted when they live in a safe, functional, supportive, and stable family environment, preferably with their parents.

Second, most children develop a lifelong psychological bond or attachment to their parents that remains even if their parents are abusive, separated from the child, or incarcerated. Third, many abused children want to continue a relationship with their parents, though they want the abuse to end and its effects remedied. The FRT protocol assumes that the child victim, offending parent, and non-offending parent have been in appropriate victim, offender, and non-offending parent therapy programs, and have progressed successfully in those therapies.

FRT outcomes (no contact, minimal contact, significant contact, or reunification) will depend upon the level of emotional connection children feel for abusive parents, their desire to maintain their family relationships in some form, and the response of the family to treatment.

The Family Resolution Therapy protocol seeks to develop a long term familial context and functional processes where children can be safe from abuse, yet continue to benefit from some type of relationship with their abusive parents. This long term familial outcome may range from family reunification and maintenance of an intact family, to family separation with unsupervised visitation, to family separation with supervised visitation, to a complete ending of the parent-child relationship.

FRT employs psycho-education and cognitive therapy procedures to change distorted thinking among and between all family members about the abuse experiences and beliefs that supported the abusive context. It employs family therapy techniques to alter the homeostatic organisational functioning, internal boundaries, and external boundaries (i.e., social isolation) of the family system that tended to support and enable the abuse.

It employs behavioral management and collateral monitoring techniques to assess, change, and monitor behaviour among all family members (particularly the offending parent) and the family system as a whole that may signal a relapse to problem behaviour patterns, abusive behaviours, and abuse supportive behaviours.

FRT attempts to change familial behaviour by altering the familial structure and power hierarchy, changing daily family processes, introducing new ways of conducting familial relationships, and carefully monitoring how new behaviours are implemented.in the family. It makes use of behavioural contracts and collateral surveillance of family functioning and individual behaviour, as well as psychotherapeutic modalities.

Integrative Developmental Model

This is a multi-faceted child and family intervention model for children with dissociative symptoms that emphasizes interrupting automatic dissociative withdrawal, teaching the child alternative communication strategies and affect management techniques, and helping the family learn new interactive patterns.

Some children with trauma histories may present with symptoms such as trance states, forgetfulness, fluctuating behaviour including rapid regressions and rage reactions, and belief in vivid imaginary friends or divided identities. Traumatic events in the child's life may precipitate these adaptations as ways to cope with a dysfunctional environment. These adaptations may be understood as difficulties in the normal developmental integration of self-capacities.

Treatment involves emphasis on self-awareness and affect regulation and encouraging the child to take responsibility for actions that the child may initially perceive as outside of his/her control. Interactions with the child emphasize acceptance of all affects, behaviours or dissociated states and the encouragement of self-acceptance as a first step towards self-management.

Development of positive fantasy for providing self-soothing illustrates to the child that fantasy, such as belief in malevolent imaginary entities, can be under the child's control. Treatment must keep in mind normal developmental expectations and avoid iatrogenic influences that support the child or family's belief in the literal reality of dissociated identities.

Family interventions involve enhancing reciprocity in communication, encouraging direct expression of feeling and avoiding the reinforcement of regressive coping. The therapist models for the child and family interactive styles that encourage wholeness, responsibility, and tolerance for the expression of feelings.

Multisystemic Therapy (MST)

Multisystemic Therapy (MST) is a treatment model that targets key factors within the youth's social ecology that relate to problem behaviour and provides multiple, comprehensive interventions that have empirical support.

The theoretical foundation underlying MST is based on causal modeling studies of serious antisocial behaviour and social-ecological and family systems theories of behaviour. Behaviour is viewed as multidetermined and, consequently, problem behaviour may be maintained by difficulties within any of the pertinent systems (e.g., family, peer, school, community) in which the youth is involved.

Thus, the scope of MST interventions is not limited to an individual youth or the family system, but includes difficulties within and between other systems. MST was originally developed in the late 1970's to address youth antisocial behaviour and has been identified as a highly promising treatment model by reviewers in the fields of substance abuse, adolescent violence, and mental health.

MST was more effective than Parent Training for improving parent-child.interactions associated with maltreatment. Abusive parents showed greater progress in controlling their child's behaviour, maltreated children exhibited less passive non-compliance, and neglecting parents became more responsive to their child's behaviour. Parent training was superior to MST on decreasing social problems. Although outcomes were promising, no follow-up was conducted.

MST is currently being tested specifically with physically abusive families in a randomized trial. Assessment to understand the "fit" between the identified problems and their broader systemic context. Child physical abuse occurs most often during periods of stressful role transition for parents, such as the postnatal period of attachment, the early childhood period of increasing socialization pressures, times of family instability and disruption, or following chronic detachment from social supports and services.

This approach is derived from attachment theory, with its emphasis on early relationship formation, and social learning theory's principles of behavioural and cognitive learning. Training parents in effective childrearing methods is based on practical applications of learning principles: educating parents about very basic contingency management principles (e.g., reinforcement, punishment, consistency, etc.); modeling for the parents (via films or live demonstrations) new ways of problem-solving and increasing child compliance; rehearsing the desired skills in non-threatening situations, with increasingly more and more realistic applications (i.e., practicing in the home with the therapist); and providing feedback (verbal or videotaped) to the parents regarding their performance.

The goals of intervention involve the development of strong positive child-rearing abilities by strengthening the early formation of the parent-child relationship, improvement in the parent's abilities to cope with stress through exposure to a mental health support system, and the development of the child's adaptive behaviours that will contribute to his or her emotional and psychological adjustment. These methods emphasize education and guidance in a format that is flexible and responsive to the needs of families and individuals.

Intervention is often re-directed toward important issues that families face during each of the emerging developmental stages that the child and parent must endure. For example, parents who require concrete demonstration of methods to promote child compliance, are socially-isolated, or demonstrate anger control problems are offered individual or group intervention designed to teach skills such as nonviolent discipline methods, self-control, and ways to access community resources.

Parent-Child Interaction Therapy (PCIT)

This intervention is a behavioural and interpersonal dyadic intervention for children and their parents or caregivers that is focused on decreasing externalized child behaviour problems, increasing positive parent behaviours, and improving the quality of the parent-child relationship. There are many underlying factors that contribute to the development of physically abusive families. Foremost among these factors is the nature of the parent-child relationship.

Abusive parents are characterized by high rates of negative interaction, low rates of positive interaction, and limited and ineffective parental disciplining strategies. At the same time, physically abused children have been reported to be aggressive, defiant, non-compliant, and resistant to parental direction. These patterns of interaction result in a negative and coercive parent-child relationship that may escalate to the point of severe corporal punishment and physical abuse.

This pattern eventually can become a relatively stable form of resolving parent-child conflicts that also generates ongoing risk for child maltreatment. While it is likely that there are many different types of physically abusive parent-child relationships, this particular cycle may explain a substantial portion of physical abuse situations, especially those that evolve from routine daily interactions around compliance and discipline.

Parent-Child Interaction Training (PCIT)

It is an intervention that is especially appropriate for use in physical abusive situations because it targets the specific deficits often found within physically abusive parent-child dyads that can lead to maltreatment. The approach incorporates both the parent and the child (and other involved family members) in the intervention process. It provides an in vivo opportunity to alter the pattern of interactions within abusive relationships, and it serves as a mechanism to directly decrease negative affect and control - while promoting greater positive affect and discipline strategies.

The interventions combine elements of family systems, learning theory and traditional play therapy. The emphasis is on restructuring parent-child patterns, not modifying behaviours. The therapist takes an extremely active and directive role in the process. The intervention consists of an initial set of approximately six sessions devoted to enhancing positive interactions, and then another six that focus on improving disciplinary practices. Progress is tracked and once parents achieve competence in one area they shift the treatment focus.

Physical Abuse-informed Family Therapy

This treatment approach is a family systems intervention for children and physically abusive parents that seeks to reduce violence and improve child outcomes by promoting cooperation, developing shared views about the value of non-coercive interactions, and increasing skills of family members. The family-ecological model views child physical abuse from a systemic perspective emphasizing the interrelationships among individual, family, and social support factors.

Treatment seeks to address various child (e.g., feelings), parent (e.g., poor empathy, physical punishment) and/or family issues (e.g., role reversal). Most interventions involving family therapy (FT) or multiple services directed toward the family system have not been formally evaluated. Family-centered services have been associated with improvements in child developmental status, parenting skill, and family relationships.

Abuse-informed FT is designed to enhance family functioning and relationships, in accord with the interactional or ecological model approach to child maltreatment. Treatment seeks to enhance the cooperation and motivation of all family members by promoting an understanding of coercive behaviour, teaching the family positive communication skills and how to solve problems together. The treatment has been shown to be superior to routine community service in reducing violence and improving child outcomes.

Parents United Programme

Parents United is a clinically based, integrated treatment programme which provides direct clinical services as well as a variety of non-clinical support for victims, offenders, adults molested as children, and their support persons. The clinical services are provided by the clinical sponsoring agency for the Parents United chapter and the non-clinical support services are provided by the Parents United membership itself.

Parents United is based on the idea that all individuals affected by sexual abuse will benefit from a variety of supportive, adjunctive services in addition to formal clinical interventions. The services include immediate access to information and a supportive response from others who have had similar experiences, as well as concrete assistance with some of the impacts following discovery of abuse.

Groups targeted for various sub-populations, including adults molested as children, offenders, denying offenders, offenders who are also victims, parents of abused children and teenage child victims and their offenders, provide a place of mutual recovery, allow participants to address and listen to each other, and serve as a vehicle for developing insight, empathy and understanding. Support persons are also included to enhance the available support system for the involved individuals.

Variations on psychoeducation, support, enhancement of interpersonal skills, and cognitive behavioural techniques are used. Some of the groups are progressive; clients move from one to the other as they achieve certain goals. Others are specific to a particular purpose. Most groups meet once a week for eight weeks.

In addition, Parents United serves the community at large through a speaker's bureau. Participants create awareness and understanding through sharing their experiences. Parents United is a non-profit, membership driven organization which provides most nonclinical support functions for the programme. These functions include child care, attendance records, speakers bureaus, support person registry, literature on the programme, orientation of membership, etc.

Parents Anonymous

Parents Anonymous, Inc. is an organization designed to strengthen at-risk and abusive parents or adults in parenting roles through mutual support, shared leadership and personal growth. The ongoing, open-ended groups offer the opportunity to learn new skills, transform attitudes and behaviours, and create lasting change.

Parents Anonymous is based on the idea that through participation in groups parents learn to identify and build on their strengths, increase their ability to deal with stress, expand their social support networks, and develop realistic expectations of themselves and their children. Parents are encouraged to take responsibility for their own problems and give and get support from one another to find solutions.

Parents Anonymous groups provide support, a safe and caring environment, encouragement to parents for taking charge of their lives and their families, and opportunities for attitude change and the integration of new knowledge and skills. Providing opportunities to develop friendships reduces isolation. The three essential components needed to create long-term behavioural change are the opportunity to: (1) examine attitudes and childrearing practices and learn new skills and behaviours, (2) practice newly learned skills and behaviours within the safety of the group and at home, and (3) incorporate the new skill or behaviour into their daily life.

Parents Anonymous encourages parents to ask for help early, whatever their circumstances, in order to effectively break the cycle of abuse and strengthen their families. Parents or adults in parenting roles (e.g., grandparents, aunts, uncles, foster parents, stepparents, or older siblings) who are concerned about their parenting abilities and seeking support, information and training are welcome at Parents Anonymous groups, whatever the age of their children or their current circumstances.

Concern for the welfare of children, particularly those who are abused or neglected, has been longstanding among medical and health professions, social service providers, and the general public. Legislation which defines child abuse and determines the appropriate role for child welfare agencies has been a part of state statutes for nearly 30 years (U.S. Department of Health and Human Services, 1999).

In 1974, the Federal government adopted a more direct role in child abuse policy with the passage of P.L. 93-247, the Child Abuse Prevention and Treatment Act (CAPTA). Although the passage of this legislation established a set of uniform operating standards with respect to the identification and management of child abuse cases, states are able to determine definitions of maltreatment, investigative procedures, service systems and data collection procedures.

Moreover, implementation of CAPTA at the state levels emphasizes treatment over prevention. Documenting the problem is a necessary but insufficient step in preventing child abuse and neglect.

Efforts to prevent child abuse and neglect (CAN) include a wide range of activities with the goal of helping families of our nation's youngest children receive the support and education necessary, so that their children will not be subjected to maltreatment. To be effective, prevention efforts require an understanding of the types and causes of maltreatment.

Prevention and intervention activities must address the risks and strengthen families and communities to create healthier environments for raising children. Prevention promotes the actions, thoughts and interactions that lead to families' well-being and healthy, optimal development of children.

The most notable actions taken by states were in the following four areas:

(1) Providing more services to facilitate adoption

(2) Enhancing partnerships with public agencies and community services

(3) Considering an expedited system for terminating parental rights

(4) Conducting comprehensive assessments of child's development and service needs

The least notable actions taken by states were in the following four areas:.

(1) Improving family reunification efforts without increasing re-entry to system

(2) Enhancing foster care and other out-of-home options

(3) Improving quality of foster parents

(4) Achieving competent practices with all cases

The areas in which states most frequently took some action:

(1) Enhancing foster care and other out-of-home options

(2) Improving quality of foster parents

(3) Achieving competent practices with all cases

(4) Improving family reunification efforts without increasing re-entry to system

(5) Establishing best practices for operations of out-of-home options and monitor compliance with standards

Paying greater attention to unique services of domestic violence, substance abusers, developmental disabilities, and mental health seems to be the most challenging strategy for CPS states to put into action. Of the 35 liaisons responding to questions on prevention services, 23 (45%) are allocating Temporary Assistance for Needy Families (TANF) or Child Health Insurance Program (CHIP) funding to support CAN prevention efforts and another state is in the planning stage, while 24 (47%) of 39 respondents are leveraging TANF funds to expand prevention services.

Among the most common prevention services cited by respondents are HFA (8), parenting skills (6), child care services (6), substance abuse programmes (3), community programs to strengthen families (2) and domestic violence services (2). In addition to using existing child welfare funding to support child abuse prevention services, eight states are also utilizing Maintenance of Effort (MOE) funds, Medicaid, and state department funds for prevention services.

In order to ease the transition from welfare to work, states are required to sustain spending levels at 80% of their FY 1994 allocations regardless of the size of their welfare caseload. State liaisons were asked what type of programmes they funded. Types of programmes most commonly reported include expanded day care, home visitation and job training.

The most common prevention programme reported was funding HFA or other home visiting programmes (eight of the 25 states, 32%). Prevent Child Abuse America launched a nationwide prevention initiative HFA to offer voluntary home visiting services to parents of newborns (see www.healthyfamiliesamerica.org). The purpose of HFA is to ensure that all new parents, particularly those at high risk for child maltreatment, have access to the support they need to care for their babies.

As of January 2001, this initiative has resulted in the establishment of 417 affiliated programmes in 39 states and the District of Columbia, up from 311 programmes in the same number of states in 1998. HFA offered parenting education and support services to nearly 40,000 parents nationwide. Most other states have established task forces to explore the development of these efforts and funding opportunities. Funding of prevention programmes, such as HFA, may look to federal and state agencies to supplement current funding in order to serve an extensive base of families.

Thirty states responded to questions pertaining to new or innovative programmes or practices to achieve outcomes of safety, permanency and well-being for children, with 28 states reporting that they had implemented programs and initiatives. Of these programs and practices, 68% reported they were focusing more closely on involving family members in the planning and providing of services for the protection of their children. Thirteen liaisons indicated that their states had instituted programmes related to kinship and foster care to increase permanency outcomes and thirteen liaisons identified infrastructure and systems redesign to assure positive child welfare outcomes.

These innovative programmes and practices include:

1. Family group decision making (FGDM) - Ohana Conferencing in Hawaii -
2. Family support projects;
3. Kinship care adoption; and foster care initiatives
4. Whole communities engaged as resources to families

An increased public awareness that was related to a number of events including: a new statewide intake programme, increased child fatalities, abandoned infants, legislation related to a professional's responsibility to report; and the development of an improved risk assessment instrument. Other changes had to do with the implementation of the Statewide Automated Child Welfare Information Systems (SACWIS), the CAPTA appeals, changes regarding TANF, and implementation of a structured decision-making process. Lastly, four state liaisons indicated changes in structural or ecological (e.g., economics, employment factors, traumatic event) factors.

These changes underscore the variability in reporting statistics over time and the sensitivity of the child welfare system to changes in social, political and administrative conditions or procedures. To help determine whether changes in reporting rates represent an actual increase/decrease in child abuse or merely reflect a more accurate assessment of the problem, we asked each liaison to name the two most significant factors that accounted for the reporting trends in their state.

These responses are based on CPS caseloads and provide a descriptive appraisal of those factors CPS administrators consider the most relevant. Of the 18 states that witnessed an increase in child maltreatment reports, 10 responded to this question. Six of the responding states attributed the rise in reports to increased public awareness through media and education about their reporting system which made the public, as well as mandated reporters, more aware of their responsibility to report suspected child maltreatment. Six states also cited substance abuse as a major contributor to growth in reports.

With respect to the decline in reports, 14 of the 25 states with a decrease in reports gave an explanation for their decline. The most commonly noted factor, indicated by five of the responding states, was changes in reporting system and procedures, such as centralized intake, more effective intake assessments, and the use of standardized screening tools. Additionally, increased public awareness regarding child welfare and child protection issues was reported by four states as a factor contributing to the decrease in reports.

To provide appropriate prevention and treatment services, it is necessary to determine the prevalence of different types of maltreatment as well as other characteristics of the CPS caseload. Each state liaison was asked to provide a breakdown of all reported and substantiated cases by type of maltreatment for 1998 and 1999. Six categories were requested: physical abuse, sexual abuse, neglect, emotional maltreatment, witnessing domestic violence and other types of maltreatment.

One interpretation would be that states are using the "other" category for more detailed behaviors of child maltreatment that are not categories provided in this survey. For example, behaviors included under the "other" category are abandonment, multiple types of maltreatment, imminent risk, substance abuse, dependency, threat of harm and bizarre discipline.

In the 1980s and early 1990s, the greatest difference between the reported and substantiated distributions involved sexual abuse and neglect cases. Overall, substantiated cases tended to include a larger percentage of sexual abuse and a lower percentage of child neglect than was observed in reports.

In recent years however, the similarity in the distribution of reported and substantiated cases in terms of primary type of abuse suggest that type of abuse, alone, may not be as important as in the past in determining whether a case will be substantiated. Sexual abuse reports have fluctuated only slightly over this period, within one to two percentage points of 10%, although they were higher in the early 90s with fewer states reporting.

Families reported for child maltreatment often display a number of problems, which can contribute to their likelihood for engaging in abusive and neglectful behavior. Identifying these problems is a first step toward prevention.

Child fatality estimates are based on the number of children who have died as a result of child abuse and neglect as confirmed by CPS agencies nationwide. One of the greatest tragedies is the death of a child from abuse or neglect. Although such deaths are relatively infrequent they have risen 11% over the past 5 years. Data from other studies and anecdotal information from liaisons strongly suggest that official records under-count the actual incidence of maltreatment fatalities in the United States.

Research has consistently found that some percentage of accidental deaths, child homicides and sudden infant death syndrome (SIDS) cases might be more appropriately labeled as child maltreatment deaths if comprehensive investigations were routinely conducted. They found that child maltreatment fatalities remained relatively stable, with between 949 to 2,022 deaths each year, from 1979 through 1988. They also concluded that 85% of deaths due to parental maltreatment were coded as due to some other cause on the child's death certificate.

A recent study that thoroughly reviewed death records of children in North Carolina further pointed out the coding problems involved in the vital records systems. To better understand how and why child abuse fatalities occur, we examined three characteristics of these deaths for the past three years: 1) prior involvement of the victim with CPS agencies, 2) type of maltreatment leading to death, and 3) the ages of the child victims.

According to information from at least 28 states, an average of 39% of children who died between 1997 and 1999 had prior or current contact with CPS agencies. This substantial percentage may reflect the fact that many states only investigate deaths of children with current or prior CPS contact, thereby ensuring that a high percentage of the reported deaths will involve such children.

On the other hand, the inability of child welfare agencies to provide sufficient services to all victims or to conduct comprehensive investigations of all reports most likely contributes to this pattern. At least 33 states were able to report the type of maltreatment that caused the child's death. These percentages remained fairly stable over the past several years.

The ability of the child protection system to respond to the continued increase in reports and child abuse fatalities largely depends on the resources available. The amount of funding CPS agencies receive dictates whether reports are investigated, victims receive services or efforts are made to prevent maltreatment before a family enters the system.

Compared to 1998, there was improvement in state funding for child protective services in 1999. In 1993, all states were provided new funding for child welfare intervention and prevention services when Congress approved the Safe and Stable Families Programme (formerly the Federal Family Preservation and Support Services Programme). As part of this legislation, states were required to initiate a comprehensive planning process to determine how best to allocate these revenues, FY 1999 appropriations of $275,000,000.

Battered Child Syndrome

Battered child syndrome is a tragic and disturbing phenomenon. Unfortunately, it is a crime that is often successfully hidden by its perpetrators. Law enforcement has an important role to play in uncovering cases of battered child syndrome and gathering evidence for their successful prosecution.

Many jurisdictions are beginning to develop training programmes to help police investigate this crime more effectively. Battered child syndrome is defined as the collection of injuries sustained by a child as a result of repeated mistreatment or beating. If a child's injuries indicate intentional trauma or appear to be more severe than could reasonably be expected to result from an accident, battered child syndrome should be suspected.

A full investigation requires interviewing possible witnesses about other injuries that the child may have suffered, obtaining the caretakers' explanation for those injuries, and assessing the conclusions of medical personnel who may have seen the victim before. The issue of whether information on the victim's prior injuries or medical conditions will be admissible at a trial should be left to the prosecutor. However, an investigator's failure to collect such information leaves the prosecutor without one of the most important pieces of corroborative evidence for proving an intentional act of child abuse.

Evidence of past inflicted injuries also may be the only information available to help the prosecutor distinguish between two or more possible perpetrators in the current case, and may help refute claims by the child's parents or caretakers that injuries suggestive of physical abuse were caused by an accident. Investigators confronted with a case of possible child abuse or child homicide must overcome the unfortunately frequent societal attitude that babies are less important than adult victims of homicide and that natural parents would never intentionally harm their own children.

When battered child syndrome is suspected, investigators should always:

— Collect information about the "acute" injury that led the person or agency to make the report.

— Conduct interviews with the medical personnel who are attending the child.

— Review medical records from a doctor, clinic, or hospital.

— Interview all persons who had access to or custody of the child during the time in which the injury or injuries allegedly occurred.

The investigator must contact all medical personnel who had contact with the family, such as doctors, nurses, admitting personnel, emergency medical technicians (EMT's), ambulance drivers, and emergency room personnel:

—Talk with those who provided treatment for the child about what diagnoses and treatments were used. The attending physician will often be able to express at least an opinion that the caretakers' explanation did not "fit" the severity of the injury. Failure to obtain an opinion from the attending physician should not end the investigation.

— Speak with any specialists who assisted the attending physician.

— Have someone knowledgeable about medical terms translate them into laypersons' terms so that the exact nature of the injuries is clear.

— Obtain available medical records concerning the injured child's treatment, including records of any prior treatment.

Most clinics and hospitals have established procedures for photographing injuries in obvious cases of abuse, but when the injuries are more subtle, they may overlook the need for photographs. The investigator should make sure that the medical personnel take and preserve photographs or that the investigating team takes them. In a child homicide investigation, an autopsy must be performed. Most States mandate that such autopsies be performed when the death of any child under a certain age is undetermined or suspicious.

In States without such a statutory mandate, the medical examiner or local prosecutor often has the authority to order an autopsy. This authority should be used whenever there is an unexplained death of a child. Interview siblings, other relatives, neighbors, family friends, teachers, church associates, and others who may know about the child's health and history. People who surround the child and are part of his or her life are sometimes overlooked as sources of background information for a child abuse or homicide prosecution.

Collect additional family history concerning connections between domestic violence and child abuse, substance abuse and child abuse, and other such connections, even apparently unrelated arrests or charges. These records may be helpful in piecing together the complicated picture of what happened to the child this time and who was responsible. Identifying experts is as important to the child abuse investigator as identifying and cultivating street informants in other types of investigations.

If the investigator does not have a basic knowledge of the causes of young children's injuries, experts may be difficult to identify. Attending training conferences can provide the investigator with a great deal of basic knowledge and help establish a network of experts. A major trait of abusive caretakers is either the complete lack of an explanation for critical injuries or explanations that do not account for the severity of injuries. The investigation must not be dictated solely by caretakers' early explanations, because once they learn those do not match the medical evidence, they will come up with new ones.

In child homicide cases, for example, investigators will learn quickly about "killer couches," "killer stairs," and "killer cribs." Abusers frequently use these items in their explanations of a child's death. However, studies show that children do not die in falls from simple household heights; they do not even suffer severe head injuries from such falls. In nearly every case of actual abuse, the caretakers will not be consistent in their explanations of the injuries over time.

Sometimes the changes are apparent from statements abusers have made to others. Additional interviews may be needed to document the changing explanations and to follow up on additional information that the investigation uncovers. Caretakers' changes in explanations often mean investigators must visit the home or the scene of the injury more than once.

The ideal time to obtain such evidence is immediately after the child's injury is reported, before caretakers have an opportunity to tamper with the scene. If the caretakers do not consent to a search of the scene, a search warrant may be necessary. The strongest evidence of the need for such a warrant will be the medical evidence of what probably happened to the child and the caretakers' inconsistent or absent accounts of the events.

Whatever explanation caretakers offer for the child's injury or injuries, it is vital that the investigator secure physical evidence. Be thorough in obtaining photographic evidence of the location where the injury took place. Physical evidence and records that must be preserved include:

— The crib from which the child allegedly fell.

— The child's "environment," including bedding within the bed or crib and other beds in the home.

— Any toys or objects the child allegedly landed upon.

— In cases where the child was apparently burned, a record of any sinks, bathtubs, and pots or pans containing water.

In addition to testing the temperature of the standing water, test the temperature of water from the water heater and from each tap. Check the temperature setting of the water heater. This may help disprove an allegation that the child accidentally turned on the hot water. Other sources of heat in the home should be documented, regardless of the caretakers' initial explanation of what burned the child.

A complete photographic or video-taped record of the home or other location in which the injuries allegedly occurred. Focus on areas that the caretakers already have identified as the site of the particular trauma (i.e., stairs, beds or crib, or bathtub). Investigators should be trained by their local crime laboratory personnel on the types of evidence that can and should be processed and preserved in these cases:

— If the child apparently suffered cigarette burns, collecting cigarette butts found in the home may facilitate analysis of the burn patterns.

— If the case involves a combination of sexual and physical abuse, collecting the child's clothing and bedding may allow identification of what happened and who was involved.

— If the child shows evidence of bite marks, saliva swabbing should be done to allow positive identification of the biter.

— If the child has suffered a depressed skull fracture, any objects the approximate size of the fracture should be seized for appropriate analysis.

It is not always readily apparent that a child's death was the result of homicide. In some cases, homicide is evident:

— It is fairly obvious that the child's death was caused by an abusive injury.

— The person who had custody of the child at the time the abusive injury was inflicted is known. Most infant deaths occur when the baby is in the care of known individuals.

— The injuries themselves are obviously the result of a deliberate intent to do harm-that is, there is really no debate that someone abused the child and that the abuse caused the child to die. Such cases include strangulation, beating, severe inflicted burns, such as scalding, and the use of a weapon.

Unfortunately, the more careful and planned out the killing is, the less likely it is that a medical explanation for the death will be found. Most fatal injuries resulting from abuse are much more subtle than poisoning, beating, bludgeoning, shooting, or strangulation. Suffocation, for example, often leaves absolutely no medical sign of the cause of death. Most infant deaths are related to head injuries, some of which leave no external sign of trauma.

Investigators must be aware that children do not die of simple falls. However, everyone who handles child fatalities must have a basic understanding of the following conditions:

— Shaken baby syndrome.

— Munchausen syndrome by proxy.

— Sudden infant death syndrome (SIDS).

Shaken Baby Syndrome

The classic medical symptoms associated with infant shaking are:

— Retinal hemorrhage (bleeding in the back of the eyeball), often bilaterally (in both eyes).

— Subdural or subarachnoid hematomas (intracranial bleeding, most often in the upper hemispheres of the brain, caused by the shearing of the blood vessels between the brain and the dura mater or the arachnoid membrane).

— Absence of other external signs of abuse (e.g., bruises), although not always.

— Symptoms including breathing difficulties, seizures, dilated pupils, lethargy, and unconsciousness.

According to all credible studies in the past several years, retinal hemorrhage in infants is, for all practical purposes, conclusive evidence of shaken baby syndrome in the absence of a good explanation. Good explanations for retinal hemorrhage include:

— A severe auto accident in which the baby's head either impacted something with severe force or was thrown about wildly without restraint during the crash.

— A fall from several stories onto a hard surface, in which case there are usually other signs of trauma, such as skull fractures, swelling, intracranial collection of blood, and contusions.

Simple household falls, cardiopulmonary resuscitation (CPR), and tossing a baby in the air in play are not good explanations for retinal hemorrhage. There simply is not enough force involved in minor falls and play activities to cause retinal hemorrhage or the kinds of severe, life-threatening injuries seen in infants who have been shaken.

In most cases of shaken baby syndrome, there are no skull fractures and no external signs of trauma. The typical explanation given by the caretakers is that the baby was "fine" and then suddenly went into respiratory arrest or began having seizures. Both of these conditions are common symptoms of shaken baby syndrome.

The shaking necessary to cause death or severe intracranial injury is never an unintentional or nonabusive action. These injuries are caused by a violent, sustained action in which the infant's head, which lacks muscular control, is violently whipped forward and backward, hitting the chest and shoulders. The action occurs right in front of the shaker's eyes. Experts say that an observer watching the shaking would describe it as "as hard as the shaker was humanly capable of shaking the baby" or "hard enough that it appeared the baby's head would come off."

In almost every case, the baby begins to show symptoms such as seizures or unconsciousness within minutes of the injury being inflicted. The baby may have difficulty in breathing, or breathing may stop completely. Often, but not always, when shaking causes death or severe injuries, it has been followed by sudden deceleration of the action caused by throwing the child down onto a surface that may be either soft or hard.

Shaken baby syndrome occurs primarily in children 18 months of age or younger. It is most often associated with infants less than a year old, because their necks lack muscle control and their heads are heavier than the rest of their bodies. An infant cannot resist the shaking, but a toddler can, to some extent. Although the collection of injuries associated with shaken baby syndrome is sometimes seen in toddlers, it is rare and is always a sign of extremely violent and severe action against the child.

Munchausen Syndrome by Proxy

Munchausen syndrome is a psychological disorder in which the patient fabricates the symptoms of disease or injury in order to undergo medical tests, hospitalization, or even medical or surgical treatment. To command medical attention, patients with Munchausen syndrome may intentionally injure themselves or induce illness in themselves.

In cases of Munchausen syndrome by proxy, a parent or caretaker suffering from Munchausen syndrome attempts to bring medical attention to themselves by injuring or inducing illness in their children. The parent then may try to resuscitate the child or to have paramedics or hospital personnel save the child. The following scenarios are common occurrences in these cases:

— The child's caretaker repeatedly brings the child for medical care or calls paramedics for alleged problems that cannot be medically documented.

— The child only experiences "seizures" or "respiratory arrest" when the caretaker is there-never in the presence of neutral third parties or in the hospital.

— When the child is hospitalized, the caretaker turns off the life-support equipment, causing the child to stop breathing, and then turns everything back on and summons help.

— The caretaker induces illness by introducing a mild irritant or poison into the child's body.

Sudden Infant Death Syndrome

Sudden infant death syndrome (SIDS) is not a positive finding; rather, it is a diagnosis made when there is no other medical explanation for the abrupt death of an apparently healthy infant. When a baby dies from shaking, intracranial injury, peritonitis (inflammation of the peritoneum, that is, the membrane that lines the abdominal cavity), apparent suffocation, or any other identifiable cause, SIDS is not even considered a possibility.

SIDS rarely occurs in infants older than 7 months and almost never is an appropriate finding for a child older than 12 months. A SIDS death is not a homicide, and apparent SIDS cases must be approached with great sensitivity. However, before SIDS can be ruled the cause of death, the investigator must ensure that every other possible medical explanation has been explored and that there is no evidence of any other natural or accidental cause for the child's death.

An investigator's suspicions should be aroused when multiple alleged SIDS deaths have occurred under the custody of the same caretaker. Statistically, the occurrence of two or three alleged SIDS deaths in the care of the same person strongly suggests that some degree of child abuse is involved. Whenever there is evidence that the child who has died was abused, or that other children in the family have been abused, SIDS is not an appropriate finding.

Even when there is no affirmative medical finding of the cause of death, prosecution may still be possible. In some circumstances, experts can explain what occurs when a child is suffocated and can render a medical opinion that suffocation is one of the ways someone could cause the child's death without leaving obvious medical signs.

Appendix

Child Protection Bill 1998

Objectives of the Legislation

The object of the Bill is to provide for the protection of children.

The Bill responds to increased community expectation that:

— children be protected from abuse and neglect;

— children who are removed from home receive safe alternative care; and

— children who suffer abuse and neglect receive quality services which promote their emotional, physical, social and educational development.

In achieving its objective of protecting children, the Bill aims to:

— ensure that all children are protected from harm and the risk of harm, irrespective of the cause of the harm;

— assist families, including extended family members, to protect their children from harm;

— ensure that the views of children and families are taken into account when making decisions about the protection of children and that children and families have information and access to review of decisions affecting them;

— provide a range of orders to achieve the protection of children when, because a child does not have a parent able or willing to protect them, the State must discharge its obligation to intervene at the least intrusive level to ensure protection;

— promote a partnership between the State, non-government entities including Aboriginal and Torres Strait Islander entities, and the

— community in taking responsibility for and providing services for the protection of children and support of families;

— recognise and articulate the entitlements and duties owed by the State to children and young people in care;

— regulate standards for the care of children placed in alternative care by the State so that children being cared for away from their own home receive a standard of care which meets general community expectations and the needs of the individual child.

Reasons for the Bill

This Bill will replace in its entirety the outdated and severely limited Children's Services Act of 1965. Enormous advances have been made in the understanding of the problem of child abuse and in the enactment of the Children's Services Act over 30 years ago. Legislative reform will reflect improved service delivery methods and changing community values, including increased accountability for the exercise of statutory authority.

The introduction of new child protection legislation in Queensland will more adequately define the role of Government in protecting children and supporting families. New legislation will emphasise the role of families in protecting children, and recognise the need to involve parents and children in making decisions about meeting the child's needs. Provisions are required to ensure that the child's voice is heard throughout the child protection process, and that children are not further disadvantaged when they are placed in the custody or under the guardianship of the State.

The Bill ensures that families are supported and appropriately involved in ensuring the protection of their children. A range of orders are provided so that the least intrusive protective option can be used in each case.

The expectations of contemporary society about the quality of care which should be provided to children who are unable to live with their family are not reflected in the provisions of the Children's Services Act 1965 relating to the regulation of alternative care. In addition, a variety of community services not envisaged by that Act are now available for children who must live away from their families for protective reasons. New legislative provisions are required to ensure that minimum standards of care are met when children in the custody or under the guardianship of the State are placed in alternative care.

New legislation will address the significant over-representation of indigenous children in care. The nationally accepted principles of the Aboriginal and Torres Strait Islander Child Placement Principle for the provision of child protection services to indigenous children and families will be given a legislative base.

The Children's Services Act 1965 does not meet the requirements of the Legislative Standards Act 1992. New legislation will clarify appeal processes and emphasise accountability in planning and decision-making.

Estimated Cost for Government Implementation

Additional funds will be required for the legislation to be implemented effectively. New legislation is one component of the child protection reform which is needed to ensure Queensland children are adequately protected from abuse and neglect. A review of existing resources and service delivery is currently underway to identify additional resource requirements. It is anticipated that additional funds required to support the implementation of the legislation will be sourced from existing departmental funds and through the budgetary process.

Consultation

Consultation has occurred with the key government departments responsible for implementation of the Bill, namely the Department of Families, Youth and Community Care (DFYCC), Queensland Police Service (QPS), Department of Justice and Attorney-General (DJAG), and Queensland Health, as well as with the Brisbane Childrens Court Magistrate, Legal Aid Queensland, the Queensland Children's Commissioner and Education Queensland. In addition, extensive community consultation took place during September and October 1998.

The consultation has occurred on four levels:

— ministerial forums with key stakeholders;

— consultation with peak bodies and relevant government departments;

— regional community consultation meetings; and

— promotion of the consultation process to the general public.

In total, approximately 250 people attended ministerial information seminars and approximately 400 people attended 36 consultation meetings, in communities around the State. Participants represented the following interest groups:

— Child and family welfare sector

— Careproviders and care services

— Client representatives

— Non-government education sector

— Youth sector

— Health sector

— Legal sector

— Tertiary institutions

— Child care sector

— Aboriginal community

— Torres Strait Islander community

Extensive consultation with departmental staff has also occurred throughout each of the regions of the DFYCC.

The Exposure Draft of the Bill was made available via the DFYCC internet page to allow interested persons to access copies electronically. An e-mail address was also set up to allow interested persons to send submissions and comments electronically.

The Bill brings into effect the reforms which were seen as important by the community and key stakeholders.

Consistency with Fundamental Legislative Principles

Comment on consistency with the fundamental legislative principles of the Legislative Standards Act 1992 is required in relation to the following provisions:

— clause 16 (Contact with child at immediate risk of harm)

— clause 17 (Contact with child in school, child care centre, family day care etc) of clause 18 (Child at immediate risk may be taken into custody)

— clause 92 (Report about person's criminal history etc)

— clause 143 (Inquiries about certain persons' suitability)

— clause 94 (Carrying out medical examinations or treatment).

All instances of departures from the fundamental legislative principles under the Bill have occurred in the context of a tension between the rights of individuals as safeguarded by the fundamental legislative principles and the competing right of a child to protection from harm. It is considered that in these specific circumstances, the right of a child to be protected from harm override other fundamental legislative principles. DJAG has expressed its view that the provisions of these clauses are reasonable, in all the circumstances, given the vulnerability of children and the overriding principle of the Bill that the child's right to protection is paramount.

The relevant clauses are discussed briefly below. They are outlined in more detail, including examples of their use, in the "Notes on Clauses" section of these Explanatory Notes.

Clause 16 (Contact with child at immediate risk of harm)

Clause 16 gives officers authority to enter premises without an order in certain defined circumstances. These powers are limited to specific circumstances where the child is at immediate risk of suffering significant harm and it is not appropriate to leave the premises to obtain an order because to do so is likely to:

— expose the child to harm while the officer is away; or

— result in the family leaving the premises with the child (or the child leaving) to avoid the investigation. When this occurs, it may be a considerable period of time before the family or child is located.

It is considered that in these circumstances, the rights of a child to be protected from immediate harm or current on-going harm override the fundamental legislative principle that power to enter premises should be conferred only with a warrant issued by a judicial officer.

When an officer uses these powers, the details including the actions taken and reasons must be recorded in a way which is accessible for inspection.

Clause 17 (Contact with child in school, child care centre, family day care etc)

Clause 17 allows officers to have contact with a child for the purpose of investigating an allegation of harm, while the child is at school or in child care and before the parents are made aware that investigation of an allegation is occurring. These are situations where prior knowledge by the parents of the contact with the child is likely to impede the investigation and result in the child remaining unprotected.

It is considered that in these circumstances, the rights of a child to be protected from harm override fundamental legislative principles in regard to the rights of individuals (in this case those of the parents). Whenever an officer uses these powers, the details including the actions taken and reasons must be recorded on a register.

Clause 18 (Child at immediate risk may be taken into custody)

Clause 18 confers a power to take a child into the protective custody of the chief executive without first obtaining an order. The circumstances when this is authorised are specifically limited to those where an officer believes a child is likely to be harmed if the officer does not take immediate action to remove the child. This section also confers an authority to obtain a medical examination or treatment of the child without the consent of the parents while the child is in protective custody under this section. (See clause 94 about undertaking medical assessment).

When an officer takes a child into custody under this clause, they must apply for a temporary assessment order for the child within 8 hours of taking the child into custody. The effect of this clause is to limit the circumstances where an officer can take a child into custody without an order to those instances when an officer must take immediate action to protect a child from current significant harm. Action under this clause can be taken only in those minority of cases where it is not appropriate for an officer to "go away and come back with an order".

It is considered that in these circumstances, the power exercised under the Bill is sufficiently defined and is subject to appropriate review and is therefore consistent with the requirements of the Legislative Standards Act 1992.

Clause 92 (Report about person's criminal history etc) and clause 143 (Inquiries about certain persons' suitability).

Clause 92 and clause 143 allow information to be obtained which may be relevant to a recommendation or decision about a person's suitability:

— to be granted custody or guardianship of a child under a child protection order (clause 92); or

— to have a child in the custody or guardianship of the chief executive placed in their care (clause 143).

The clauses enable the commissioner of police to provide relevant information from police records which includes charges as well as convictions. Information from police records about domestic violence history is able to be provided. Also under these clauses the chief executive of the Transport Department is able to provide information about certain traffic violations.

It is considered that the provision of this information is justified in the context of making decisions about whether a child will be safe with a proposed carer and about the standards of care which that person could provide. It is particularly relevant in relation to charges of sexual offences against children where convictions are difficult to obtain, e.g. because of the need to rely upon child witnesses.

Clause 92 (7) also allows evidence from police records (i.e. records of interview and formal police statements) to be provided for the purposes of assessing suitability of persons to whom the court is considering granting custody or guardianship of a child. This includes evidence about allegations against the person, limited to relevant offences, ie offences against a person (such as assault and sexual offences), related to illegal drug-taking or dealing, and certain offences against this Bill relating to unlawfully removing a child from custody.

Without this provision, the situation could arise where a vulnerable child, one who has been found to be in need of protection because of abuse or neglect, could be placed in the custody of a person known to the police as having been the subject of numerous allegations of sexual abuse of children but who has not been convicted because the children involved were too young to be reliable witnesses.

It is considered that the State's duty of care to children who have been found by the court to be in need of protection cannot be properly discharged.if significant information about persons in whose care these children may be placed cannot be made available to the DFYCC. These children are especially vulnerable because of their history of abuse or neglect and it is imperative that precautions are taken to ensure that they are not placed in further danger by arrangements made by the court or the DFYCC for their care.

It is considered that in these circumstances, the rights of a child to be protected from harm override fundamental legislative principles relating to consistency with the principles of natural justice.

Clause 94-carrying out medical examinations etc.

Clause 94 authorises doctors to carry out examination and treatment of a child when the child has been taken into custody under clause 18, even though the child's parents have not consented to the examination. Medical examination and treatment under a court order are also covered by this clause.

The ability to provide medical examination and treatment pursuant to the child being taken into custody under clause 18 is a departure from the general fundamental legislative principle that sufficient regard be given to the rights of individuals (in this case those of the parents). This is considered justified in situations where:

— the child needs to be given immediate medical care and it would be inappropriate to delay this until a temporary assessment order was obtained; or

— significant medical evidence relating to abuse or neglect of the child may be lost or destroyed if medical examination cannot commence immediately, ie prior to obtaining a temporary assessment order.

This clause also recognises the practical consideration that urgent medical treatment cannot be carried out without appropriate examination. However, clause 94 stipulates that the doctor may only carry out medical treatment that is reasonable in the circumstances.

This clause does not effect any rights held by the child, for example the common law right of children who are competent to make their own decisions to refuse medical treatment or examination.

Notes on Provisions

Chapter 1- Preliminary

Part 1-Introduction

Clause 1 sets out the short title of the Bill.

Clause 2 provides for commencement of the provisions of the Bill. Clause 3 provides information about the where abouts in the Bill of the "Dictionary" and of key terms and concepts which are central to an understanding of the Bill.

Part 2-Purpose and Administration of Act

Clause 4 states the purpose of the Bill which is to provide for the protection of children.

Clause 5 sets out the principles which will guide the administration of the Bill. The guiding principles reflect national and international child protection practice directions.

The Bill's administration will be founded on the principles that every child has a right to protection from harm and that therefore the welfare and best interests of the child are paramount.

The Bill establishes the responsibility of the State to intervene to protect children while recognising that the primary responsibility for the care and protection of children rests with the family. The principles clarify how these competing factors should be balanced. For example, the Bill indicates that intervention should be at the least intrusive level necessary to protect the child and that intervention should be aimed at supporting the child's family to meet the child's protective needs.

The key principles outlined in clause 5 are reflected throughout the Bill.

Clause 6 sets out additional provisions which apply throughout the administration of the Bill in relation to Aboriginal and Torres Strait Islander children and families. If the child is an Aboriginal or Torres Strait Islander child, decisions of an officer or court under this Bill should only be made after consultation with a "recognised Aboriginal or Torres Strait Islander agency". This term is defined in the Schedule 4 as the agency which reaches agreement with DFYCC that they are the appropriate agency for a particular community. The term "recognised Aboriginal or Torres Strait Islander agency" includes an organisation or an individual.

This clause recognises the special needs of indigenous children and their families and communities to receive services which meet the cultural and identity needs of indigenous children, and to avoid dislocation of children from their communities. It recognises the unique needs of Aboriginal and Torres Strait Islander families stemming from their history as indigenous Australians, as evidenced by the over-representation of indigenous children in care. The principles of the Aboriginal and Torres Strait Islander Child Placement Principle are embedded in this provision, which has application throughout the Bill.

This provision has been drafted in consultation with representatives of relevant indigenous organisations, including the State Aboriginal and Islander Child Care Agency (State AICCA), who support its intent. Clause 7 outlines the functions of the chief executive which provide the framework for the proper administration of the Bill. These functions are part of the broader context within which the powers and obligations set out in the Bill are effected. The duties of the chief executive relate to the provision of services to prevent harm to children, to intervene at an early stage to assist vulnerable families, and to respond to the needs of children and families when harm or risk of harm occurs. The provision of all of these services occurs through administrative programs and does not require specific legislative powers. The powers of the Bill to protect children relate to the small percentage of circumstances where the chief executive is required to assume protective custody of children, or take action without the consent of parents.

Part 3-Basic Concepts

Clause 8 clarifies that the Bill applies to all children and young people.under 18 years old. The term "child" can be read as "young person" where the young person is under 18.

Clause 9 clarifies the meaning of the term "harm" as being any detrimental effect on the child's well-being, ie its common usage. However for the purposes of this Bill, "harm" is to be read as "significant" harm, ie the injury or other detrimental effect must be significant in nature. The type of harm .may be physical, psychological or emotional. It may be the result of physical, psychological or emotional abuse or neglect of a child, or the result of sexual abuse or exploitation, but is not limited as to its cause.

Clause 10 defines the concept of "a child in need of protection" which is used particularly in Chapter 2, Part 4. A court must find a child "in need of protection" before making a child protection order in relation to the child.

The intention of the words "does not have a parent able and willing to protect the child from harm" is to limit the circumstances when the State can remove children from the custody and guardianship of their parents. If the child's protection can be achieved by the parents (possibly with support and help from the State), it is not warranted to make an order for the State to assume custody or guardianship of the child.

This definition includes situations where the risk of harm is caused by the child's own actions or someone outside the home. It includes circumstances where, despite a parent's conscientious efforts and through no neglect or action on their part, the child remains exposed to risk of harm. It also includes circumstances where the parent does not have the capacity to care safely for the child despite a desire to do so, and circumstances where a child has no parent or family available to them.

Risk of harm includes circumstances where no harm has yet occurred but is likely to occur if no action is taken to protect the child. This may include circumstances where past evidence relating to other children indicates risk to the current child. It also includes circumstances where a child is abandoned, or where actions of the child or parent expose the child to risk of harm by others.

When determining whether a child is "a child in need of protection" the main focus of the court is upon the child's needs and whether an order is required to meet them, rather than upon the parents' actions, omissions or incapacity which may have led to the harm or risk of harm.

Clause 11 defines the meaning of the term "parent". Throughout most of the Bill, the word "parent" has a broad meaning and can include anyone caring in an ongoing way for the child like a parent, eg step-parents, or grandparents with whom the child lives.

"Parent" does not include temporary carers, eg relatives with whom the child stays for a few weeks or neighbours who mind the child each day. It does not include persons standing in temporary "loco parentis" for the parent, for example school principals.

The definition for Aboriginal and Torres Strait Islander parents is able to be interpreted broadly to include customary relationships within a community or tribal grouping.

Clause 12 describes the meaning of the term "custody" as it is used throughout this Bill.

A child may be in the custody of the chief executive or a relative:

— under the authority of the Bill alone (this is only possible under clause 18); or

— under an assessment order or a child protection order.

For a child in protective custody under the Bill, the officer taking the child into custody or person granted custody can do things and make decisions that relate to day-to-day matters concerning the child's care. This may include obtaining necessary medical care.

Clause 13 describes describes the meaning of the term "guardianship" as it is used throughout this Bill.

A child may be under the guardianship of the chief executive or a relative under a child protection order. A person who is granted guardianship of a child under this Bill has the right to make decisions that relate to day-to-day matters concerning the child's care, and has all the rights, powers and responsibilities in relation to the child, including making decisions about the long term care and development of the child, as does a person having parental responsibility under the Family Law Act 1975. When the child is under the guardianship of the chief executive as the result of an order under the Bill, the chief executive becomes the legal guardian of the child, instead of the parents, for the term of the order.

Similarly, if a relative becomes the guardian of the child as a result of an order under the Bill, the relative then becomes the only guardian for the.term of the order. "Guardian" means a person having parental responsibility as defined in part 7, division 2 of the Family Law Act 1975.

Chapter 2- Protection of Children

Part 1-Children at risk of harm

The preferred way of protecting the well-being of children is through the provision of information and support services to families. However, despite the provision of preventative and early intervention services, and support services to families, some children will still be exposed to the risk of harm. These children and families require a transparent system of assessing and responding to the needs of the child and family.

The system used to protect individual children includes:

— receiving reports of alleged harm to a child;

— investigating these reports and assessing a child's need for protection; and

— if a child needs protection, determining what level of intervention if any is required to ensure the child's safety.

In most cases, action to assess reports of alleged harm (e.g. contact with the family and child, and if necessary medical examination) is carried out with the consent of the child and the child's parents. In a minority of cases, parents object to officers having contact with a child for the purpose of investigating an allegation of harm, or will not consent to procedures which may be considered necessary, e.g. medical examination of a child's injuries. In these cases, officers require the legal authority to take action to assess the child's need for protection and to safeguard the child's immediate welfare.

Officers administering the Bill are obliged to use all reasonable means to gain the consent and co-operation of parents in taking action to protect children (e.g. moving the child to a safe place if necessary while the matter is assessed) and usually such actions are taken with parental consent. Where it is not possible to gain the voluntary consent and co-operation of a parent or child the Bill provides the means for authorised officers and police officers to fulfil the State's responsibility to protect children. This part outlines these authorities and defines and limits their use.

Clause 14 obliges the chief executive to take appropriate action when in receipt of allegations of harm to children. This may be through investigation and assessment of the allegations, or taking other appropriate action. Allegations are usually received as reports of concerns about a child and may include mandatory notifications.

Responses include investigation and assessment through contact with the child and family. When the allegation does not relate to significant harm, "other action" may be taken through the provision of protective advice to assist the notifier respond to the family's needs. For example, the notifier may be given information about resources which could be accessed by the family.

This clause also requires that departmental officers becoming aware of a possible criminal offence against a child must report the suspected offence to the police. When a criminal investigation and a child protection assessment are occurring in relation to the same matter, the responses of police and authorised officers are co-ordinated.

Clause 15 ensures that parents are given information about allegations concerning their child, and about the outcome of a child protection investigation, but also allows information to be withheld in certain circumstances.

The requirement that authorised officers or police investigating an allegation of harm must tell at least one of the child's parents what the allegations are does not include details about the person who reported the concerns (the notifier). Officers are not obliged to give details of matters to each of a child's parents because:

— in some cases where a child has four or more parents as defined in the Bill, this poses an onerous requirement; and

— in some cases the privacy of one parent would be violated without sufficient cause if the other parent was told of unsubstantiated allegations.

DFYCC practice standards require that all parents who are implicated in the allegations are told about them, that the primary carer is always told, and that both parents are told if the allegations are substantiated. However, an officer is not required to tell parents all details of the allegations or investigation if to do so may jeopardise a criminal investigation of the matter, or if telling them would place the child at risk of harm.

Clause 16 gives authorised DFYCC officers and police officers authority to enter premises without an order in certain defined circumstances. These powers are limited to specific circumstances where the child is at immediate risk of significant harm and it is not appropriate to leave the premises to obtain an order because to do so is likely to:

— expose the child to significant harm while the officer is away; or

— result in the family leaving the premises with the child (or the child leaving) to avoid the investigation. When this occurs, it may be a considerable period of time before the family or child is located.

For example:

Officers investigating a report that a small child has been left alone in a house can hear sounds of a distressed child inside the house and no adult responds to their knocks on the door. A family is known to officers as having in the past "gone into hiding" with the child to avoid investigation of concerns about the child. If, on locating the child, officers are denied contact with the child, they must act immediately. If they go away to obtain an order, the family is likely to have left the premises by the time the officers return.

It is considered that in these circumstances, the rights of a child to be protected from immediate harm or current ongoing harm override other legislative principles.

When an officer uses these powers, the details including the actions taken must be recorded in a register administered for that purpose. DFYCC officers will record this information using the centralised child protection information system administered by DFYCC; police officers will record the information on a register administered by the Queensland Police Service (QPS).

Clause 17 allows officers to have contact with a child for the purpose of investigating an allegation of harm, while the child is at school or in child care and before the parents are made aware that an investigation is occurring

These are situations where prior knowledge by the parents of the contact with the child is likely to impede the investigation and result in the child remaining unprotected. Examples include:

— A child tells someone about his or her sexual abuse by a parent and the allegations are notified to the DFYCC. Because of the dynamics involved if the child is being sexually abused, the parent is likely to pressure the child into not talking to the officer about the alleged abuse. The officers investigating the matter decide to initially talk to the child at school.

— A child in childcare tells a group leader about serious emotional abuse by a parent. The child is very afraid of reprisal by the parent for having told someone. The officer believes the child will refuse to talk about the abuse if the parent is present or talks to the child before the officer does. The officers assessing the matter decide to initially talk to the child at childcare.

Officers will negotiate with the person in charge of the school or child care centre e.g. the school principal, about a suitable time to visit the school and talk to the child. As with clause 16, whenever an officer uses these powers, the details including the actions taken must be recorded. DFYCC officers will record this information using the centralised child protection information system administered by DFYCC; police officers will record the information on a register administered by QPS.

Clause 18 confers a power to take a child into the protective custody of the chief executive without first obtaining an order. The circumstances when this is authorised are specifically limited to those where an officer believes a child is likely to be harmed if the officer does not take immediate action to remove the child. For example:

— An officer investigating an allegation that a parent has physically harmed a child find the child has considerable bruising. The parent is angry about the child having told someone about the abuse. The officer believes the child will be beaten by the parent again if left in the parent's care that day.

— A child tells officers about being sexually abused by a parent. The parent denies the allegation and places a good deal of pressure on the child to retract the statement. The officers believe that the child will be subject to emotional abuse if left in the care of the.parent when they leave. A young person is located by police late at night in circumstances where there is considerable danger of sexual assault. The young person objects to going with police to a safe place. It is likely to be too late to act if police go away to obtain an order. The police take the young person into protective custody in order to remove her from the danger.

This section also confers an authority to obtain a medical examination or treatment of the child without the consent of the parents while the child is in protective custody under this section.

When an officer takes a child into custody under this clause, they must apply for a temporary assessment order for the child within 8 hours. The effect of this section is to limit the circumstances where an officer can take a child into custody without an order to those instances when an officer must take immediate action to protect a child from current harm. Action under this clause can be taken only in those minority of cases where it is not appropriate for an officer to "go away and come back with an order". The temporary assessment order can be applied for by contacting a magistrate by telephone, facsimile, radio or any other electronic means.

Clause 19 ensures that when a child is taken into custody because of the need to act immediately, this overrides any other custody or guardianship order under the Bill which may be in existence. For example, a relative may have long-term guardianship of the child under a child protection order. If an officer believes immediate action is necessary to protect the child, the child may be taken into custody under section 18 despite the existing child protection order. However, the existing order only ceases to have effect for the time the child is in custody under clause 18.

Clause 20 ensures that if a child is taken into protective custody parents are given information about why this has occurred and what it means, ie that for a period of up to 8 hours or until a decision is made about an order, the child is in the custody of the chief executive.

Parents will usually be informed of where their child has been taken and in whose care they have been placed while in custody. However this clause, while it requires that the parents be given general information, does not require that they be given the details of the person with whom the child is.placed. When there is doubt as to whether giving this information could place the child or care provider in jeopardy, the information can be withheld.

Clause 21 allows action to be taken to protect the child in circumstances when the child needs to be moved from an unsafe situation but it is not considered necessary to override any of the parents' legal rights in relation to the child. This may apply when there is no parent present with the child, and the child is at risk if left where they are. For example:

— a child is found wandering alone at night and the parents' circumstances are unknown; police attending a domestic violence incident find young children who were staying with friends in the home. Because of the violence occurring, they believe the children will be at risk of harm if left in the household. The children's parents are away.

This section allows the child to be moved to a safe place and cared for until a parent or family member can collect the child. It can not be used if a parent is present with the child.

This section is an enabling section; it does not confer powers on the officers taking the action to override parental consent or to override the objection of a child whose level of maturity would enable him or her to consent to being moved, i.e. a child who is aged 12 years or older. "Safe place" is not defined-it has its everyday meaning. The safe place to which a child may be taken until parents are located and resume care of the child will vary depending on the child's options, the circumstances and the geographic location. For many children it will be the home of a relative, friend or neighbour. For others, depending on the circumstances, it could be a hospital, childcare facility, or other formal or informal emergency care arrangement. A safe place for a child cannot include a watch-house-by law it is not permitted for a child who has not been charged with an offence to be placed in a watch-house.

Clause 22 protects notifiers of alleged harm to children from legal liability related to making the report of alleged harm. It also protects persons who give information in answer to questions asked of them in relation to an investigation of alleged harm to a child.

In addition, a person is not considered to have breached any code of professional conduct or ethics by notifying the DFYCC that they suspect a child has been harmed or is at risk of harm.

Protection from liability is not given if the person who notified alleged harm did so knowing that the allegations were false. This section does not make reference to malicious allegations or allegations which are unsubstantiated, because there is no correlation in most cases between the intent of the notifier and the accuracy of a report. A report which was made for malicious reasons may nevertheless be accurate and lead to the protection of children who were at risk. On the other hand, a report found to be unsubstantiated may have been made with good intentions by a caller who honestly suspected a child needed protection.

Part 2-Temporary assessment orders

The purpose of temporary assessment orders is to authorise actions considered necessary as part of an investigation and assessment of harm, where it has not been possible to obtain the parents' consent. These are a new type of order which do not involve going to court. The term "assessment orders" denotes that these orders apply during the process of assessing whether or not a child needs protection. They allow a short period of investigative intervention without locking the family into an unnecessary court process when the level of ongoing protection required (if any) is not yet known. Temporary assessment orders apply the principle that intervention to protect a child should not include any action which is unwarranted in the circumstances.

Clause 23 limits the meaning of the term "parent" in this part to include only parents or others who by law have parental responsibility for the child. The term includes parents or others who would currently have legal parental responsibility if it were not for a child protection order granting custody or guardianship of the child to the chief executive or someone else.

The meaning of parent has been limited in this part because it deals only with parents whose legal rights may be affected by the provisions of this part, eg by the granting of custody or guardianship to the chief executive. Elsewhere in the Bill, "parent" is afforded a broader meaning to be inclusive of other persons parenting the child, eg step parents who care for the child but may not have legal parental responsibility.

Clause 24 explains that the purpose of a temporary assessment order is to facilitate the process of investigation and assessment by enabling necessary actions to be taken when a parent's consent cannot be obtained.

Clause 25 sets out the procedure for an officer (authorised officer or police officer) to apply for a temporary assessment order. The application must indicate which powers are sought under the order, and the reasons for the application. The application is made to a magistrate, not to a court.

Clause 26 allows for an application for a temporary assessment order to be heard "ex parte". Many such orders will be made by telephone contact with a magistrate. The purpose of these orders would in many cases be defeated if they could not be made promptly without notice to the parents. Clause 27 sets the matters to be considered by the magistrate in making the temporary assessment order. It ensures that an order is made only if it is necessary and only if it is not possible to obtain parental consent to do the things sought under the order. It also allows an order to be made in circumstances where parental consent can not be validly obtained (eg because a parent is psychiatrically ill).

Clause 28 sets out the provisions which may be included in a temporary assessment order. An order may include one or more of these provisions if warranted. If custody of the child is granted, the magistrate must be specifically satisfied that it is necessary to remove the child from home during the period of investigation and assessment. The order may direct a parent not to have contact with the child, or allow contact only when a stated category of person is present, e.g. "one of the mother's family", or "a worker from 'xyz' agency". The ability to direct a parent in this way presents an alternative to a custody order, in circumstances when a child has a protective parent but that parent needs assistance to enforce restrictions on an allegedly abusive parent.

The order may also give a power of entry if the court agrees that it is necessary, to enable contact with the child.

Clause 29 limits the duration of a temporary assessment order to 3 days. An order may however be made for a lesser time, and may be extended by application under clause 29. Three days will usually be sufficient time to enable a brief assessment of the child's circumstances to be completed, so that decisions about initial responses (if necessary) to the child's and family's needs can be taken.

Clause 30 provides for making the application by phone or by other electronic means. This may be necessary in many circumstances when an officer is unable to go to the magistrate to obtain the order, eg when the application must be made over the weekend to a magistrate on call, or when the officer is in a location some distance from the courthouse. The procedure to be followed ensures that the original written application and the signed order are filed. At the same time, it provides that a copy of the order, completed by the officer after telephone consent by the magistrate, can be used to authorise powers exercised by the officer.

Clause 31 requires that an officer using a power of entry under a temporary assessment order must follow the procedure generally required for the exercise of power of entry under a warrant.

Clause 32 outlines the obligations of the officer to inform at least one of the child's parents about the order, the terms and effect of the order and their right of appeal. Clause 189 outlines the general obligations of officers to explain the terms and effects of orders to parents, a child's carer (in certain circumstances) and to the child themselves if of an age and capacity to understand.

Clause 33 ensures that the DFYCC is advised of any temporary assessment order obtained by police.

Clause 34 allows an officer to apply for one extension of a temporary assessment order if it is decided that a court assessment order or child protection order is required to protect the child but it is not possible to apply for the court assessment order or child protection order before the temporary assessment order would end (e.g. because the decision is made on Saturday and the order ends on Sunday). The order can be extended to the end of the next business day so that the safe custody of the child continues.

Clause 35 provides that a temporary custody order takes precedence over any other custody or guardianship order under the Bill which may be in existence (e.g. a relative may have custody or guardianship of the child under a child protection order) for the duration of the temporary custody order.

Part 3-Court assessment orders

These are a new type of order, the purpose of which is the same as that of temporary assessment orders discussed above. Court assessment orders may authorise actions considered necessary as part of an investigation and assessment of harm where it has not been possible to obtain the parents' consent and it is considered that a period of more than a few days is required to complete the assessment about the level of ongoing protection (if any) required by the child.

Like temporary assessment orders, court assessment orders apply the principle that intervention to protect a child should not include action which is unwarranted in the circumstances. However they are for a longer period-up to four weeks-and for that reason must be made by a Childrens Court. This allows parents to make submissions to the court about the application.

Clause 36 limits the meaning of the term "parent" in this part to include only parents or others who by law have parental responsibility for the child. The term includes parents or others who would currently have legal parental responsibility if it were not for a child protection order granting custody or guardianship of the child to the chief executive or someone else. The meaning of parent has been limited in this part because it deals only with parents whose legal rights may be affected by the provisions of this part, e.g. by the granting of custody or guardianship to the chief executive.

Elsewhere in the Bill, "parent" is afforded a broader meaning to be inclusive of other persons parenting the child, eg step parents who care for the child but may not have legal parental responsibility.

Clause 37 explains the purpose of a court assessment order as identical to that of a temporary assessment order, ie to facilitate the process of investigation and assessment by enabling necessary actions to be taken when a parent's consent cannot be obtained. Court assessment orders are used for this purpose when a period of longer than 3 days is considered necessary, and because their duration may be for four weeks, an "ex parte" order is not appropriate.

Clause 38 allows an authorised officer or police officer to apply to the Childrens Court for a court assessment order. The application must state the reasons for the order and the types of powers sought. Clause 39 provides for the court registrar to set the date for hearing the application. The registrar must set the date as early as possible to minimise the detrimental effects of time delays in planning for the child.

Clause 40 provides that each of the child's parents must receive a copy.of the application. The child must also be given information. Young persons who are the subject of an application would usually be given a copy of the application. Clause 166 also provides that notice need not be served on a parent if it is not practicable to do so, e.g. because the parent cannot be located. DFYCC practice standards require that the application is fully explained to the parents and the child.

Clause 41 names the parents as respondents. The child is not a respondent but is a party to the proceeding.

Clause 42 ensures that the Childrens Court can not proceed with hearing the application unless the parents have had reasonable notice. "Reasonable notice" is not defined because it may vary in specific circumstances, for example to allow access to legal advice and travel time which may vary in different parts of the state. This clause also recognises that in some cases it will not be practicable to give a parent notice, eg if they can not be located.

Clause 43 provides for the court to make a court assessment order and states the matters about which the court must be satisfied before making the order.

Clause 44 sets out the provisions which may be included in a court assessment order. An order may include one or more of these provisions if warranted. If custody of the child is granted, the magistrate must be specifically satisfied that it is necessary to remove the child from home during the investigation. The order may direct a parent not to have contact with the child, or allow contact only when a stated category of person is present, eg "one of the mother's family", or "a worker from 'xyz' agency".

The ability to direct a parent in this way presents an alternative to a custody order, in circumstances when a child has a protective parent but that parent needs assistance to enforce restrictions on an allegedly abusive parent. The order may also give a power of entry and search if the court agrees that it is necessary, to enable contact with the child. Clause 45 requires that an officer using a power of entry under a court assessment order must follow the procedure generally required for the exercise of power of entry under a warrant.

Clause 46 limits the duration of a court assessment order to 4 weeks. The total time of 4 weeks includes any adjournment period. The order may be made for a lesser amount of time. An order may be extended once by application under clause 48.

Clause 47 outlines the obligations of the chief executive to provide the parties to the application with a copy of the order and information in writing that explains the terms and effect of the order and their appeal rights. Clause 189 outlines the general obligations of officers to explain the terms and effects of orders to parents, a child's carer (in certain circumstances) and to the child themselves, if of an age and capacity to understand.

Clause 48 allows for extension of a court assessment order but only for reasons to do with the best interests of the child. For example:

A relative is able to assume the child's care with agreement of the child's parents, and this could represent a resolution of the child's safety needs. However further time is required to assess the suitability of the relative who has only recently made the offer. It is in the child's interests to extend the court assessment order to allow assessment of the relative, rather than make application for a child protection order as the only other way to ensure interim protective custody of the child.

The order can not be extended for reasons unrelated to the child's interests, eg because an officer was on leave and therefore unable to complete the assessment. The court assessment order can be extended for no longer than 4 weeks. The application procedure for an extension is the same as for the original order. Clause 96 provides that if the original order would end before an extension application is heard, the child's custody continues until the application for extension is heard.

Clause 49 allows an authorised officer to apply to vary or revoke a court assessment order. The procedures are the same as for the original application. Variation or revocation may be sought if the circumstances of the case change during the term of the order and some of its provisions are no longer required. There is no provision for a parent to apply to vary or revoke the order because of its short duration. The hearing of an a application by a parent which was contested by the DFYCC could take as long as the term of the order, and deflect the efforts of all concerned from the purpose of the order, ie to assess the child's and family's needs.

Part 4-Child Protection Orders

When, as a result of assessing a child's need for protection, the chief executive decides that it is necessary to take action to ensure the child's protection, this action will usually occur with the voluntary consent of the family. When intervening to protect the child, the chief executive will whenever possible work with the family to assist them to protect and guide the child. In most cases action taken to protect children does not require their removal from home and occurs with the co-operation of the child and child's family.

However, if a child needs protection and the use of voluntary options to work with the family to protect a child is not possible or not appropriate, a child protection order may be required to ensure the child's safety. This may occur, for example when:

— the level of harm to the child is such that the child can not remain safely with his or her family; or

— the family disagrees with a delegated officer's decision about the child needing protection.

In such cases, a Childrens Court may be asked to determine whether the child is a child in need of protection, and, if so, what type of child protection order will best meet the child's need.

Clause 50 limits the meaning of the term "parent" in this part to include only parents or others who by law have parental responsibility for the child. The term includes parents or others who would currently have legal parental responsibility if it were not for a child protection order granting custody or guardianship of the child to the chief executive or someone else. The meaning of "parent" has been limited in this part because it deals only with parents whose legal rights may be affected by the provisions of this part, eg by the granting of custody or guardianship to the chief executive. Elsewhere in the Bill, "parent" is afforded a broader meaning to be inclusive of other persons parenting the child, eg step parents who care for the child but may not have legal parental responsibility.

Clause 51 explains that the purpose of a child protection order is to secure the protection of a child when the Childrens Court has found the child to be in need of protection. A "child in need of protection" is defined in clause 10. Although child protection orders vary in type, effect and duration, all have this common purpose.

Clause 52 allows an authorised officer to apply for a child protection.order and sets out the procedure for application. Only officers of the Department of Families, Youth and Community Care can make application for a child protection order. This recognises the role of the department as responsible for the protective custody of children, for the ongoing statutory intervention with children and families, and for determining which of the department's responses best meets the needs of the child and family.

Clause 53 provides for the court registrar to set the date for hearing the application. The registrar must set the date as early as possible to minimise the detrimental effects of time delays in planning for the child.

Clause 54 provides that each of the child's parents must receive a copy of the application. The child must also be given information. Clause 189 provides that notice need not be served on a parent if it is not practicable to do so, eg because the parent cannot be located. Clause 189(4) provides that the child is to be given information appropriate to their age and ability to understand. Under clause 189(5) young persons who are the subject of an application would usually be given a copy of the application. Departmental practice standards require that the application is fully explained to the parents and the child.

Clause 55 names the parents as respondents. The child is not a respondent but is a party to the proceeding.

Clause 56 ensures that the Childrens Court can not proceed with hearing the application unless the parents have had reasonable notice. "Reasonable notice" is not defined because it may vary in specific circumstances; for example to allow access to legal advice and travel time which may vary in different parts of the State. This clause also recognises that in some cases it will not be practicable to give a parent notice, eg if they can not be located.

Clause 57 provides for the court to make a child protection order if it is satisfied that a child is in need of protection ("a child in need of protection" is defined in clause 10), and that an order is the appropriate way in the circumstances of protecting the child. Clause 47 also sets pre-requisites to the making of a child protection order by the court. These aim to ensure that a child protection order is not made before there have been opportunities for the family to hear and discuss the reasons for the application, explore family options for the child's safety, and where possible resolve issues related to the application.

Clause 57(2) also seeks to ensures that if the court grants custody or guardianship to a relative, steps have been taken to assess the suitability of the relative to have custody of the child.

Clause 57(3) sets additional pre-requisites for the making of a long-term guardianship order (i.e. to 18 years) because such orders are meant to achieve a long-term safety and care for the child. A long-term order can be made only if:

— the court is satisfied that it appears unlikely that a parent will be able to resume care of the child; or

— the order best meets the child's need for emotional security in the long-term (e.g., if an older child in care has been with the same care provider family for many years, it may best meet the child's emotional needs in the long-term to remain with the care providers, even though the child may now have a parent able to provide adequate care. To move the child now may cause lasting emotional damage to the child).

Clause 57(4) guards against children growing up in long-term care as "wards of the state" if a suitable alternative order can be made.

Clause 58 sets out the child protection orders which the court may make. The following are illustrative examples:

a) an order may direct a parent not to leave the child in the care of a particular person convicted of seriously harming a child;

b) an order may direct a parent who has harmed the child not to have contact with the child, or allow the parent contact only when a stated category of person is present, eg "one of the mother's family", or "a worker from 'xyz' agency";

c) an order may require the chief executive to supervise the parents' care of the child in relation to necessary medical care for the child; d)(i) an order may grant protective custody of the child to an aunt for twelve months; d)(ii) an order may grant custody of the child to the chief executive for eighteen months;

e) an order may grant long term guardianship of the child (ie to 18 years of age) to the chief executive;.f)(i) an order may grant long term guardianship of the child (ie to 18 years of age) to a grandmother; f)(ii) an order may grant long term guardianship of the child (ie to 18 years) to a person who has been the child's careprovider for a number of years.

Clause 59 provides for the duration of child protection orders. Orders which direct a parent and orders for protective supervision by the chief executive may be up to one year in duration. Orders granting custody or guardianship may be up to 2 years duration, except for long-term orders granting guardianship, which expire when the child turns 18.

Clause 60 describes the chief executive's obligation to provide copies of the child protection order to the parties and to give them information in writing that explains the terms and effect of the order and their appeal rights.

Clause 61 allows for authorised officers to apply for extensions of child protection orders (other than long-term guardianship orders). The application procedure is the same as for the original child protection order. Clause 96 provides that if an application is made to extend a child protection order for custody or guardianship and the order would end before the extension application is heard, the child's custody or guardianship continues until the application is decided.

Clause 62 allows any party to an order, including parents, the child, or a person granted custody or guardianship of the child, to apply to vary an order, to revoke an order, or to substitute another less stringent order in place of the existing order.

Clause 62(2) (a) and (b) prevent any party other than the chief executive DFYCC applying for a more stringent order to replace an existing order, or for an extension of an existing order.

Clause 62(2) (c) and clause 62(3) limit the making of "repeat" applications by parties for revocation or variation of orders.

Clause 62(5) sets procedures to be followed if a parent or other "interested person" applies to revoke or vary the order. Other interested persons (e.g. the other parent) must be advised by the chief executive about the application. This is to ensure that notice is properly given to all parties entitled to it.

Clause 62(6) ensures that the court must consider the child's protective needs before deciding to revoke an order. Part 5-Adjournments of proceedings and court ordered conferences

Clause 63 enables the court to adjourn proceedings; however the court must state the reason for the adjournment and give directions. This seeks to ensure that adjournment periods are effectively used and do not occur unless necessary. The court is required to adhere to the principle that applications should be decided without undue delay because it is detrimental to children to have decision-making about their lives "put on hold".

Clause 64 enables the court to make interim orders to apply during a period of adjournment. For the period of the adjournment, these orders have the same effect as the corresponding child protection orders (see clause 58). However custody of a child during adjournment for a court assessment order can not be given to anyone other than the chief executive because of the purpose and short length of those orders.

Clause 65 enables the court to make procedural orders about actions to be carried out during a period of adjournment. These are actions to assist with the clarification and resolution where possible of issues related to the child's protection, and may result in reports for the information of the court in deciding the application.

Clause 65 also provides that the court may order the child be separately legally represented (see clause 107).

Clause 66 provides for the arrangement of a court ordered conference. Clause 67 provides that all parties to an application (i.e. the applicant, the parents and other respondents if any, and the child) may attend a conference with their legal representative, and a representative of a recognised Aboriginal or Torres Strait Islander agency if the child is an indigenous child. Children do not usually attend but would be represented by their separate legal representative if they have one.

Clause 68 aims to ensure that parents can hold open discussion at conferences without fear of what they say being used in any criminal hearing relating to the harm to the child.

Clause 69 provides for the filing of a report on the outcome of the conference with the court and for the immediate recommencement of the hearing before the court if practicable.

Part 6-Obligations and rights under orders

Clause 70 places a responsibility on the chief executive to service child protection orders. For all such orders (other than for long-term guardianship) the chief executive must work with the child's family towards resolving the child's protective needs and for this purpose must have regular contact with them. (Contact must also occur with children subject to long-term guardianship of the chief executive. However in these cases, resolution of the child's protective needs is seen as having been achieved through the making of the order).

If the child is in custody or short-term guardianship, the child's protection needs will be met by returning the child home if this is possible and in the child's best interests. In some cases, work with the family will result in the child's needs being met in another way, eg the parents supporting a decision in favour of a long-term order for the child. The responsibilities of the chief executive under clause 70 also apply when custody has been granted to a relative.

Contact with family members may be by telephone, or similar means, when it is not practicable to have face-to-face contact, eg because the person lives too far away.

Clause 71 obliges the chief executive to ensure the charter of rights for a child in care is complied with for children in the custody or under the guardianship of the chief executive. The Charter is contained in schedule 1. All children in care must be told about the Charter, and given a written copy unless they are too young to understand it.

Clause 72 states that the chief executive will provide assistance to a child or young person, who has been in the custody or guardianship of the chief executive, in the transition to independence. This assistance may include, for example:

— providing information about identity and personal history

— assistance in finding suitable accommodation

— assistance to access income support (e.g. Custudy)

— assistance in accessing education or training

— financial assistance.

Clause 73 describes the application of division 2 as relating to child protection orders requiring supervision.

Clause 74 sets out the obligations and powers relating to orders for the chief executive to supervise the parents' care of the child in relation to stated matters. This clause aims to ensure that an authorised DFYCC officer is able to have access to the child for the purpose of the order.

Clause 75 authorises a delegated officer supervising a child's care under a child protection order for protective supervision to issue directives to a parent to do (or not to do) certain things. Any directive must be in writing and must directly relate to the matters stated in the order as requiring supervision. The following are illustrative examples:

The stated matter may be to ensure the safety of a child, through proper supervision-the directive under clause 75 may require the parent to ensure the child does not have unsupervised contact with a particular person considered a risk to the child;

The stated matter may be the child's need for therapy to address significant developmental delays-the directive under clause 75 may direct the parent to ensure the child attends for medical appointments at a specialist clinic;

The stated matter may be the child's need for adequate physical care while an infant-the directive under clause 75 may require a parent who has seriously neglected their baby to accept the services of a resource worker in order to learn about a baby's physical needs.

Because a direction under this clause is given for the purpose of fulfilling the requirements of a child protection order, which can be appealed to the court if parents oppose it, grounds for administrative appeal are limited to arguing that the direction does not relate directly to the matters stated in the order as requiring supervision. The direction cannot be stayed pending outcome of an appeal because it is grounded in the order of the court and a stay may frustrate the intent of the court order.

Clause 76 obliges family members who are granted custody of a child under a child protection order (other than long-term) to allow authorised DFYCC officers to service the order by having access to the child, and by working with them and with the child's parents to resolve the child's protection needs.

Clause 77 obliges family members who are granted custody or guardianship of a child under a child protection order to give information to the child's parents and to facilitate contact between the parents and the child. This obligation applies to child protection orders granting long-term guardianship, as well as orders for custody. However the court may approve non-compliance with this provision if compliance would risk the child's or care provider's safety. This authority is vested in the court rather than the relatives' discretion because the parents would not otherwise be able to appeal the decision to prevent or limit contact.

Clause 78 outlines the application of division 4.

Clause 79 notes the authority of the chief executive to make decisions about where a child who is under the custody or guardianship of the chief executive will live, ie in whose care. This clause mentions the most common placements, i.e. licensed care services, approved careproviders (foster parents), and others such as relatives. Clause 79 does not limit where the chief executive may place a child.

Clause 80 gives effect to the principle that placements for Aboriginal and Torres Strait Islander children in protective custody must be culturally appropriate and maintain the child's cultural identity (as stated in clauses 5 and 6). It gives a legislative base to the intent of the Aboriginal and Torres Strait Islander Child Placement Principle. This includes consultation with a recognised Aboriginal or Torres Strait Islander agency and adherence to the hierarchy of placement options when making decisions about where to place the child.

Clause 81 states that when an approved careprovider agrees to care for a child, the careprovider and the chief executive will enter into a written agreement for the child's care. This "placement agreement" contains terms about matters relating to meeting the child's particular needs and also generic terms which put beyond doubt the right of the authorised DFYCC officer to have contact with the child.

Clause 82 obliges a delegated officer to inform parents where a child has been placed while under an assessment order (temporary assessment order or court assessment order), unless telling the parent/s where the child is would be a risk to the child's or care provider's safety.

Clause 83 obligates a delegated officer to inform parents where a child has been placed and with whom, while under a child protection order. The child's parents, and the child, have the right to appeal the placement decision to a tribunal. Information about the placement can be withheld if giving it would risk the child's or care provider's safety. The child's parents also have the right to appeal the decision to not inform them of where their child is placed.

Clause 83 also provides that the chief executive is not obliged to provide written notice of where the child is living if the child is in a placement for a brief period only. This decision not to provide notice is not appealable because appeal would be irrelevant given the short length of the placement.

For example:

It would be impracticable to give written advice to the parents when a child is placed with care providers for a week only as an emergency placement (though verbal information may be provided); the child will have been moved by the time any appeal is started.

Clause 84 relates to the chief executive's obligation to provide opportunity for contact between the child and family members. However the chief executive is not required to take unreasonable steps and is not compelled to allow physical contact if this would risk the child's or care providers' safety. It is also recognised that it may sometimes by impracticable for the chief executive to comply with a request for contact.

For example:

it may be impracticable to arrange contact with the child while the care providers have the child away with them on holidays; if contact has to be supervised, it may be impracticable to provide it every weekend.

Parents may appeal against a decision to limit contact with the child. This clause does not compel the chief executive to meet the costs of family contact as part of providing "opportunity for contact".

Clause 85 obliges the chief executive to review the arrangements in place for a child's care, at least every 6 months. This clause applies to instances where the chief executive has custody or guardianship of the child under a child protection order.

Clause 86 describes the chief executive's right to move a child from a carer if it is considered to be in the child's best interests. The term "carer" includes both approved careproviders (foster parents) and others such as relatives with whom a child is placed.

Clause 87 states that when the chief executive has decided to remove a child from a carer, the carer and the child (depending on age and capacity to understand) must receive written notice which outlines the reasons for the decision and advises of appeal rights when appropriate (refer to clause 88). The chief executive need not provide the written notice if the child has been with the carer for less than 7 days or removal of the child has been planned with the carer as part of the careprovider agreement (refer to clause 81).

Clause 88 outlines the rights of carers to appeal decisions to remove a child from their care. In all instances appeal is allowed if the stated reason for the removal of the child is that the carer is no longer considered to be a suitable person to care for the child. In other circumstances, approved careproviders may appeal the removal of a child only if the child was placed with them under a long term child protection order, ie the intent was that the placement would be long-term.

The lack of appeal against the removal from approved careproviders of children under short-term orders is because the intent of such orders is to safely reunite children with their family whenever possible. A decision to return a child home necessarily involves removal of the child from the careprovider and in such cases appeal against the removal is inappropriate.

Clause 89 advises the application of division 4.

Clause 90 enables the chief executive to arrange for the public trustee to manage the property of a child in care. This may occur, for example, if the child is the beneficiary of an estate which gives the child real estate property or substantial money. The term "incapacitated person" is a defined term under the Public Trustee Act 1978.

Clause 91 enables section 60 of the Public Trustee Act 1978 to be applied in relation to a child in care at the request of the chief executive. This may occur if, for example, the child is a beneficiary of an estate managed by someone on the child's behalf, and the chief executive has reason to suspect that the trust is being managed to the detriment of the child.

Part 7-General

The provisions under this part are general provisions used to give effect to the requirements of other provisions.

Clause 92 allows information to be obtained which may be relevant to a recommendation or decision about a person's suitability to be granted custody or guardianship of a child under a child protection order. It enables the commissioner of police to provide relevant information from police records which includes charges as well as convictions. Information from police records pertaining to criminal matters and domestic violence history is able to be provided. Also under this clause the chief executive of transport is able to provide information about certain traffic violations.

It is considered that the provision of this information is justified in the context of making decisions about whether a child is likely to be safe with a proposed carer and about the standards of care which that person could provide. It is particularly relevant in relation to charges of sexual offences against children where convictions can be difficult to obtain, eg because of the need to rely upon child witnesses.

The following are illustrative examples of information which may suggest that a person is not suitable to care for a child under an order for their protection:

— a person may have been charged with sexual offences against children where the evidence is compelling but police were unable to obtain a conviction because the court considered the children too young to give reliable evidence;

— a person has had a number of domestic violence orders made against them, but does not disclose this in discussion with officers assessing his or her suitability to have the care of a child. The existence of the orders and the circumstances in which they were made may indicate that a child placed with the person may be at risk of exposure to domestic violence;

— a person's criminal history may show some convictions for serious offences (eg burglary) and that numerous other similar charges which were not proceeded with after plea bargaining in relation to the most serious offence-the total history may suggest that the person is a habitual offender;

— a person's traffic history may show that they have lost their license a number of times for drink driving-this may indicate a history of alcohol abuse which is inconsistent with a suitable standard of care for children and a further practical concern that they will not be licensed to drive the child to appointments etc.

Clause 92(7) also allows evidence from police records (ie records of interview and police statements) to be provided by the police commissioner to the chief executive for the purposes of assessing suitability of persons to be given custody or guardianship of a child who has been abused or neglected. This includes evidence about allegations against the person. This evidence is limited to relevant offences, ie offences against a person (such as assault including sexual assault), related to illegal drug-taking or dealing, and certain offences against this Bill relating to unlawfully removing a child from custody.

The words "to which the commissioner has access" enable the provision of information from police records in other States, territories or countries.

Clause 93 obliges a delegated officer to convene a family meeting when the officer has decided to intervene to protect a child and is able to take this action without a court order (ie it is possible and appropriate to work with the family while the child remains in their custody). In these circumstances, when an officer has, in their role as a statutory child protection officer, assessed a child as requiring protection by the state, a family meeting is required to provide a formal opportunity for the family to be advised of the reasons for the officer's decision, to have their say about the matters, and to receive relevant written information.

A delegated officer is also required to convene a family meeting if one is ordered by the court. Family meetings cannot be held unless at least one parent attends. A representative of a recognised Aboriginal or Torres Strait Islander agency may attend if the child is an indigenous child. The child will attend only if this is considered by the convening officer to be in the child's interests (younger children do not usually attend), but the child must be given appropriate information. The attendance of other persons is at the officer's discretion because of the primary purpose of family meetings to facilitate involvement of the child's parents in making decisions about their child's future safety. In practice, relatives and support persons usually attend.

Clause 94 authorises doctors to carry out the actions required by a court order or authorised under the Bill. This relates to medical treatment, examination or assessment under clauses 18, 28, 44 and clause 65. A parent's or guardian's consent (including the chief executive's) is not required. However this clause does not effect any rights held by the child, for example their common law rights, if they are competent to make.decisions for themselves, to refuse treatment.

A medical practitioner can not be held liable in relation to the preparation of the report (eg for its contents, if they are the honest professional opinion of the author). However, he or she has the same liability as would have applied if the examination etc had been carried out with consent (eg, the doctor could still be held liable for a negligent medical, action).

Clause 95 authorises a qualified practitioner (eg, a psychologist or social worker) to carry out a social assessment of the child and family required by a court order under clause 65. A qualified practitioner can not be held liable in relation to the preparation of the report (eg for its contents, if they are the honest professional opinion of the author).

Clause 96 applies throughout chapter 2 "Protection of children" to circumstances when a child is already in custody or guardianship under an order which is due to expire, and application for another order for custody or guardianship or extension has been made but cannot be heard by the magistrate or court before the existing order ends. This clause allows the custody or guardianship of the child to continue until the application for a further order or extension is heard. This protects the child by ensuring there is no "gap" in the protective custody between one order and the next.

Chapter 3-Childrens Court Proceedings

Part 1-Preliminary

Clause 97 describes the application of part 1.

Clause 98 clarifies meaning of the word "order" in chapter 3.

Part 2-Jurisdiction

Clause 99 outlines how the Childrens Court must be constituted when exercising its jurisdictions. Appeals from the decisions of Childrens Court.magistrates can be heard only by a Childrens Court judge. The jurisdiction of the Childrens Court when constituted by two justices of the peace (magistrate court) is limited to deciding applications for court assessment orders or making interim orders, and does not include deciding a child protection application.

Clause 100 allows the hearing of a matter in the Childrens Court to proceed even though a criminal matter relating to the same circumstances is pending. This is to ensure that decisions related to a child's need for protection are not delayed and take precedence if necessary over the timing of a criminal hearing on the same matter. This is in line with the principle in clause 63(3).

Part 3-Procedural provisions

Clause 101 states that the paramount consideration of the court in exercising jurisdiction under the Bill must be the welfare and best interests of the child. This principle applies to all decisions made within the court's jurisdiction under this Bill. In addition, the court is required to adhere to the provisions of clause 6(3) in relation to Aboriginal and Torres Strait Islander children.

Clause 102 provides that the court is not bound by the rules of evidence and need only be satisfied of matters on the "balance of probabilities" (rather than satisfied "beyond reasonable doubt"). The court is inquisitorial, and may use whatever means it wishes to inform itself. For example, the court may accept a submission from interested family members, or may ask to speak to the child in the magistrate's office.

Clause 103 requires the court to take reasonable steps to ensure that the child (if present in court), the parents and other parties understand the proceedings. This includes the appropriate use of an interpreter if any party experiences difficulty communicating in English and a person to facilitate communication if a party has a disability which would limit their taking part in the proceedings.

Clause 104 provides that the court can receive expert advice to assist it in its deliberations. For example, in a highly complex medical matter the court may request a medical expert to clarify the implications of material before.the court.

Clause 105 allows the child, the child's parents and any other party, (eg a relative who has been granted custody of the child) to be legally represented. It also allows for the parent or other party to appoint someone as an agent to "stand in" as their proxy, eg if they are unable to attend court, and to present their views and wishes to the court.

Clause 106 ensures that the court does not proceed with hearing of an application unless the parents have had a chance to arrange legal representation. The parents will have had "reasonable opportunity to obtain legal representation" if they have had time to apply for legal aid, even if they have not been granted legal aid.

Clause 107 provides for the separate legal representation of a child. The court may order that the child be separately represented in any case, but is obliged to consider whether such an order should be made in all cases in which the parents or the child oppose the application. The style of separate representation is similar to that which is provided by separate child's representatives in the Family Court. The separate representative has an obligation to the court to act in the child's interests, and is not obliged to act on any instructions of the child.

Clause 108 allows for a lawyer to represent more than one child (e.g., within the same family) unless the court orders otherwise.

Clause 109 protects a child from being called to appear in the court and give evidence, unless the court permits this to happen. The clause also restricts the circumstances in which the court can grant permission. This clause recognises the extreme emotional distress and damage that can occur for a child when they are asked to testify against their own parents or in relation to harm which they have endured. It also recognises that it is contrary to strengthening positive family relationships for this to happen. The child's statement (if any) and views must be put before the court, but in an appropriate way which does not call the child to give evidence in court.

Clause 110 enables the court to take submissions from persons who are not parties to the proceedings, if court considers the person has useful information to provide. (However, this does not imply that any person who is not a party can be present in court without leave of the court).

Clause 111 allows a Childrens Court magistrate to transfer proceedings to another Childrens Court. This may be appropriate, for example, if the.child and family have moved.

Clause 112 enables the court to hear two or more applications together (e.g. for two children in the same family).

Clause 113 provides for each party to pay their own costs. There is no provision for costs to be ordered against the State as the applicant because of the complexity of this statutory role on behalf of the people of Queensland. If an application results in withdrawal or is dismissed because an order is considered by the court to be unnecessary, this does not mean that the application was unwarranted. It may represent a positive resolution of the protection issues during the court process, an outcome which may have been aided by the court application.

If costs were to be awarded against the State as applicant, financial considerations could become the determinant factor in deciding whether to make application for an order, instead of the child's current need for protection.

Part 4-Court Appeals

Clause 114 allows any of the parties to appeal a decision of a court on an application for an order. This includes the child who may appeal in their own right, or through a separate legal representative.

Clause 115 sets out the procedure for making an appeal.

Clause 116 allows for the appellate court to stay a decision which is being appealed. If an appealed decision is not stayed, it can be implemented even though it is being appealed.

Clause 117 provides for the appeal to be decided on the Childrens Court records of the original hearing, except that a Childrens Court judge hearing the appeal can order a new hearing or partial hearing.

Clause 118 lists the powers of the appellate court to confirm, vary or set aside decisions and to make new decisions.

Chapter 4- Interstate Transfers of Guardianship and Custody of Children

Clause 119 defines the meaning of "parent" for the purpose of this chapter.

Clause 120 outlines the procedure for the chief executive to accept a transfer of a custody or guardianship order for a child from another state. When the chief executive assumes custody or guardianship by signing a declaration, the interstate order becomes a Queensland child protection order as if made under this Bill. The duration of the order is translated to be consistent with a child protection order under this Bill.

Clause 121 requires the chief executive to advise the child and the child's parents of the making of the declaration, i.e. that the order is now a Queensland child protection order.

Clause 122 enables the chief executive to arrange a transfer of guardianship of a child under the chief executive's custody or guardianship from Queensland to another state. Written notice of the planned transfer must be given to the child, the child's parents, and, if applicable, the carers. The chief executive must consider any submissions they make that the transfer should not be made. Transfer of guardianship decisions can be appealed to a tribunal.

Chapter 5-Regulation of Care

Part 1-Standards of care

Clause 123 obliges the chief executive to ensure that when a child is placed with an approved care provider or in a care service, the care is of an adequate standard. The Statement of Standards requires the chief executive to, as far as possible, meet the material, educational, psychological and other needs of children placed in out-of-home care by the DFYCC.

The Statement of Standards is a central provision of the part dealing with regulation of care because adherence or ability to adhere to those of the standards which are within the care provider's means are used to assess the suitability of care providers and services.

The Statement of Standards is consistent with the provisions of the United Nations Convention on the Rights of the Child. Corporal punishment or punishment which frightens or threatens a child is prohibited because, among other reasons, children in care for protective reasons may have experienced treatment of this type and are particularly vulnerable.

Part 2-Licensing of care services and approval of care providers

Clause 124 establishes the purpose of this part.

Clause 125 ensures that a license can only be held by an organisation, not by an individual.

Clause 126 sets out the procedure for application or renewal of a license to provide a care service. The organisation must name an individual as the "nominee" for the license, ie the person administratively responsible for the license.

Clause 127 prohibits the chief executive from granting the application for license unless satisfied that the organisation, and those persons managing and providing the services (i.e. caring for children) are suitable. In assessing whether persons are "suitable", the chief executive may consider criteria under a regulation, including their ability to meet the stated standards, and can take into account information about a person's criminal and other histories (clause 143). Any child protection records about the person held by the department may also be taken into account.

Clause 128 requires a license to be issued if approval of the application is granted and enables a license to include reasonable conditions (for example, limiting the type of care which can be provided-a care provider may be approved only to care for babies).

Clause 129 limits the duration of a license to 3 years.

Clause 130 sets out the procedures to be followed if the chief executive refuses a license.

Clause 131 establishes that the nominee of a license holder is responsible for ensuring suitable standards of care.

Clause 132 provides that only an individual can be an approved care provider (foster parent), although two or more individuals can be jointly approved. If a couple is to care jointly for the child, both must be approved as care providers.

Clause 133 sets out the procedure for application or renewal of a certificate of approval as a care provider.

Applicants for approval as care providers must make application to the DFYCC.

Clause 134 prohibits the application being granted unless the applicant is suitable to be a care provider and all adult members of their household are suitable to associate on a daily basis with children. In assessing whether persons are "suitable", the approving officer may consider criteria under a regulation, including the applicants' ability to meet the stated standards, and can take into account information about a person's criminal and other histories (clause 143). Any child protection records about the person held by DFYCC may also be taken into account.

Clause 135 requires a certificate of approval to be issued if approval as a care provider is granted. Conditions may apply to the approval.

Clause 136 sets the duration of the initial and subsequent certificates of approval.

Clause 137 sets out the procedure for refusal of an application for a certificate of approval.

Clause 138 sets out the procedure for licensees or approved care providers to apply for an amendment to the conditions of their license or approval. Throughout the rest of this division both licenses and certificates of approval are referred to generically as "authorities". Clause 139 enables licenses and approvals to be amended by the chief executive, for example if standards of care are not being met or conditions are not being adhered to. The procedure for amending the license or approval is set out.

Clause 140 sets out the grounds on which a license or approval may be suspended or cancelled.

Clause 141 sets out the procedure for suspending or cancelling a license.or certificate of approval. The holder of the license or approval must be given written notice of the reasons for the proposal to suspend or cancel the license and have at least 28 to respond. Decisions to suspend or cancel licenses or approvals may be appealed to a tribunal.

Clause 142 outlines the procedure to be followed if a license or approval is to be amended, suspended or cancelled. The amendment, suspension or cancellation takes effect on the day the new authority is given out (or later if stated) and cannot be backdated.

Clause 143 authorises criminal history and other checks to be made by the chief executive for the purpose of determining the suitability of persons to provide care for children. It applies to persons managing and providing care services at a licensed service, to care provider applicants and to the adult members of their household. It authorises the commissioner of police to provide information about a person's criminal history and domestic violence history and the chief executive for transport to provide information about a person's traffic history (see clause 92 and discussion under the heading "Fundamental legislative principles" about why such checks are justified). Departmental child protection records may also be considered in determining the suitability of persons.

Clause 143 does not enable the provision of police records about alleged offences, as is possible under clause 92(7), because children placed with approved care providers will have regular contact by authorised DFYCC officers (clause 92(7) applies when persons may be granted custody or guardianship of children).

Clause 144 provides that failure to advise of a decision about an application within 90 days may be taken as notice of a decision to refuse the application.

Clause 145 makes it an offence to contravene a condition of a license or a certificate of approval.

Clause 146 enables an authorised officer to request a licensee or approved care provider to produce their license or certificate of approval.

Clause 147 provides for an authorised officer to enter and inspect the premises of a licensed care service at any reasonable time to ensure that the provisions of the Bill are being complied with.

Chapter 6-Administration

Part 1-Authorised officers

Clause 148 provides for the chief executive to appoint authorised officers (DFYCC employees and other persons by regulation) for the purpose of carrying out duties under the Bill.

Clause 149 provides for the powers of an authorised officer to be limited.

Clause 150 provides for stating an authorised officer's conditions of appointment.

Clause 151 requires an authorised officer to have a departmental identity card for the period of their appointment.

Clause 152 requires an authorised officer to show their identity card before exercising a power under the Bill or, if this is not practicable, as soon as possible afterwards.

Clause 153 provides that, if something is damaged when exercising a power under the Bill (for example if something in the home is broken when a child is being taken into custody), an authorised officer must give written notice about the damage to the owner.

Clause 154 provides that if a person incurs loss or expense to property because a power was exercised under this Bill, they can claim compensation. This clause does not relate to indirect loss or loss other than property, eg it does not include loss of income or the incurring of medical or legal expenses.

Part 2-General

Clause 155 enables the chief executive to delegate powers under the Bill to departmental employees.

Clause 156 enables the chief executive to approve forms for use under this Bill.

Clause 157 relates to co-ordination of government departments and community agencies involved in providing child protection services. It makes the chief executive responsible for ensuring that roles and responsibilities of departments and agencies are co-ordinated at a broad policy and planning level; and at the level of taking action to protect individual children.

This clause ensures that mechanisms to co-ordinate statutory child protection intervention services, such as the proposed Child Protection Council, the inter-departmental Co-ordinating Committee on Child Abuse and existing Suspected Child Abuse and Neglect (SCAN Teams), must exist.

Clause 158 allows for the financial support by the chief executive of children in the chief executive's custody or placed in alternative care for reasons related to their protection and welfare. There is provision for the chief executive to help meet expenses of the transition of a child from custody or guardianship under the Bill to independence. These expenses may in some cases be incurred after a young person turns eighteen years, and may include, for example, a contribution towards establishing a household or towards tertiary education costs.

Chapter 7-Enforcement and Legal Proceedings

Part 1-Offences

Clause 159 makes it an offence to obstruct an officer exercising powersunder this Bill. However it is expressly allowed that a child who resists being taken into custody for the child's own protection cannot be charged with an offence under this section.

Clause 160 makes it an offence to impersonate an authorised officer.

Clause 161 makes it an offence to remove a child under custody or guardianship of the chief executive from the care of the person with whom the child has been placed.

Clause 162 makes it an offence to remove a child from someone who has custody or guardianship under this Bill. It is also an offence to keep a child whom someone else has unlawfully removed.

Clause 163 makes it an offence to unreasonably refuse to allow an authorised DFYCC officer to enter a house to check on the well-being of a child under an order giving custody or guardianship to the chief executive.

Clause 164 makes it an offence to take a child under a custody or guardianship order interstate, with the intention of preventing this Bill from applying to the child.

Clause 165 makes it an offence for a parent to contravene an order directing that they not have contact with the child. A person who has been given notice of an order, e.g. by it being sent to their last known address, is taken to know about the order.

Part 2-Warrant for apprehension of child

Clause 166 enables an authorised officer or police officer to apply for a warrant for the retrieval of a child. This may be necessary when a child has been unlawfully taken from the person with whom they were placed, or when it has not been possible to take custody of a child even though an order granting custody or guardianship has been made.

Clause 167 allows the issuing of a warrant by a magistrate. The warrant authorises the officer to enter any places where the child is thought to be. It may not be known exactly where the child is at the time of issuing the warrant, and therefore its authority must enable the officer to enter any place the child is thought to be while searching for the child. It would not be practicable to have to seek a specific order relating to another place each time the child was moved.

Clause 168 sets out the procedure to be followed after a warrant is issued by phone or fax etc. It ensures that the sworn application and signed warrant are filed and allows a copy of the warrant to be used by the officer in the same way as a the signed warrant.

Clause 169 requires that an officer using a power of entry under a warrant must follow normal procedure for the exercise of power of entry under warrants.

Part 3-Powers of authorised officers

Section 170 clarifies the application of part 3.

Section 171 authorises DFYCC officers, in the circumstances outlined in clause 170, to seize (ie take with them, as evidence) anything that may otherwise not be available at a later date as evidence.

Section 172 sets out the procedure to be followed if a thing has been seized by an authorised officer. These are standard procedures.

Section 173 allows the court to order the forfeiture of a seized thing.

Section 174 deals with the status of forfeited things.

Section 175 allows authorised DFYCC officers to take photographs as evidence, in the circumstances outlined in clause 148, i.e. the same circumstances as they are authorised to seize things.

Part 4-Evidence and legal proceedings

Clause 176 provides that proof is not required for a Childrens Court to accept that an authorised officer is authorised under this Bill or that a document tendered under the signature of an authorised officer or the chief executive is in fact signed by them.

Clause 176 also provides a list of statements which, if certified by the chief executive, can be taken as evidence that the statement is true. For example:

If a statement signed by a delegated officer certifies that a licence was issued on a particular date, this can be taken as evidence of the matter-no further proof is required.

Clause 177 provides for offences under the Bill to be dealt with as summary offences.

Clause 178 limits the time within which a proceeding for an offence can be commenced.

Part 5-Confidentiality

Clause 179 provides some definitions used in this part only. "Publish" can mean any public means of communication, e.g. speaking at a public meeting, but does not include communication which is not accessible by the public. "Act" in this part includes reference to the Children's Services Act 1965 so that records created under that Act are covered by the Bill's confidentiality provisions.

Clause 180 ensures that confidentiality is maintained about the identity of persons who notify statutory authorities of their concerns about possible harm to a child. The clause prohibits officers who are aware of the notifier's details from disclosing them, except to others requiring the information to perform duties under this Act, or if ordered by a court or tribunal. It also prohibits the questioning of an officer in a court or tribunal proceeding about the identity of the notifier unless the court or tribunal gives leave. The identity of the notifier is also protected during the process by which the court or tribunal considers whether to grant leave to disclose the information.

This clause is essential for the effectiveness of the system for the protection of children in Queensland. Statutory authorities with responsibility to protect children rely upon members of the public to report concerns about children. In most cases, notifiers will not report or disclose information unless they can be assured that their identity will be protected. Any lessening of this standard would erode public confidence in Queensland's child protection system.

Clause 181 is the central confidentiality clause of the Bill. It prohibits DFYCC employees, police officers, and other persons performing duties under the Bill who obtain personal information, for example information from child protection case records, from disclosing the information. The prohibition applies to persons both directly and indirectly involved in the administration of the Bill, e.g. staff of the department and Minister, employees of licensees, and approved careproviders.

However the clause allows disclosure for purposes related to a person's duties under the Bill, and for purposes directly related to the welfare of any child. Such disclosure may not be directly related to the protection of the child it concerns, but may be disclosed in relation to the protection or welfare of another child or children. For example:

A parent may have seriously neglected an infant in their care, and now a second child is about to be born. Information about the first child can be disclosed for the purpose of ensuring the protection of the second infant.

Clause 181 also enables disclosure of personal information if the disclosure relates to co-operating with other government entities which have responsibilities relating to the protection of children. For example:

A family where the children are considered at risk of harm moves interstate. Information about the family may be disclosed to the other state welfare department when they locate the family, to assist that department to protect the children. Similarly, information about a child may be disclosed to a non-government agency. For example:

An agency provides protective services to children referred by the DFYCC. To enable them to provide the assistance required to help the family meet the child's needs, the DFYCC provides information held by the department about the child's needs.

Information may also be given to a person if it is information about them.

Clause 182 ensures that personal information which is given to someone under clause 181 must be treated confidentially by that person. However the person may give the information to someone else if this is necessary for the protection or welfare of the child. For example:

A school principal given information by an officer about a child may pass on necessary parts of it to teachers of the child to enable them to help support and safeguard the child.

Under this clause "purposes directly related to a child's protection and welfare" can include purposes related to assessing or reviewing a child's need for protection, and may relate to other members of the child's family whose welfare is linked to that of the child.

Clause 183 makes it an offence to publish information which would identify a child living in Queensland as being a child who has been harmed by someone within their own family. This provision recognises the emotional trauma to a child (even many years later) of seeing or hearing themselves publicly identified as a child whose family mistreated them. The repercussions extend to the attitudes of others with whom the child has contact, e.g. a child being embarrassed or bullied because other children at school, for example, have had access via the media to very personal information about what happened within the child's home.

For the same reasons, clause 183 also makes it an offence to identify a child as the subject of investigation of a child protection allegation under this Bill or the subject of an application or order under this Bill, unless approved by the chief executive for publication.

Clause 184 protects personal client records by ensuring that subpoenas are targeted to the documents required and do not catch up irrelevant personal documents. This clause also protects the confidentiality of documents which have been supplied in response to a subpoena, when in the control of the court registrar or other agency.

Clause 184(1) (b) provides that records or documents from the department which are in the possession of another government entity are included in the provisions of clause 184 relating to subpoena of records.

Clause 185 allows an officer involved in administering the Bill to refuse to disclose certain information to a court or a tribunal. The circumstances relate to the safety of a child or family member, or to identifying a notifier, or to the disclosure of highly personal information and jeopardising the trust of the child or family member. Provision exists for the court or tribunal to order the disclosure if it is satisfied that the information is relevant to the proceedings, and that the arguments in favour of disclosing it outweigh the arguments against. However this clause does not override clause 180 in relation to the identity of a notifier.

Clause 186 prohibits the public reporting of proceedings under this Bill in the Childrens Court (which is not open to the public), unless approved by the court. The Childrens Court is a closed court to protect the privacy of children.

Clause 187 prohibits the publication of any identifying information about a child who is a victim or witness in a court proceeding about a sexual offence. A court may also order the prohibition of identifying information about a child in any other court proceedings relating to offences against the child or in which the child is a witness.

Clause 188 enables personnel of a health service under the Health

Services Act 1991 (e.g. a hospital or public clinic) to release information from the health service records to give to the chief executive. This may be.necessary, for example, when a hospital has information directly relevant to the assessment of a child's protection needs. It may include information about another person (e.g. a parent) when the information relates to the child's welfare.

Part 6-General

Clause 189 provides that when required to explain an order or declaration or to serve notice on someone, the chief executive need only comply to the extent "reasonably practicable" in the circumstances. For example, in the circumstance where a parent cannot be located or contacted it is not reasonably practicable to serve notice.

Children must be told or notified of matters, but in a way which is appropriate to their age and ability to understand the information. This includes the child being entitled to receive the information in writing if:

— the child is entitled to be told about matters where notice to parents is required in writing, and

— the child or young person is considered by the authorised officer to have the maturity and competence to deal appropriately with the written information.

Clause 190 provides that if a police officer or authorised officer is required to do something, the task can be performed by another officer with the same delegations or powers.

Clause 191 provides protection from civil liability for a police officer or authorised officer (or someone acting under their direction) acting properly and honestly in an official capacity under the Bill.

Chapter 8-Miscellaneous

Clause 192 enables an aggrieved person for an appealable decision to appeal to the Children's Services Tribunal.

Clause 193 enables the Governor in Council to approve regulations under this Bill and lists the matters about which a regulation may be made.

Chapter 9-Repeals, Savings and Transitional Provisions

Part 1-Repeals

Clause 194 repeals the Children's Services Act 1965 in its entirety. Clause 195 permits a reference to the Children's Services Act 1965 in existing Acts or documents to be read as a reference to this Bill, if relevant.

Part 2-Savings and transitional provisions

Clauses 196 to 203 provide for the transition of existing orders under the Children's Services Act 1965. These are existing 'care and protection' orders, 'protective supervision' orders, 'care and protection' orders under a section 47 or section 134 declaration, 'care and control' orders under section 61 and 'supervision' orders under section 61. Provision is also made for the transition of existing licenses for care services and certificates of approval for care providers.

Chapter 10-Amendments

Clause 204 states that schedule 3 lists consequential and other amendments to other Acts.

Schedule 1-Charter Rights for a Child in Care

Schedule 1 describes the obligations of the chief executive to children and.young people who are in the custody or guardianship of the chief executive under a child protection order. The Charter acknowledges the special vulnerability of children who do not have a parent able and willing to protect them and reflects the obligation of the State to provide care for these children in a way that ensures their rights, as documented in the Charter, are met. The matters stipulated in the Charter are provided for in other sections of the Bill. Their listing in the Charter using language which may differ from that used elsewhere in the Bill can not be taken to limit any of the provisions contained in the body of the Bill.

Schedule 2-Appealable Decisions and Aggreived Persons

Schedule 2 lists all decisions under the Bill which are able to be appealed to the Children's Services Appeals Tribunal. The aggrieved persons, ie the persons entitled to appeal, are listed alongside each decision.

Schedule 3-Amendment of Acts

Schedule 3 lists the Acts which are amended by the Bill.

Schedule 4-Dictionary

Schedule 4 defines terms used in the Bill.

Bibliography

American Association for Protecting Children (AAPC). (1988). Highlights of official child neglect and abuse reporting - 1986. Denver, Co: American Humane Association.

Briggs, Freda and Hawkins, Russell, Child Protection: A Guide for teachers and Child Care Professionals, Sydney, Allen and Unwin, 1997.

Britton, J. 2001, Federal funding for child abuse and neglect prevention. Chicago, IL: Prevent Child Abuse America.

Broadbent, Anne and Bentley, Rebecca, *Child Abuse and Neglect Australia 1995-96, Child Welfare Series,* Number 17.

Brown, Pat and Jones, Elizabeth D, Help for Adult Survivours of Child Abuse, Chicago, NCPCA, 1990.

Browne, Kevin D and Lynch, Margaret A, Child Abuse Review, Vol 6 Issue 3 August 1997

Calvert, Gillian, Ford, Adrian and Parkinson, Patrick, eds, The Practice of Child Protection: Australian Approaches, Sydney, Hale and Iremonger, 1992.

Clarke, P and Milne, R (eds), *Child Rearing Patterns: Background Information,* Free Kindergarten Association Multicultural Resource Centre, 1996.

Commonwealth of Australia, 1997, Report of the Commission of Inquiry into Abuse of Children in Queensland and Institutions Queensland , 1999.

Courtney, M. E. 1999, The economics. *Child Abuse and Neglect,* 23(10), 975-986.

Daro, D., & Harding, K. A., 1999, Healthy Families America: Using research to enhance practice. *The Future of Children.*

Domestic Violence Resource Centre, *Walking on Eggs: A Video and Workbook for Young Children Affected by Domestic violence,* South Brisbane, Domestic Violence Resource Centre, 1996.

Harding, K. A., *Child abuse prevention efforts: Strengthening families, protecting children.* In A. Giardino & E. Giardino (Eds.), Recognition of child abuse for the mandated reporter. St. Louis, MO: G. W. Medical Publishing.

Hartley, Robyn (ed), *Families and Cultural Diversity,* St Leonard's, Allen and Unwin, 1995.

Herman-Giddens, M. E., Brown, G., Verbiest, S., Carlson, P. J., Hooten, E. G., Howell, E., & Butts, J. D., 1999. Underascertainment of child mortality in the United States. The Journal of the American Medical Association.

Patton, Michael Quinn ed., *Family Sexual Abuse,* Newbury Park, Sage, 1991.

Perry, Garry Pand Orchard, *Janet Assesssment and Treatment of Adolescent Sex Offenders,* Sarasota, Professional Resource Press, 1992.

Schofield, Ann, *Signposts of Change: A Chronology of Australian History and World Events,* Melbourne, Aird Books, 1987.

Vocational Consumer and Family Education Network, *The Bruises Don't Always show,* White Bear Lake, Minnesota Curriculum Services Centre, NDP.

Watson, Lilla, 'Our Children: Part of the Past, Present and Providing a Vision for the Future: *A Murri Perspective',* Australian Child and Family Welfare, 38, 8, 1989.

Watts, Vivienne, *Responding to Child Abuse: A Handbook for Teachers,* Rockhampton, Central Queensland University Press, 1997.

Willis, Diane J, Holden, E Wayne and Rosenberg, Mindy, eds. , *Prevention of Child Maltreatment: developmental and Ecological Perspectives,* New York, John Wiley, 1992.

Index